Management and Industrial Relations Series

1

Lost managers

867 - B3R - 220

00

Management and Industrial Relations Series

Edited for the Social Science Research Council by

DOROTHY WEDDERBURN
Principal of Bedford College, London

MICHAEL BROMWICH
Professor of Finance and Accounting, University of Reading

and

DOUGLAS BROOKS
Director, Walker Brooks and Partners

Social science research has much to contribute to the better understanding and solution of problems in the field of management and industrial relations. The difficulty, however, is that there is frequently a gap between the researcher and the practitioner who wants to use the research results. This new series is designed to make available to practitioners in the relevant fields the results of the best research which the Social Science Research Council (SSRC) has supported through its Management and Industrial Relations Committee. The subjects covered and the style adopted will appeal to managers, trade unionists and administrators because there will be an emphasis upon the practical implications of research findings. But the volumes will also serve as a useful introduction to particular areas for students and teachers of management and industrial relations.

The series is jointly produced by the Cambridge University Press and the Social Science Research Council.

Lost managers
Supervisors in industry and society

by

JOHN CHILD

Professor of Organizational Behaviour,
University of Aston in Birmingham

and

BRUCE PARTRIDGE

Lecturer, Department of Management Studies,
University of Leeds

CAMBRIDGE UNIVERSITY PRESS

Cambridge
London   New York   New Rochelle
Melbourne   Sydney

Published by the Press Syndicate of the University of Cambridge
The Pitt Building, Trumpington Street, Cambridge CB2 1RP
32 East 57th Street, New York, NY 10022, USA
296 Beaconsfield Parade, Middle Park, Melbourne 3206, Australia

© Cambridge University Press 1982

First published 1982

Printed in Great Britain at the
University Press, Cambridge

Library of Congress catalogue card number: 81–17979

British Library Cataloguing in Publication Data

Child, John
Lost managers. – (Management and
industrial relations series; 1)
1. Industrial management – Great Britain
I. Title   II. Partridge, Bruce
III. Series
658′.00941   HD70.G1

ISBN 0 521 23356 9 hard covers
ISBN 0 521 29931 4 paperback

Contents

		Page
Editorial introduction		vii
Preface		xi
Abbreviations		xiv
I	**Introduction**	**1**
1	The supervisor in changing perspective	3
2	The research setting and method of study	17
II	**Supervisors' jobs**	**33**
3	One and many supervisory roles	35
	Appendices 3.1 to 3.6	56
4	The shaping of supervisors' jobs	63
	Appendices 4.1 to 4.4	84
5	Coping and surviving	90
	Appendices 5.1 to 5.3	119
6	Assessing supervisory performance	122
	Appendices 6.1 to 6.3	138
III	**Social identification**	**141**
7	Supervisors at the class divide	145
	Appendix 7.1	167
8	Looking to management or to union?	169
IV	**Conclusion**	**189**
9	Lost managers – will they be found?	191
	Appendices	
A	Sample of 16 supervisors in the food plant who were directly observed	219

Contents

B Twelve statements on 'the supervisor's role today' which were evaluated by supervisors and managers   220

C Items used to form the composite measure of supervisors' 'personal flexibility'   221

D Twenty statements employed for assessing supervisors' views on trade unions   221

Notes   223
Bibliography   227
Name Index   235
Subject Index   238

Editorial introduction

The Social Science Research Council (SSRC) awards grants, through its Management and Industrial Relations Committee (MIRC), for research and postgraduate training in a wide range of management and industrial relations topics and functions. MIRC is concerned with the development of research in a specific area of social activity. Management and industrial relations deal with issues arising in the organization of economic activity both public and private. The problems which call for analysis in this field are vast and varied. The range includes such issues as how to establish criteria of efficiency and effectiveness in economic performance, the factors influencing organization structure, the motivation of individuals participating in an organization, the impact of public policy on industry, as well as that set of relationships which is generally subsumed under the heading of industrial relations. Thus, MIRC's remit covers research on activities within organizations as well as relations between them. In doing this it draws on functional specialisms – production, personnel, finance, marketing; techniques – statistics, computing, market research, operational research; and a number of basic disciplines – accountancy, economics, sociology and psychology. Indeed, many would argue that inter-disciplinary and integrative research is vital for effective study of the management and industrial relations field.

SSRC has a duty to provide for the dissemination of the research it supports. Because of its particularly close contacts with the world of industry and administration, MIRC has for long actively sought ways of making research results as widely available as possible. Seminars with potential 'consumers' of research have been held to explore problems and needs. In 1977 an innovative scheme called the Open Door Scheme was launched. This encourages groups of practitioners in the management and industrial relations area to approach SSRC if they feel they have particular problems which might benefit from research. They are then helped with more precise formulation and are put in touch with researchers possessing the necessary expertise and interest to approach SSRC or other bodies for funding. But publication remains an essential vehicle for dissemination and MIRC was fortunate enough to interest the Cambridge University Press in the idea of a joint publication series. It is designed to make available to a general reading audience the results of the best research which the Committee is supporting. This is the first volume of this new series.

We are aiming at a style which will be attractive to the non-specialist, avoiding the use of academic jargon or the overloading with statistical detail. At the same time a simple description of the basic research methodology will be provided. Most importantly there will be an emphasis upon the practical implications of the research.

Lost Managers by John Child and Bruce Partridge is dealing with a subject of wide interest. It is a study of first-line supervisors of manual workers in manufacturing industry, those whom it has been common to refer to as the 'men in the middle', squeezed between the manager proper above, and the work force they supervise below. Arguably a better understanding both of the task that the supervisor is expected to perform and of the pressure which he perceives to surround his role would contribute much to an improved utilization of production capacity. Child and Partridge argue, among other things, that their findings reveal a discrepancy between, on the one hand, the supervisors' lack of managerial authority and on the other, the responsibility which they carry for the performance of their sections.

They believe that management must make efforts to understand better the tasks which supervisors actually perform and they seek to provide a framework of analysis within which this can be achieved. This will then face management with choices about the way in which the supervisory role can be developed, appropriate to the characteristics of particular organizations. A certain urgency attaches to this reconsideration, because Child and Partridge suggest that, while still identifying with management goals, most supervisors feel that they cannot rely upon management to look after their interests and that it is necessary for them to belong to a trade union on pragmatic grounds. How long the remaining good will towards management will last is therefore uncertain.

Forthcoming volumes in this series will deal with such topics as equal pay and discrimination in the workplace, the role of management strategy in industrial relations, participation and decision making in top management and recent changes in trade union organization. In one way or another all of these studies will contribute to a better understanding of the complex set of factors underlying Britain's industrial decline and contemporary problems of adjustment.

DOROTHY WEDDERBURN
Bedford College
Former Chairman of the Social Science Research Council's Management and Industrial Relations Committee

Preface

This book presents and discusses findings from a study of first-line supervisors in industry. It launches a new series which is intended to make research funded by the Social Science Research Council available to a wider readership than those who have access to specialized academic journals.

The need for a compact presentation permits us to treat certain aspects of the research only. We have attempted to discuss its findings in the light of previous investigations and also with reference to present-day concerns. It will, however, become apparent that despite the large number of articles which continue to appear on supervision, there are still only a handful of substantial studies into the central questions of what supervisors' jobs actually amount to and what their position is within the industrial system. Much previous discussion has been based upon stereotypes of the supervisor rather than on close examination. A disproportionate amount of attention has been given to one facet of supervision – the 'leadership style' adopted towards workers – and this mainly within the one culture of the United States. The more fundamental issue of where supervisors are located within the overall system of organizational control, and whether their role and identification is managerial or not, has been neglected by comparison. With this imbalance in mind, we have chosen to allocate the larger part of this book to the substance rather than the style of supervisors' jobs, and to their relations with management rather than with the shopfloor.

Although much of the book is taken up with findings from our research, we are also concerned to address these to the so-called 'problem of supervision'. The opening chapter traces the historical roots of this problem, while the final chapter examines the policy options that are now available. For those who might wish to delve into our work in greater detail, the bibliography lists the authors' papers which have so far become available, together with other literature referred to in the text.

The research involved quite a lot of new methodology which we had to develop as we proceeded. Its results are therefore exploratory rather than definitive; nor can they be offered with any assurance that they are representative of British industrial supervisors as a whole. Nobody appears to know the precise characteristics of supervisors in British industry, and the problem is not made any easier by the lack of generally-accepted definitions for jobs called supervisor, foreman, chargehand, and the like. The main part of our research was confined to two factories in Birmingham, and we do not therefore have a 'sample' in the technical sense. Nevertheless, we have found in our wider contacts with industry that the issues and problems which emerge from our study are much the same as those which are of concern more generally.

There is some use of statistics and statistical tests in the book. We have normally confined details of tests to footnotes or appendices. Indeed, with a probably unrepresentative sample of supervisors we could be accused of using certain tests in unwarranted circumstances. We decided that, on balance, there was a case for their use as a complement to the provision of purely descriptive information. A statistical treatment obliges the researcher to tell the reader more about the nature of any patterning which appears in his data than is the case when the reader has to rely totally upon the writer's own interpretative account. The former need not, however, exclude the latter. One can also take heart from the robustness of many parametric tests, particularly the correlation coefficient, when applied to data which do not perfectly satisfy the stringent assumptions that statistical theory lays down. Our argument is, in short, a pragmatic one: statistical tests can be useful in the presentation of data from the kind of research we have conducted. They must be interpreted conservatively, and always with a clear understanding that their results in no way indicate the substantive and analytical significance of relationships.

Any progress we may have made in our investigations owes a great deal to other one-time members of the research team in the University of Aston Management Centre. Dr. Julia Kiely, Professor Victor Oubridge and Michael Brock played an important role in preliminary studies which were conducted within the Midlands-based division of a large British metal processing company. These studies were first undertaken at the prompting of David Dolton, Divisional Personnel Director at the time, who believes that academics can and should contribute to the resolution of practical industrial problems. Stuart Bell and Beverley Lawson conducted MBA (Master of Business Administration) projects closely related to our work, and which helped to inform our thinking. Lisa King, Sandra Pearce and Betty Roderick were at various stages heavily involved in the study reported in this book. It is only their new full-time commitments which have precluded their participation in its writing. It also goes without saying that there would have been very little to write about if the Social Science Research Council had not funded the project.

A number of colleagues have given generously of their time to comment on an earlier draft. We owe a special debt of gratitude to Professor Dorothy Wedderburn who forsook some of the delights of Copenhagen in order to write us a detailed and incisive commentary from which we learned a great deal. Adrian Atkinson, Douglas Brooks, Tony Chapman, Elizabeth Child, Ray Loveridge, Aubrey Silberston, Ted Stephenson and Godfrey Williams all made valuable comments and observations on our shortcomings. Mary Maybank must be relieved that, after coping so patiently with many changes, she has now at last typed a final product. Our greatest debt of gratitude, however, must go to all the supervisors, managers and union representatives who found the time and patience to answer our questions. We only hope that they have found it worthwhile.

JOHN CHILD
BRUCE PARTRIDGE
Birmingham and Leeds
November 1980

Abbreviations

ACTSS	Association of Clerical, Technical and Supervisory Staffs
APEX	Association of Professional, Executive, Clerical and Computer Staff
ASTMS	Association of Scientific, Technical and Managerial Staffs
AUEW	Amalgamated Union of Engineering Workers
BIM	British Institute of Management
BIOSS	Brunel Institute of Organization and Social Studies
HMSO	Her Majesty's Stationery Office
IDS	Income Data Services
IPM	Institute of Personnel Management
K–R	Kuder–Richardson
NALGO	National and Local Government Officers' Association
NBPI	National Board for Prices and Incomes
NGA	National Graphical Association
NIIP	National Institute of Industrial Psychology
SOGAT	Society of Graphical and Allied Trades
SPSS	Statistical Package for the Social Sciences
TGWU	Transport and General Workers' Union
TSA	Time Span Analysis
TSD	Time Span of Discretion
USDAW	Union of Shop, Distributive and Allied Workers

PART I

Introduction

1

The supervisor in changing perspective

'We are not the bosses we used to be.' (Birmingham supervisor)

This book is about the first-line supervisors of manual workers in manufacturing firms. It presents the findings of investigations carried out in two Birmingham factories into the jobs supervisors perform and into how they view their position in industry and society today. The role that supervisors play in management and their standing in relation to managers was a particular interest throughout these investigations. The position of the first-line supervisor is, indeed, usually claimed by British companies to be a managerial one, as the person who has direct and undisputed authority over employees engaged in shopfloor, office or service operations. The reality, however, can be very different. First-line supervisors are in practice given various titles, including foreman and chargehand, but they will be referred to here as 'supervisors'.

There are no exact figures for the total number of supervisors in Britain. It is, however, safe to say that they are not a particularly large group. The latest Census figures at the time of writing are for 1971, and these show that there were 600,000 'foremen and supervisors' of manual workers in Great Britain or 2.5 per cent of the total working population. These numbers were projected to rise to about 650,000 by 1981 (Department of Employment, 1976), but recession has almost certainly caused this to be an overestimate.

It is probably because supervisors form a small part of the total working population and have not in the past been able to exert much social pressure, that they have been relatively neglected both by academic investigators and by the framers of industrial policy. As Thurley and Wirdenius (1973) point out in introducing one of the few major studies of supervision, the subject has not ranked high in the priorities of governments, trade unions, employers or managers. The

TP

explanation for this low ranking, they suggest, lies in the modest status and marginality of supervisors, as well as in the view that problems of supervision, persistent though they may be, are not the cause of dramatic industrial crises.

A diminution of the relative status enjoyed by supervisors within their employing organizations, and an increase in their marginality in the control of the labour process, is the product of a historical transformation from the very different position enjoyed by many of their equivalents a hundred years ago. It is important to note this transformation, since from it stem many of the elements in the so-called 'problem of the supervisor' today. The past may well live in the present so far as supervisors are concerned, by providing them with a definition of supervision which they accept as legitimate but which is at variance with contemporary conditions. Any proposal to change the present-day role of supervision has to take the influence of history into account, and it is a point of reference when deciding whether to reverse, modify or continue the historical trend.

Historical transformation

The historical transformation in the position of supervisors has to be understood in the context of changes in the control and organization of the labour process. In the early development of factory organization and large-scale construction ventures, many employers enforced control over the conduct and performance of workers through the medium of determined, and often ruthless, supervisors. The advancing division of labour, the increasing interdependence between jobs, and the extension of firms' operations to cover a wider range of types of production, broadened the knowledge required for supervision beyond the capacity of the employer. The growth in the scale of business and in the attention required by its commercial aspects also hastened the process of delegating workplace control.

During much of the nineteenth century, the supervisor in Britain and America could typically be characterized as 'the man in charge' of the workshop or of the construction site. Edwards (1979), writing of the United States, has called this the system of 'simple' hierarchical control. Under this system 'each supervisor was simply assigned the task of directing the work within his shop or division and making his subordinates work as hard as possible. And in enforcing his orders, the supervisor could call upon most of the powers exercised by the capitalist in an entrepreneurial firm.' (p. 33) These powers included the hiring and firing of workers, the docking of pay and, on occasion, even physical force.

In Victorian Britain, supervisors were often accorded delegated powers, as in many staple industries (Melling, 1980) and on building sites (Bendix, 1956) where even today they can play an important role in the selection and control of labour. At the time, writers on workshop management considered it appropriate for the supervisor to have complete authority in the workplace, without undue interference from the employer, and to have sole charge over the hiring and dismissal of labour (e.g. Smith, 1878). However, closer examination also reveals that this pattern of supervision was not uniform, and where sub-contracting or piecework systems were used the duties of supervision would be undertaken by the contractors or leading workmen (Melling, 1980: 191). Moreover, where supervisors did enjoy extensive delegated powers, they were under orders from above and expected to secure desired results in order to preserve their own jobs. They were in this respect placed 'in the middle' between employers and labour, though in a hierarchy where the main flow of power and authority was downward. In contrast to more recent characterizations, nineteenth-century supervisors were not often caught between two powerful opposing parties since employers generally held the advantage and backed supervisors in carrying out their purposes.

In the early stages of industrialization in Britain, it was sometimes the case that supervisors of operatives were not paid appreciably above the level of skilled craftsmen and their pay could even be inferior. In other industries, such as mining, where supervisors were promoted from the ranks of skilled workers and where the work to be supervised required some technical knowledge or carried considerable responsibility, their pay was appreciably higher than that of ordinary wage-earners (Pollard, 1968: 172). Later in the nineteenth century, supervisors are frequently found to have an education and a life-style superior to those of manual workers. Supervisors are known often to have owned modest houses and rented rooms to workers in their departments, in addition to being careful savers and investors (Melling, 1980: 192; Williams, 1915). The bowler hat, donned by many foremen, had become a symbol of superior status as well as of authority.

In the late nineteenth century, new industries and new methods of production began to spell significant changes in the role of supervision. Factors leading to these innovations in Britain included the pressures of increasing international competition and the hold that collectively-organized labour had on working practices in certain industries. In America, the plentiful availability of cheap and compliant immigrant labour was also significant.

One important new development was the attempt to break the hold that the skilled crafts had upon working methods and productivity norms. The thrust by employers here was towards a reduction of the skilled job into specialized tasks for which management could define methods and output norms. These new jobs were a fragmentation of the closed structure of craft work and, when introduced, provided employers with significantly greater control over the productive process. Such jobs were in some industries harnessed to flow-line or assembly technology, which added the further discipline of a pace and sequence of tasks designed by management into the very equipment with which employees had to work: Edwards (1979) has called this 'technical control'.

The scientific management movement which provided the techniques as well as legitimation for such changes claimed to be substituting the engineer's rule of measurement for the craftsman's rule of thumb. Many supervisors were craftsmen and therein lay the justification for their widely-embracing control within workshops which depended primarily upon the quality of skilled workers. Scientific management challenged this supervisory role and instead argued for its breakdown into the various elements prescribed in F. W. Taylor's concept of 'functional foremanship'. Activities such as selection, planning of work, costing, procurement of materials, and quality control, Taylor argued, could now be made subject to scientific procedures under the charge of appropriately qualified staff personnel.

The growth in scale and complexity of major British firms encouraged the employers concerned to establish functional departments to support the greater burden of administration that resulted. Relatively well-educated technical and administrative specialists were recruited. This development strengthened the argument in favour of reallocating to specialist experts activities previously under the supervisor's control. Increasingly, centralized staff functions planned the work passing through supervisors' departments, substituted standard selection procedures for the judgement (and patronage) that supervisors had exercised, and made other inroads into the supervisory role (Melling, 1980: 196). The introduction of individual incentive schemes based on time study also reduced the requirement for supervisors to extract sustained effort from employees. While the application of new management methods was often assisted by the spread of machinery and newly-integrated forms of technology, they had a significant impact upon supervision in their own right. They are components of what Edwards (1979) identifies as a third 'bureaucratic' system of control.

The systematic selection of employees and their training in the new methods of work was a major principle of scientific management. In Britain, this emphasis on selection and training became fused with the movement to invest in employees' welfare. Interest in employee welfare was partly altruistic and partly a recognition of the benefits that could accrue from a higher level of worker identification with the enterprise. In these beginnings of personnel management, there was an awareness of the need to reform and restrict what was perceived to be the abuse and arbitrariness of supervisors' powers over workers. Thus the power which supervisors enjoyed over the shopfloor began to be further constrained with the introduction of embryonic personnel departments even before the 1914–18 war. After the war, the supervisor was singled out as the culprit for much of the industrial unrest and hostility to employers which then prevailed (a theme to be repeated after the Second World War). He was now urged by writers on management to moderate his control, so as to substitute leadership for domination (Child, 1969: Chapter 3).

These were the beginnings of the often-noted decline in supervisors' authority and of the erosion of their managerial functions. The trend has been particularly apparent in large-scale industry, although even there it has not been identical across all sectors. It has been reinforced in more recent times by the changed balance of industrial power and by the collective organization of employees. The advent of relatively full employment in the 1940s in both Britain and the United States considerably enhanced the power of labour. By and large, the days were now gone when workers depended upon the supervisor for holding on to their job, and when the workers' loyalties would attach primarily to him. His ability to enforce authority on the shopfloor was now uncertain, while his very position of leadership over the employees he supervised was increasingly being challenged by their own chosen and union-accredited representatives, the shop-stewards.

By the 1940s it was widely recognized that these changes in the supervisor's position within the organization had created 'a supervisory problem' – particularly from the perspective of American management which faced supervisory unionization and strikes even in key war industries. The supervisor was now seen to be the 'man in the middle' (Roethlisberger, 1943) caught between the opposing forces of management and shopfloor, torn by competing demands and loyalties. The supervisor's role had become more stressful and his capacity to achieve what management expected of him progressively more limited. The continued development of centralized functional departments, laying down a framework of procedures which governed many shopfloor parameters, and the encouragement they gave for shop-stewards to bypass the supervisor, led other commentators to conclude that he no longer occupied a position of special importance in the management system. He was more a transmitter of management decisions than an active participant in them. This view was captured by the notion of supervisors as 'the marginal men of industry' (Wray, 1949). As the same writer put it, being held accountable as managers of employees while being excluded from many management decisions, supervisors are 'special victims of the disparity between social norms and social reality' (p. 301). More recently still, it has been suggested that under certain conditions, such as the automation of production processes (Crossman, 1960; Taylor, 1971) or the development of autonomous working groups (Gulowsen, 1972), there is little if any role for the supervisor any more. Development and experimentation along these lines has been accompanied by supervisory redundancies. The 'end of management' which Fletcher (1973) predicted began to enter into many supervisors' minds as a distinct possibility. If they were now marked as 'men on the way out', it is not surprising that many in Britain decided to unionize and put up a fight first.

The historical transformation of the supervisor's position raises the empirical question as to what degree of authority and discretion actually remains to supervisors, and whether their job retains any managerial attributes. Despite the tendency for supervisors to become excluded from control over many parameters of workplace management, it remains a basic tenet in management ideology to claim their comradeship as first-line *managers* (e.g. British Institute of Management (BIM), 1976). It is possible therefore that supervisors today experience something of a double standard when they compare how the ideology expresses their relationship to management with the way this actually operates.

Another potential double standard arises from the way that, over time, management has formally removed responsibilities from supervisors to specialists, without necessarily recognizing that those supervisors still have to deal with the application of specialist activities to the shopfloor or office under their charge. As a consequence, the full scope and burden of work remaining with supervisors may not be fully appreciated by higher management. Supervisors may actually have to make good deficiencies in management's formal organization, such as poor co-ordination between specialists, and this only adds to the problem. There is a danger, then, of incongruence between the limited formal recognition given to a supervisor's role and the complex, stressful realities of carrying out that role. These realities may well entail compensating for shortcomings in formal procedures and systems, co-ordinating different specialist interventions and services at the point of their operational application, and dealing with contingencies so as to keep crises away from management's door. The possibility of such double standards speaks for the need to investigate supervisors' discretionary responsibilities and of ascertaining whether they are similarly perceived by both supervisors and managers.

The appreciation which managers have of shopfloor activities may have been further weakened by another historical development. The old-style supervisor embodied an intimate understanding of production and its technical requirements in the control of the labour process. Technologies were, of course, still relatively rudimentary in the nineteenth century and skill plus experience could stand in good stead against academic training. Today, this integration in the one role of planning and control with an intimate understanding of the workplace situation has often been fractured by the reservation to members of management of planning, and the determination of work schedules, methods and equipment. Other functions may be performed by specialists, who are again removed from the workplace and not necessarily well co-ordinated among themselves. As is noted shortly, a decreasing proportion of these managers and specialists are likely to have had significant direct experience of the shopfloor, and this further limits their ability to appreciate the shopfloor situation. It has been argued by Mant (1979), among others, that the separation of career managers from the realm of making things (production) and

9

its technologies is particularly marked in Britain and constitutes a significant reason for the nation's poor productive performance. The question is raised, therefore, how far in practice supervisors are excluded from decisions on technology and other basic parameters of operational design and planning. Do supervisors have expertise and knowledge based on intimate experience which is no longer made available to, or recognized by, management?

The gap between supervision and management has come to have a social aspect as well. Promotion from the shopfloor to supervision was, a hundred years ago, often regarded as a significant step up in the world. The superiority in social status which many supervisors enjoyed over workers in the later nineteenth century has been noted. When management hierarchies first developed, there were often good opportunities for supervisors to gain further promotion – experience was still valued rather than paper qualifications and qualified people tended to avoid industry anyway. Since the Second World War, however, recruitment into management has come increasingly to require graduate or higher diploma qualifications and a decreasing proportion of managers have significant shopfloor or first-line supervisory experience. An educational barrier has grown up between the members of management proper, with its ladders of advancement, and members of supervision, particularly on the production side where many supervisors do not even possess apprenticeships. In Britain, educational barriers tend to become social barriers as well. At the same time, promotion from worker to supervisor now represents a less significant upward move with the decline that has taken place in the authority, standing and differential rewards and privileges that supervisors enjoy.

This historical trend both points to the scope for misunderstanding between managers and supervisors who now inhabit different realms of personal development and future orientation, and it also raises the wider question of where supervisors' social identity now lies. Do they today retain a working-class identification with the group from which they were made up; or does becoming a supervisor still represent a qualitative social advance in their eyes? Is the social identity of supervisors within their place of work linked to a perception of where their interests now lie, and can it account for the interpretations they give to trade union membership?

Consideration of supervision in historical perspective thus brings to the fore certain questions about supervisors' jobs and social identity which provide the framework for this book. Over the past ten years, these questions have been raised with a new urgency, spurred on by action which supervisors themselves have taken in protest and as protection.

Contemporary interest in supervisors

Since the mid-1960s, supervisors in Britain have given notice in increasing numbers that their loyalty to, and willingness to depend upon, their employer can no longer be taken for granted. The erosion of their differentials and privileges over shopfloor workers, the vulnerability of their authority to pressures from organized employees, and the threat of redundancy, have all been powerful reasons for supervisors to unionize. It has sometimes only taken a small straw to break the camel's back of mounting concern over their declining position. For example, the visit of the Group Personnel Director of a large engineering group to one of its Midlands factories was followed by an instruction that foremen should stop taking their tea in cups and saucers and instead use vending machines, like their workers. A week after this attempt to revoke a minor supervisory privilege, all the foremen had joined the Association of Scientific, Technical and Managerial Staffs (ASTMS) and they had submitted a claim for more pay. The percentage of British supervisors who are now members of a trade union has been estimated at around 40 per cent (Institute of Supervisory Management, 1979). The unionization of supervisors, and instances of their involvement in industrial action, raises the question of how far they now perceive their interests to be at variance with those of the company as represented by senior management.

Investigation into the identification and commitment of supervisors should also inform continuing sociological discussion on the composition and attitudes of the so-called 'white-collar' sector and on the location of its boundaries with the working class. Supervisors are in a formal sense members of the white-collar sector and they have been classified as belonging to an 'intermediate' stratum between manual workers and higher levels of the class structure (Goldthorpe, 1980). However, by origin (for the most part), and perhaps increasingly by the real nature of their position, they can be more correctly located within the working class. Where supervisors see their interests and commitment to be located must also enter into any consideration of improvements to workplace productivity. For supervisors can either serve as important catalysts for change or they can provide a focus for resistance to developments aimed at increasing productivity (Weir and Mills, 1973). If they perceive change to threaten a further erosion of their position, they may well generate shopfloor opposition to management's proposals.

Over the past few years, the debate about the poor performance of British manufacturing industry has shifted focus. Previously it was generally believed, particularly by outsiders to the manufacturing workplace, that better productive performance was most likely to come from increased investment in plant and machinery. Then it came to be realized that the problem lay at least as much in poor utilization of investment, due to inefficiencies in the workplace with which supervisors are directly concerned. A potential link could therefore be discerned between the dissatisfaction of rapidly unionizing British supervisors and poor performance at the point of manufacture. A number of companies, to the writers' own knowledge, for this reason began to make internal enquiries during the 1970s into the 'problem' of supervisors in their plants. The British Institute of Management established a working party on supervision which reported in 1976. The possibility that supervisors in practice performed a greater range of indispensable functions than management had realized was also brought to its attention by the difficulties which arose following attempts, particularly in Norway, to abolish first-line supervision when quasi-autonomous work groups were set up (Swedish Employers' Confederation, 1975: Chapter 4). Perhaps there was more to supervisors' jobs than managers and academics had generally appreciated.

Further impetus has been given to the study of supervisors' jobs, activities and problems by the realization that the particular characteristics of each workplace and company situation have to be taken into account. Earlier discussion of supervision had assumed that the role was basically the same in most industries, and this view was reflected in much of the literature as well as in principles of selection, training and organization for supervision. Case study investigations conducted in Britain by the National Institute of Industrial Psychology (NIIP) (1957) and by Thurley and Hamblin (1963) demonstrated that there is actually considerable variation between supervisors' tasks and activities in different work situations. Both investigations suggested that technology and the style adopted by a supervisor's own manager might contribute to this variation. Joan Woodward's (1958) early report on management and technology noted that the number of employees under a supervisor, his span of control, varied systematically according to the general type of manufacturing production system. There was, however, surprisingly little follow-up to the lead which these investigations provided, and the situational (or 'contingency') perspective only gained widespread acceptance in the 1970s. Today, it is seen to present a new challenge for the understanding of supervision and the design of supervisory training by indicating the potential variety both in supervisors' jobs and in the organizational conditions which may affect the performance of those jobs (cf. Bates and Hosking, 1977).

Research perspective

When we began the investigations described in this book, the historical transformation which supervision had undergone was very much in our minds. It appeared to raise largely unanswered questions about the authority and functions remaining to supervisors, and about the ambiguities, problems and stresses which might now attend their role. A further puzzle was whether any pattern could be discerned in the apparently great variety of supervisory jobs. We had also been alerted to the subject by the concern which many managers were expressing over dissatisfaction among supervisors and their supposedly diminishing commitment to management objectives and company performance. The manner in which supervisors had flocked to join unions seemed to denote a watershed in their relations with management.

The design of our research, which was first set under way in 1974, was therefore influenced by an interest in these questions and it rested upon a number of assumptions which we recorded at the time. These are now listed, in order to clarify the initial perspective of the investigations, and they are arranged in an order that corresponds to the order of chapters which report our findings (Chapters 3 to 8 inclusive). A basic assumption was that it is not fruitful to generalize about supervisors away from the situations in which they work. This is likely to be particularly true of their jobs and how these are performed. It might also be true of their social identity in the absence of a strong common occupational identification shared with supervisors in other places of work. Research on supervisors should therefore be sensitive to each situation and of sufficient depth to discern the particular nature of each supervisor's position. Further, more specific, assumptions were that:

(1) The relationship of supervisors to management and the managerial scope of their job has been neglected in most previous studies, yet it appears central both to historical trends and to contemporary concerns. Research on supervisors should therefore have regard to their authority and influence over decisions and the extent to which the managerial component of their jobs has now been restricted. This implies granting priority to investigation of the discretionary elements in supervisors' jobs rather than to repeating the descriptive classifications of supervisory behaviour which were prominent in previous studies – for example, the time supervisors spend communicating, doing paperwork, walking around and so forth. Our findings on supervisors' authority and influence are reported in Chapter 3.

(2) The 'task system' (the technology and organization of tasks performed) in which supervisors work is likely to be an important situational influence upon the content of their jobs. Previous research had suggested that supervisors' spans of control vary according to the type of production system, and there was reason to believe that the nature of supervision required also depended upon the design and efficacy of managerial control systems (Woodward, 1970). Thurley and Hamblin's (1963) studies had pointed to the relevance of task system contingencies (variation in operations, complexity in operations, degree of mechanization and span of control) for explaining variations in supervisors' jobs, but they also illustrated how the outlook and practices of the managerial superior could be influential. Attention was thus directed again at the supervisor's relationship upwards with his manager.

The historical transformation in supervision, however, suggests that it will today be set at some distance from management proper. It was also noted how Nealey and Fiedler (1968) had concluded from their review of American middle-managers' jobs that the largest gap in the industrial hierarchy lay between the first-line supervisor and the manager above him. Any such discontinuity is likely to give supervisors some *de facto* discretion in how to carry out their jobs. The probability that managers would not have a detailed understanding of supervisors' work or of any norms of conduct shaped by occupational socialization, would in practice lend a degree of freedom for supervisors to determine the conduct of their jobs, and perhaps encourage variation despite the presence of situational contingencies. Chapter 4 takes up this issue and examines how far supervisors' jobs, in particular their discretionary content, appear to be shaped by identifiable aspects of the work situation.

(3) The supervisor may also be regarded as an actor in the work situation and not simply as someone whose behaviour is shaped by the situation. That is, supervisors are likely to put their own stamp upon their activities, the more so when a lack of managerial familiarity with shopfloor conditions gives supervisors some scope to develop their role as they see fit. This implies that it may not be possible to discover a limited number of types of supervisory role accounted for straightforwardly by different combinations of major contingencies. Viewing the supervisor as an actor in his work situation also means understanding him as a person. This generates an interest in problems as he sees them, and in any dissatisfaction and stress he may experience, since these will affect his wellbeing as an individual. Bearing in mind previous characterizations of the supervisor as subject to conflicting pressures, marginality or even redundancy, Chapter 5 examines the problems and strains that supervisors experience and how they decide to cope with these.

(4) The possibility, already mentioned, of discontinuity between supervision and management raises questions about the basis on which management assesses supervisors' performance. Here, differences in expectations between a supervisor and his manager over priorities, the proper scope of the job, or the style of its execution, might influence how his performance in the job is evaluated by the manager. The closeness of contact between the two parties, and the extent to which they share personal similarities, might also be expected to influence performance ratings given by the manager. Chapter 6 reports on the factors found to be associated with managers' ratings of supervisors' performance.

(5) If there is some distance today between supervision and management, which may be reinforced by the exclusion of most supervisors from managerial career opportunities, then the question arises as to whether this gap is reflected in the supervisor's social identification. Does he now see himself as closer to manual workers and the working class than to managers and the middle class? We assumed that this might well be the case, despite the persistence of managerial claims that supervisors belonged to them. We also

thought that the supervisor's own social origins and whether he had experienced non-manual employment would help to shape his perspectives on these matters. Our findings are discussed in Chapter 7.

(6) Finally, it was impossible to ignore the rapid growth in the unionization of supervisors in British industry. It is possible that this movement itself reflects a shift of loyalties and identification away from management. On the other hand, specific local events may have provided the impetus for supervisors to join a trade union at the time that they did. Chapter 8 is concerned with the process of supervisory unionization and with the meaning that supervisors attach to membership of a union.

These preliminary assumptions provide the rationale for the central chapters of this book. Part II contains those chapters (3 to 6) which are mainly concerned with supervisors' jobs. Part III consists of two chapters (7 and 8) on class and union memberships, which are concerned with the social identification of supervisors. This division, while logical, is to some extent arbitrary since it will become evident that the conditions of supervisors' jobs, especially the extent to which they see their work role treated as a managerial one, are associated with their social identification. Part IV contains one concluding chapter (9), which addresses the findings of the research to the so-called 'problem of the supervisor', and then goes on to delineate the main policy options available for supervision in the future.

This chapter has outlined the roots of contemporary concern about supervisors in industry and the research questions which we formulated with this background in mind. Before proceeding to the findings of the research, we need to indicate how we went about the investigations and to describe both the supervisors involved and the context in which they were working. This is done in Chapter 2.

2

The research setting and method of study

By 1970 the importance of studying the special characteristics of each workshop and company situation was generally recognised. (Thurley and Wirdenius, *The Influence of the Supervisor in Organizations* (1980:3))

The initial assumptions described in the previous chapter shaped the design and method of investigation adopted. The assumption that there would be variation in supervisors' jobs spoke in favour of sampling a sufficiently large number of supervisors located in sufficiently different areas of work and places of employment for such variation to be recorded. On the other hand, it was also thought that the supervisory situation was a complex one and that the limitation of many previous studies in restricting their investigations to a few variables should be avoided. Not only would such restriction be likely to understate the complexity of supervision, but it would also make it difficult to investigate at one and the same time both the work situation and the supervisor as an actor within that situation. The practicalities of investigating a wide range of variables and of understanding the nature of connections between them spoke in favour of concentrating the research on to relatively few supervisors in a limited number of work situations.

In the event, the design adopted for the research was an attempt to satisfy both criteria: that of investigating possible variation and that of investigating complexity. The original intention was to study a selection of at least six different companies and/or plants. However, preliminary studies pointed to the presence of differences in supervisors' jobs within individual plants, and this was confirmed within the two Birmingham factories to which we eventually decided to confine the research. We abandoned a plan of extending the investigations to other types of industry such as quarrying, construction and process production in favour of devoting the time available to conducting direct observations of supervisors at work. The research reported in this book is therefore limited to two Birmingham plants which are located within the batch production sector of manufacturing industry. The contribution that this research may make rests upon its ability to analyse reasonably comprehensively issues which are of general interest for current discussion about supervision, while drawing upon research settings that cannot be said to provide a representative sample.

Preliminary studies

During 1974 and 1975 preliminary studies were carried out in four Midlands non-ferrous-metal manufacturing plants belonging to a division of a large British company. These studies extended to 58 supervisors. They proceeded initially through exploratory interviews with each supervisor and also with most managers in the plants. The opportunity was subsequently taken to pilot some standardized research measurements through further questioning.

The preliminary enquiries provided valuable experience in (1) developing appropriate methods for gathering data on matters such as priorities, authority and influence; (2) formulating an interview approach especially towards more sensitive issues, and (3) the reporting back of results to all those participating in the research. They exposed a number of problems in each plant, and formed the basis for subsequent discussions which led supervisors and management to decide on changes. The research also provided an opportunity for associated studies conducted by post-graduate students into managers' and supervisors' job satisfaction, the assessment of supervisors' performance, and the positions and perspectives of technical staff.

There is only space here to make two general points arising from the preliminary studies in the metal plants. First, supervisors in these plants had recently experienced an accelerated version of the historical transition from being 'the man in charge' of the workshop to occupying the greatly-eroded role more typical of today. Each plant had previously been an independent small family company until its acquisition by the present owning group during the 1960s. Supervisors had tended to act in a 'general foreman' capacity. The small size of each company (total employment figures in 1974–75 were 242, 288, 446 and 477) and the lack of well-developed management hierarchies had permitted personal contact between owners and supervisors. Incorporation into the larger company had led in a few years to:

(1) 'rationalization' of production supervisors' jobs, tying them to particular sections, accountable for the work of those sections, and subject to many new standard procedures;

(2) considerable growth in staff departments impinging on the supervisor's role in respect, for example, of disciplining employees, safety, production scheduling and quality control;

(3) increased pressures for production and productivity, accompanied by some factory closures within the division to which the plants belonged, and a fear (which later materialized) of supervisory redundancies;

(4) the unionization of virtually all supervisors in ASTMS, and the subsequent issue of a 'charter' by the division, which was intended to reassure supervisors of their status, but which in fact caused further resentment because of what they saw as its divergence from actual managerial practice.

In many respects, then, it was possible to find in these metal plants a microcosm of trends which have developed elsewhere since the early years of this century.

The second point concerns the necessity for researchers to have an independent standing if they are seeking to secure valid data on issues which are regarded by respondents as sensitive. Because of the developments just described, there was a deteriorating climate of relations between supervisors and management when we began our studies in the metal plants. We had been invited to conduct research by the division's Personnel Director and the company paid for the maintenance of one research assistant. Even though management in no way determined the nature or content of our enquiries, this support from the company made it very difficult to convince supervisors of (1) the anonymity which their responses would be given and (2) our intention to provide identical and simultaneous feedback to supervisors and management so that both parties 'owned' the research output equally. Before accepting management's suggestion that we should undertake some research, we had secured the support of the ASTMS Regional Officer. This proved to be another source of concern for supervisors since they were determined to guard zealously the autonomy of their branch against the union's full-time bureaucracy. Some of this initial distrust on the part of supervisors eventually evaporated, but it greatly handicapped our ability to put questions on more sensitive topics such as union membership and social identity.

In order both to extend the research and to avoid financial dependence upon any of the parties involved in the investigations, we applied for and received a grant from the Social Science Research Council in 1975. This supported the main research study reported in this book, which was conducted according to the following four principles agreed beforehand with the managements and supervisors concerned:

(1) the research was to be financed independently of the company, and would not in any way be conducted as a commission from management;

(2) having gained the agreement of all groups involved in the research prior to its commencement, this agreement would have to be maintained as a condition for the research to continue;

(3) there would be a feedback of major findings in the same form and at the same time to *all* participants;

(4) the research team would be willing to return to the site to comment on the research findings and to join in any subsequent discussions.

It was believed to be both appropriate and necessary to have these principles agreed: appropriate in terms of the university researcher's professional ethics and necessary as a prerequisite to obtaining reasonably valid data. It is, of course, particularly difficult to maintain an 'independent' approach in the conduct of research which has implications for subsequent action within the same context: some social scientists would question whether it is possible at all. Our attempt to preserve an independent position stemmed from a recognition, reinforced by our experience of conducting the preliminary studies in the metal plants, that research such as ours is necessarily conducted within a political arena in which the legitimacy of the researcher can easily be prejudiced. In the event, we are confident that the approach we endeavoured to maintain did generate some respect for the purposes of the investigation, which was powerfully reinforced when the research was seen to be conducted, and feedback subsequently given, on the terms originally agreed. More can be said about the method of carrying out the research after a description of the two plants in which it was located and of the supervisors involved.

The research setting

Table 2.1 summarizes some background information about the two Birmingham plants in which the research was carried out between 1975 and 1977. The numbers of supervisors and managers who answered our questions are also given. The engineering plant was the major production unit and headquarters location for an electrical manufacturing company which continued to trade under its own name although it had been acquired by a much larger diversified British company in 1971. The food manufacturing plant was the largest production unit and the location of senior management for a major division of a large British company which operated in several sectors of the food and drinks industry.

1. Engineering plant

The engineering company was founded in 1908, starting with the production of switch and fuse gear. More recently its range of products has extended to embrace both industrial and domestic switchgear, in which field it is the UK market leader; motor control gear, in which it is one of several major UK producers; and domestic electrical accessories, in which market it is not one of the largest suppliers. A growing proportion of its sales has gone to export over the past few years, and this was close to 40 per cent at the time of our study. The company's management placed a great deal of emphasis upon the quality (and of course safety) of its products as a key competitive factor. This will be seen to be reflected in supervisors' priorities, and it led to a policy of, as far as possible, making every part of each product within the company. As a result a very wide range of different production operations were housed under the one roof of the plant where our research was conducted. These included a foundry, press shop and extrusion mill, plastic moulding department, a porcelain works, machine shops, paint shop and assembly sections. Ancillary sections or departments included stores, despatch and transport, toolroom, maintenance, inspection and development. Production was organized on a day and night shift system. Most supervisors worked on the day shift.

Table 2.1 *Outline characteristics of plants and supervisors sampled*

	Engineering plant	Food plant
Type of firm	Electrical engineering	Food processing
History	Founded 1908	Founded 1835
	Family firm, acquired by multidivisional group 1971	Family firm, merged with another large foods group 1969
Products	Switch and fuse gear, motor control gear	Chocolate bars, assortments, confectionery, confectionery bars
Technology	Small and large batch production	Large batch production
	Foundry, pottery, machining, assembling	Grinding, moulding wrapping, printing and packaging
Number of levels in plant production management (including supervisors)	4	5
Type of workforce	Predominantly male Semi-skilled	Even male/female mix Semi-skilled
Number of employees on site	1,100	5,200
Number of supervisors on site	66	232
Number of these supervisors in research sample	54	102
Number of these supervisors' immediate managers on site	15	30
Number of these managers in sample	14	27

At the time of our research, the main line management hierarchy in the company as a whole was organized into six levels. These were, in descending order, production director, general works manager, works managers for each plant (including the one where the research was located), a 'works superintendent', 16 departmental superintendents, and 66 supervisors.[1] Most of the supporting functions necessary for the organization of production reported to the production director. These included plant engineering (covering the maintenance of buildings and plant), production control, process engineering (covering machinery planning, methods and work study), quality control (as a design function responsible for setting quality standards), and personnel (which also covered industrial relations). Inspection, in respect of checking that quality standards were maintained, reported to the plant works manager. There was also a separate safety function reporting to the general works manager. There was no accounting function for the factory, since it produced not only its own range of products but also components that were consumed by other production plants within the company, which meant that there was no measure of value until the goods were returned in a finished and assembled form and booked into stores. Cost control was handled indirectly on the basis of yield – that is, the level of production extracted from a given quantity of materials, within a given time. Monitoring of performance in these terms came under the purview of the production control function. This arrangement should be borne in mind when noting in Chapter 5 (Table 5.5) that supervisors in the engineering plant gave relatively low priority in their jobs to the monitoring of costs *per se*.

Inspection of production quality was normally handled on a sample basis, except for motor control gear which was inspected as it was finally adjusted. Each stage of production was inspected. If a deviation from standards were found, an inspector would in the first instance draw the supervisor's attention to the problem. The supervisor would then usually call in the tool setter and the consequent three-way discussion could well resolve the problem – such as the need to adjust a piece of production equipment. If the problem appeared to be more deep-seated, the inspector would normally inform the supervisor in question, and then report the matter to his own inspector/supervisor. If the latter were concerned, the matter could pass up the inspection hierarchy and eventually involve a production superintendent or above.

The planning and scheduling of production in the engineering plant was extremely complex. Planning was done on a four-week cycle by the production control function. Production embraced a wide range of different activities, as has been noted. Around 15,000 different individual components were manufactured, and about 3,000 types of components were bought in, plus about another 5,000 raw material specifications. The company's sales catalogue at the time offered about 2,800 different articles, although some of these products were made in the company's other, smaller plants. These statistics convey some idea of the complexity of the production scheduling that was involved and of the serious re-scheduling problem that could arise in the event of an unforeseen contingency such as plant breakdown. With each product typically involving eight to ten stages of manufacture, a breakdown would often involve multiple scheduling changes and decisions to substitute one batch for another. If re-scheduling had to be carried out, this would normally be decided between superintendents and production controllers. Supervisors would not necessarily be consulted, although they would have to deal with the consequences of re-scheduling within their sections, including the impact upon workers' earnings.

Most production employees in the plant were paid on an individual output incentive scheme. A small number of employees were on a two or three person group incentive system. All non-production workers were paid on a straight time rate. Supervisors were paid according to the level of salary associated with their grade. The grade levels as a whole were collectively negotiated with the company by their union. Within this grade, supervisors' pay levels varied according to an assessment of the responsibility and ability or skill required for the supervisor's job. Supervisors could only raise their relative level of pay within the company by moving to a higher-rated supervisory position or by promotion above the supervisory level. There was a tradition of long service in the company among employees, supervisors and managers.

Production workers were organized by the Transport and General Workers' Union (TGWU), while the Amalgamated Engineering Union (AUEW) predominated among skilled ancillary functions. The company recognized and provided facilities for shop-stewards, who in turn elected up to 12 of their number to sit with company representatives on a joint consultative committee. Supervisors were not normally involved in this committee. If a shop-steward wished to leave his area of work to visit another area, the agreed procedure obliged him to seek permission not from the supervisor but from the superintendent. In the handling of claims, grievances and disputes, it was formally agreed that the first course was to raise the matter with the supervisor. If this did not resolve the problem, the agreed procedure then took it above the supervisor's head, with no provision for him to be consulted.

2. Food plant

The food manufacturing company had been founded in 1835. In the late 1960s it merged with another large British firm in the food and drinks industry. This changed the company's prevailing ethos. Up to that time, it had been a family firm whose philosophy emphasized social obligations, including employee welfare, support for the local community, and security of employment. As in the engineering company, there was a tradition of long service, and this very frequently extended to having several generations of employment from the same family. The merger was with a company which had developed a considerable financial expertise and emphasis among its senior management. Within the food plant, cost reduction now came to be given more prominence, as did the improvement of profitability in general. The food plant is a major producer of chocolate and confectionery products but these are sold under strongly competitive conditions. Some difficult trading years have caused the emphasis on cost reduction to persist, although its highly developed personnel function survived and continued to exert a major influence at all levels, including first-line supervision.

The plant in Birmingham where the research took place is a large centre of employment. The factory employed 5,200 persons at the time. It manufactured chocolate bars, confectionery bars, and assortments, including seasonal products such as Easter eggs. The manufacture and printing of wrapping and card-box for its own use was also carried out within the plant. The production areas were divided into (1) chocolate and moulding (for the production of chocolate bars and confectionery bars); (2) assortments; and (3) printing and card-box. The production of chocolate and assorted confectionery was broken down into various stages concerned with the preparation of ingredients, the moulding of bars or enrobing in chocolate of assortments, wrapping, packing and weighing. A supervisor's section located at any given stage would often contain several layouts handling different product varieties. A double day shift system was generally in operation and a supervisor would have responsibility for the section during one of the shifts. A trades area

25

covered maintenance functions for electrical equipment, plant, internal transport, and so forth. Finally a services area provided a range of miscellaneous functions ranging from cleaning services to the preparation of special samples.

The production management hierarchy within the whole Division to which the food plant belonged contained six levels of management.[2] The Division had a production director with overall responsibility for this and three other production units. In descending order below him were a factory director for the food plant, 5 divisional managers, 17 superintendents, 50 section managers, and 232 supervisors.[3] Although the hierarchical distance between the supervisor and top production management was the same in both companies, despite a considerable difference in their size, within the two plants themselves the lengths of the hierarchies were more in proportion, with three levels up to the works manager of the engineering site and four levels up to the director of the food factory.

Some production support functions in the food plant reported to the factory director. These included quality control, central maintenance services, factory accounting, and factory services such as cleaning and hygiene. The three production divisional managers enjoyed a matrix-type link to the accounting, quality control, hygiene and industrial engineering functions. Though industrial engineering formally reported to the factory director via the factory accountant, in practice the reporting relationship was primarily to divisional manager. Both routine maintenance and production control functions reported to each production divisional manager. The personnel function included personnel, industrial relations and safety, and all reported via a factory personnel manager to the factory director.

The production system and its planning was not as complex as in the engineering plant. An overall characterization would place it in the large batch category, though this would mask significant variations within the plant. Each of the three production divisions had a production planner. A number of schedulers reported to each planner,[4] and the role of each scheduler was defined according to the major task boundaries within each division. The planning and scheduling system in the division producing assortments provides an idea of the general approach. A 'long-range' production plan was drawn up for the division, which identified a six months' cycle of work to be done. The planners and the superintendents met weekly in order to consider the achievement of the plan to date both in terms of production output and labour consequence, and forward adjustments were made for as far as two months ahead. A separate meeting then ensued between each superintendent, his or her section managers and the schedulers. The superintendent would translate decisions made in the previous meeting into implications for the week's production, and also anticipate changes for the following week – a two-week horizon overall. Schedulers would have been briefed by their planner previous to this meeting. Production supervisors were not involved in these shorter-term meetings, though together with their section managers they were expected to understand what was required in the first week of the two-week cycle and to make this happen.

Quality inspection was handled in a number of stages. First, incoming ingredients and packing materials were checked on a sample basis and passed on or otherwise as fit for use. Second, from this point, each stage of the production process, from the first stage of manufacture through to final packing, was checked using a statistical sampling basis. The supervisor of each section had a responsibility to produce to quality and cost standards, and the quality services were seen to provide more of an ancillary function in this respect. The high priority which supervisors gave to quality is noted in Chapter 5. Third, further checks were made on product quality in stockrooms and depots. Management took the view that minor quality problems should be resolved directly by supervisors and quality control personnel.

The cost control system at the time produced information with a six-week backlog, which was not in tune with supervisors' time horizons or requirements. As well as information being late, it was not produced according to a categorization that was particularly relevant for supervisors. There was a gap between the supervisor's perspective on costs and the basis on which period accounts were being produced. Supervisors were evaluated against efficiency targets concerning plant performance, levels of waste and labour utilization, which were criteria alien to the content of the accounting information then being produced. Nevertheless, in contrast to the engineering plant, where costing was not applied, there were moves at the time in the food plant to adjust accounting to production management requirements and to educate supervisors in accounting and cost control principles.

Introduction

Production operatives in the food plant were normally paid on a piecework basis, except where special conditions prevailed, such as the running in of new equipment. Generally speaking the percentage of earnings which varied with individual output was about 25 per cent. Operatives in the services division also had a bonus element in their pay tied to levels of production, while maintenance employees were paid on a time basis. Supervisory jobs were allocated to one of two grades. It was possible for supervisors in charge of production sections to improve their grading by moving to another position assessed as bearing greater responsibility, but this was not possible in the craft maintenance areas, where all supervisory posts were graded at the same level. Levels of payment for the grades were negotiated collectively on behalf of supervisors by ASTMS.

Production operatives were organized into three TGWU branches (day men's, day women's, nights and evenings) and one Union of Shop, Distributive and Allied Workers (USDAW) branch. A Pay and Productivity Committee linked these branches together, through the branch officials (senior shop-stewards), into a negotiating forum with management. In addition, there was a works committee structure at which some 12 to 14 representatives sat with management. This met on a fortnightly basis, and had a number of standing committees covering areas such as fringe benefits, education and training, health, safety and suggestions. These committees comprised members of management and senior shop-stewards. This structure excluded supervisors, and senior stewards would not normally be involved in discussing issues with supervisors. Each section had a local shop-steward who would be the point of contact for supervisors and the section managers immediately above them.[5]

Supervisors were involved only on an informal basis with respect to procedure on matters of discipline and redeployment of employees. Thus a supervisor would be expected to give a first verbal warning on matters of discipline, but if the matter then entered formal procedure it would pass out of his hands. Supervisors were also expected to initiate discussions on redeployment of labour and perhaps satisfy the issues involved. Formally, an employee who had a grievance was required to consult the supervisor first, but in practice it often passed directly to the section manager who would not necessarily involve the supervisor.

To summarize, the engineering and food plants differed most in terms of their size, their industry and the complexity of their production systems. The food plant faced somewhat more competitive trading conditions. The two plants had in common a basically batch mode of production, although there were variations in size and continuity of batches within each plant. In both plants, product quality was regarded as highly important in addition to output levels. The labour force in both cases had a tradition of long service and, it should be added, low militancy.

Sample and method

There were 66 supervisors in the engineering plant, with 16 superintendents at the next level of authority above them. It was our intention to question every supervisor and superintendent. In the event, supervisors in the stores area declined to take part, and together with illness this reduced the totals to 54 supervisors and 14 immediate superiors. This still provided a coverage of all areas of production, together with dispatch, toolroom, maintenance and inspection functions. The research was then extended to the food plant where a sample of some 100 supervisors was sought in order to bring the overall scope of the study to about 150 supervisors. One hundred and two supervisors in the food plant were selected to be representative of production, trades and supporting service sections. Twenty-seven of these supervisors' immediate superiors (section managers) were also interviewed. The sample in total thus amounted to 156 supervisors who were each formally in a first line of authority over employees and who had no officially prescribed manual duties. Most of them (69 per cent) were responsible for direct production sections.

Profiles of the supervisors studied were similar when comparing the two plants. The average age of both groups was 50 years. Supervisors in the engineering plant sample had, on average, worked there for 23 years, following 12 years' work elsewhere, and had been supervisors for ten years. On average, supervisors had worked in the food plant for 26 years, following 10 years' employment elsewhere, and had been supervisors for 13 years. All but ten supervisors were men, and so the male gender will be employed throughout this book.[6]

Some assessment of how 'typical' this Birmingham sample is may be made by comparing it with other samples which have been drawn of supervisors in Britain (NIIP, 1951; Government Social Survey, 1968; BIM, 1976; Hill, 1976b; also unpublished data on 726 supervisors in the Nuffield College Social Mobility Project's 1972 sample of 10,309 employed males in England and Wales, supplied by John H. Goldthorpe). This comparison (details of which are given in Child *et al.*, 1978) suggests that the present sample is on the whole somewhat older and longer serving than is typical, which could reflect the fact that the two plants are in older, long-established, relatively low-technology industries. Only 16 per cent of the Birmingham sample possessed educational qualifications of any kind, and just ten per cent had more than an elementary or ordinary secondary school education. This educational level appears to be slightly lower than is usual for supervisors. Three-quarters (74 per cent) had fathers in manual working occupations, a proportion which compares closely with the Nuffield sample.

It was decided to use interviewing as the primary method of collecting information. This was dictated by (1) the size of the sample, (2) our aspiration to examine supervisory authority and influence across a range of decisions which might not all arise within the time-span that could be allocated to direct observation, and (3) the importance within our perspective of appreciating supervisors' expectations and perceptions, to which interviewing appeared to provide a suitable access. None the less, the problem of securing insights into how supervisors carried out and coped with their jobs which were both valid and capable of accounting for complex processes, suggested the complementing of interviewing by some direct observation.

The bulk of the investigation was conducted through two series of interviews, and further details of specific questions will be given as these are reported in subsequent chapters. The first interview with each supervisor covered his description of his job: priorities, authority and influence, job definition and formal procedures, contacts with other people on work-related matters and purely social contacts, degree of routine and variety in the job, assessment of performance, appropriate style of supervision and general opinions on the supervisor's role. On a separate occasion, each supervisor's manager was asked the same questions relating to the jobs of supervisors reporting to them; they were also asked to give a more comprehensive rating of each supervisor's performance. These first interviews normally lasted between 60 and 90 minutes. After a gap of some two to three months, we interviewed each supervisor again. Illness, retirement and death by this time had reduced total numbers from 156 to 149 supervisors. This second interview concentrated on how each supervisor saw his job in respect of possible conflicts, pressures, ambiguity, marginality and stress. It enquired about problems in the job and how supervisors coped with them. Questions also covered job satisfaction, personal orientations towards work, social and career background. Finally, there was an exploration of the supervisor's identification inside and outside the company, and of his views on unionism. This interview generally lasted about two hours, and it was considerably more open-ended than the first interview.

Some direct observation of workflows and supervisory activities had been carried out as a familiarization for the researchers prior to conducting the interviews. After the interview programme was completed, it was decided, with the active encouragement of supervisors in the food plant, to undertake direct observation of a small number of them in their work context. The objectives of the observations were: (1) to check the validity of information collected through the interviews on supervisors' priorities, authority and influence, style and problems; (2) to extend our appreciation of how supervisors actually go about their jobs; and (3) to clarify the ways in which supervisory behaviour may be a function of the work situation – especially the task system and manager's style – as opposed to being primarily a consequence of individual differences among supervisors. With these purposes in mind, 16 supervisors in the food plant were selected, so as to give coverage of different work situations and at the same time to provide four sets of comparisons where different supervisors shared similar work situations, plus four sets of paired comparisons where supervisors shared the same manager. Details of this sample are given in Appendix A. The method employed was for a member of the research team to accompany each supervisor everywhere during a series of half-day observations over a weekly period.

PART II

Supervisors' jobs

3

One and many supervisory roles

> ... the unwisdom of making general statements about foremen – about their work and its requirements, their responsibilities. (NIIP, *The Place of the Foreman in Management* (1957: 142))

The continued debate and perplexity over the role of the supervisor suggests that it has evolved as much through accident as through design. There have, admittedly, been some attempts to define supervision in the language of conscious organizational design, particularly by members of the Glacier project. For example, Brown (1960) defined the essence of supervision as performance of that component of the production job which the operator is unable to do without leaving his work station. Jaques (1976) developed this definition, regarding the supervisor as an assistant to a full manager who performs certain delegated functions without severing the manager's direct authority over employees. However, the operational translation of such definitions into the vagaries of organizational practice is far from simple.

The role of supervision might be described more realistically and substantively as that of dealing on the spot with operation contingencies unanticipated by management and its formally-designed procedures (Thurley and Wirdenius, 1973). Viewed from this perspective, the scope of supervisors' jobs will extend to those areas of *discretion* which traditionally comprised the occupationally-defined role of foremen and which have not been taken away by formal procedures, by the establishment of specialist staff functions, or by the creation of autonomous work groups. This description of supervision draws attention to what remains to first-line management authority and influence as a result of the gaps in formal procedure and the inability of other management arrangements to handle all operational requirements adequately. Though a 'negative' approach, it has the virtue of avoiding fixed *a priori* definitions of supervision. Instead, it draws attention to the need to investigate particular situations in detail.

This chapter examines the authority and influence which supervisors have in their jobs. It discusses some of the problems involved in assessing these characteristics, and it investigates how far the perceptions of supervisors agree with those of their managers in this area. A further question studied is whether the detail of supervisors' authority and influence patterns over a range of decisions can be satisfactorily simplified into a few overall measurements. We proceed on the assumption that authority and influence are key attributes for assessing the managerial content of supervisors' jobs, and in agreement with Patten (1968) that they should be included in any analysis of such jobs.

The relationship between supervisors' authority and their responsibility – in the sense of what they are accountable for – has also been central to the debate over whether they are 'men in the middle', 'on the margin', or somewhere else in modern industry. The man in the middle is caught in a position where his responsibilities exceed his authority. This argument maintains that supervisors' responsibilities are still significant, and that these may even have increased in more recent years (Boyd and Scanlon, 1965). In contrast, the man-on-the-margin thesis suggests that supervisors' responsibilities and authority have both declined to insignificant levels through their incorporation within the control of either management or the workforce. A more cautious view is that the nature of supervisory authority and responsibility has changed. Thus, while specialist departments and formal systems may have absorbed functions which traditionally came under supervisors' discretion, management still depends upon the co-operation of the supervisor at the point of operation, and upon his provision of adequate information, for the successful performance of those functions (NIIP, 1957).

Assessing authority and influence

In its common-language sense, 'authority' indicates formally designated and socially accepted command over subordinates. In the present context, we believe it is more useful to employ the term to refer to the extent of a supervisor's discretion in making decisions. There are two advantages in this approach. First, it allows the point of reference for an assessment of supervisors' jobs to be the whole system of tasks and relationships in which they may be exercising discretion, and not just their supervision of subordinates. Second, it moves away from authority simply being that which is formally designated, for supervisory discretion could also reflect informal accommodations and custom and practice.

Little research has been conducted into supervisory authority. Some of this has been concerned with the size of the supervisor's workgroup or the capital value of the machinery in his charge. Larger-sized workgroups or more expensive machinery have been taken as indicative, other things being equal, of greater authority. No attempt has been made, however, to use both these proxy variables to develop an overall scale of authority which would specify what size of workgroup represents equivalent authority to what value of machinery and plant. It has also been argued that the scope of authority should be measured either in terms of the organizational resources that an individual can commit (Crossman, 1969) or the opportunity costs of making a wrong decision (Alderson, 1976). The former tends to be limited to the formal budgetary process with which supervisors are not often involved, while the latter approach is difficult to apply empirically. A different method is therefore required for assessing supervisory authority.

The time-span approach

One alternative approach is based on the measurement of delegated formal authority. Time-span Analysis (TSA) arises from the view that work is made up of prescribed and discretionary elements (Jaques, 1956). The prescribed elements allow the job holder no choice: the duties must be carried out in the prescribed manner and subject to externally defined and observable control. In contrast, no one can know definitely if the discretionary elements of the job have been done as set out by the job holder's superior(s) until the superior reviews the result and accepts it as satisfactory or rejects it as sub-standard. No discretion is allowed to continue indefinitely without being subject to a superior's review. The Time-span of Discretion (TSD) of a job is defined as the longest period which can elapse before the superior can be sure that the job-holder has not been exercising marginally sub-standard discretion. TSD has been offered as a measure of the level of a person's work, and has been shown to be related to salary levels: the longer the TSD then the larger the salary.

There are, however, difficulties in the application of TSA. The use of TSD as a measure is based on a view of how organizations should be run, rather than how they are actually run: it depends on a clearly structured work situation (Hill, 1976a). It requires the superior to be explicit about the standards he defines for his subordinates and about the criteria to show marginally substandard use of discretion. But the superior is often uncertain (1) exactly what decisions he does expect his subordinates to make on their own initiative; and (2) how to review poor exercise of discretion. TSD is useful in emphasizing the discretionary authority of a job which can be too easily overlooked or oversimplified in a job description. But TSA runs into difficulty in practice because it is an attempt to formalize informal arrangements. TSA is not equipped to handle the intuitive understandings between the manager and his subordinates – instead it tries to make implicit communications explicit (Miller, 1976). At the level of personal interaction it is sometimes doubtful whether it is possible to distinguish between discretionary and prescribed elements (Gordon, 1976).

Time-span Analysis was an attempt to overcome the difficulty of applying traditional job evaluation techniques to a wide variety of jobs between the shopfloor and middle management, for example, supervisors, clerks and draughtsmen. It should not be forgotten that first-line supervisors in the Glacier Metal Company, where TSA was first developed, consistently rejected it as an acceptable alternative to job evaluation. TSA does not take into account such factors as the type of decisions or duties involved, the variety or number of kinds of decisions, their importance, the consequences of poor use of discretion, or the difficulty in exercising discretion (Beal, 1963; Jaques, 1967). TSA is only one facet of authority and responsibility.

The decision-making approach

An alternative way of looking at supervisors' authority is to concentrate on the formal right to make a decision (Lennerlöf, 1966). However, a supervisor's authority is only partly laid down in written form in job descriptions, procedures, and the like. Supervisors also have to rely on verbal statements from superiors and sometimes they have to infer their authority from their superior's behaviour. These cues are not without their contradictions and are open to different interpretations. Even when the formal authority system specifically denotes one individual as the decision maker on a given question, decisions in practice are usually formed by means of a complicated, continuing interaction process. The supervisor is not only aware of his formal authority to take decisions. He is also aware of the opportunities to affect others' decisions and of the influences to which he in turn is subject in making decisions: from, for example, workers, shop-stewards, other supervisors and managers. Complete formal authority is only an extreme value on the scale and it would be extremely limiting to focus just on this. To do justice to the concept of supervisory authority also requires reference to partial or shared authority, as well as to the idea of influence. It is possible for supervisors to influence decisions for which they have no recognized authority.

Abell (1975) similarly distinguishes between the formal right of decision making and influence over a decision. He regards influence as the more significant concept: he is critical of the assumption behind most of the work on decision making, that its location can be clearly defined. In reality, he maintains, 'decisions are characteristically taken collectively, either in formalized committees or in less institutionalized collective (including dyadic) interactions where influence and bargaining are a salient feature' (p. 16).

The approach we adopted was to look at supervisors' authority and influence over a range of decisions concerning the work of their sections. Our methodology was adapted from Lennerlöf. We asked each supervisor, and on a separate occasion the manager immediately above him, who decided each matter: whether it was the supervisor, his manager, a staff specialist, and so forth, or whether it was shared between various parties. For every decision, authority was coded on a five-point scale indicating whether the supervisor had sole or full authority (coded 5), whether he had no authority at all (coded 1), or whether he shared authority with others: shared with one other (coded 4), shared with two others (coded 3), or shared with more than two others (coded 2). Supervisors were also asked to rate their influence over each decision along a 21-point scale, even where they perceived that they had no authority for that decision. Thus, in contrast to Lennerlöf's method, authority and influence were treated as distinct phenomena.

The range of decisions examined was largely derived from Lennerlöf, who had started with 76 decisions grouped under 14

Table 3.1   *Decisions investigated*

Short title	Description
Systems management	
New work	Whether a new type of work is to be taken on to the section
Scheduling	Scheduling work waiting to be done
Methods	What specific operations/methods are involved in completing a job of work
Machine allocation	The choice of machines/equipment for particular jobs of work
Labour allocation	Allocating employees to machines and jobs of work
Job definitions	Specifying duties that make up employees' jobs
Manning	Manning levels of the section
Technical management	
Purchase equipment	Whether to purchase items of tools and equipment (not simply replacements)
Specify equipment	Specification of new tools and equipment
Specify plant	Specification of new plant and machinery
Requisitioning sundries	Requisitioning sundry materials
Materials quality	Whether quality of materials is acceptable
Work quality	Whether quality of work in the section is acceptable
Repair equipment	Whether repair work on tools and equipment is necessary
Repair plant	Whether repair work on plant and machinery is necessary
Accept repairs	Whether quality of repair work is satisfactory
Safety	How safety standards are to be maintained
People management	
Recruits	Whether to accept/reject applicants for a vacancy in the section
Assessment	Assessing probationary workers
Contingencies	Contingency adjustments of times/pay rates
Overtime	Allocating overtime to individual employees
Grading	Whether a worker should be upgraded/promoted

(Contd.)

Table 3.1 (*Contd.*)

Short title	Description
Training	Whether a worker should be given training
Style	How much discretion employees should be given
Discipline	Ways of maintaining discipline
Work study	Determining the time at which work study comes on to the section
Wage queries	Dealing with wage queries

headings. Using factor analysis, Lennerlöf constructed three authority indices, which he labelled production, technical and personnel. Most supervisory jobs contain (1) elements which are administrative, concerning planning, organization, the interpretation of rules and regulations, and other aspects of production systems; (2) elements which are technical, relying on specialized knowledge, skills and experience and (3) elements which are mainly concerned with handling people. Although it is possible to classify decisions in such terms, the potential interdependence of such decisions also has to be borne in mind.

Lennerlöf retained 58 of these decisions. They provided the main basis for our development of a similar schedule, which was refined down to a final list of 27 decisions, after preliminary investigations had provided evidence of their general applicability and comparability. This number of decisions appears at first sight to be low compared to the coverage of previous studies, such as Patten (1968) who used 107 'responsibilities' or Dowell and Wexley (1978) who covered 100 'work activities'. However, many of these activities are operational, requiring the expenditure of time rather than constituting a matter for decision. The 27 decisions are listed in Table 3.1, where they are grouped into the broad categories of systems management, technical management and people management.

These three categories are similar to Lennerlöf's three authority constructs. It can be argued that they point to the different skills a supervisor may be required to exercise (Mann, 1965). The categories also reflect research on the leadership behaviour of supervisors. The Ohio State University studies identified two dimensions of supervisory leadership: initiating structure and consideration. The

Michigan Survey Research Center identified two similar dimensions: production-centred and employee-centred leadership, with the production-centred subsequently being broken down into administrative and technical components. While there are these similarities in categorization, our investigation is concerned with the task functions of supervisors rather than with the socio-emotive leadership functions emphasized in the literature. Returning to the point made earlier about authority, supervisors are not just leaders of employees responsible for their morale and motivation; they are also concerned in the management of materials and equipment as well as in planning and control systems. This is not to suggest that the traditional emphasis on leadership is misplaced, rather that it has given insufficient emphasis to the system in which the supervisor has to work (Thurley and Wirdenius, 1973).

Supervisors' assessments of their authority and influence

Table 3.2 summarizes how supervisors taken as a whole rated their authority and influence for each of the 27 decisions. Decisions within each category are rank ordered by their authority score. There is close agreement in the rank ordering of decisions whether by authority or by influence, particularly within each category of decision.

Decisions for which supervisors tended to have sole authority were the allocation of employees to jobs of work, requisition of sundries, repair of equipment, style of supervision adopted, discipline, wages queries and allocating overtime. Several of these decisions fall into the people-management category, and it can be seen that the average authority score is highest for people decisions (3.1) and lowest for systems decisions (2.5). The pattern for influence scores is similar: most influence over people decisions (13.5) and least over systems decisions (11.3). When supervisors were asked to assess their influence over each of the three decision categories taken as a whole, they also tended to score people decisions as the area in which they had most influence (average: 17.2) and systems decisions as the area in which they had least influence (16.2). Although the general tendency to perceive greater authority and influence in the people-management area could be due to the decisions we selected for investigation, it is also to be expected from historical trends which have removed authority for systems and technical decisions from the supervisor rather more than authority for people decisions. Indeed, a considerable number of the books and training courses prepared for supervisors in the past few decades appear to conceive of their role as being almost totally concerned with human relations issues.

Decisions for which supervisors generally had little or no authority were in specifying new plant, deciding whether new work should come on to the section, determining manning levels, deciding whether workers should be upgraded, specifying new equipment, making contingency adjustments to pay and grading, vetting new recruits and purchasing new equipment.

Authority and influence appear to be related: the decisions for which supervisors had the most authority were the same decisions over which they had most influence: indeed correlations between authority and influence were moderately high for most decisions. The average correlation (r) between authority and influence was 0.64 but as $(r)^2$ is a better expression for accounting for the variance between two variables this means that on average approaching half (41 per cent) of the variance in influence between supervisors corresponds to the variation in authority between them. This suggests that although authority and influence are related, they are by no means identical.

The degree of correspondence between supervisors' authority and influence differed according to the level of authority. Authority and influence were most closely correlated not where most supervisors had sole authority, nor where most had no authority, but rather for the decisions in between, where the situation was mixed. A closer examination of these decisions, where the average authority scores fell between 2.0 and 4.0, revealed that the distribution of authority for these decisions tended to be bimodal: rather than the supervisor generally sharing authority for these decisions, many had sole authority, whilst many others had no authority. That is, authority for these decisions varied significantly between supervisors, and where this happened, authority and influence were closely associated. The decision where authority and influence were least closely related concerned safety matters: virtually all supervisors thought they had considerable influence over how safety was to be maintained but under half perceived that they had full authority on the matter.

These findings on authority and influence are broadly consistent with those from studies previously conducted in this country. The NIIP (1951) found that supervisors had considerable authority over the volume of production, quality of product, general discipline and allocation of overtime, but that supervisors had negligible authority

Table 3.2 *Authority and influence of supervisors* (N = 156)

Decisions	Authority (A) Mean	Authority (A) Standard deviation	Influence (I) Mean	Influence (I) Standard deviation	Correlation of (A) with (I)[a]	Full Authority %[b]	No Authority %[b]
Systems decisions							
Labour allocation	4.3	1.4	17.8	5.3	0.77	68.6	13.5
Job definition	2.7	1.8	12.6	7.6	0.74	28.8	50.6
Scheduling	2.6	1.8	12.5	7.3	0.68	25.0	51.3
Methods	2.6	1.8	11.3	7.5	0.76	28.2	55.1
Machine allocation	2.2	1.8	8.8	8.1	0.81	23.4	66.2
Manning	1.5	1.2	9.1	6.3	0.43	2.6	81.3
New work	1.3	0.8	6.8	6.2	0.43	1.9	90.4
Category average	2.5		11.3		0.66		
Technical decisions							
Safety	4.2	1.0	18.6	3.6	0.19	45.5	3.8
Requisition sundries	4.1	1.6	17.4	6.8	0.85	73.7	19.2
Repair equipment	3.9	1.5	16.6	6.7	0.78	55.8	19.2
Accept repairs	3.5	1.7	15.1	6.2	0.67	44.9	29.5
Work quality	3.3	1.6	15.6	5.8	0.63	30.1	30.1
Repair plant	2.8	1.8	13.7	7.2	0.71	27.7	46.5
Materials quality	2.5	1.7	11.8	7.2	0.68	17.9	53.2
Purchase equipment	1.9	1.5	8.6	7.6	0.68	12.5	75.7
Specify equipment	1.6	1.4	7.4	7.0	0.69	8.7	78.5
Specify plant	1.2	0.7	4.7	4.9	0.28	0.7	92.5
Category average	2.9		13.0		0.62		

People decisions

Style	4.3	1.4	17.1	6.0	0.69	73.5	12.9
Discipline	4.3	1.2	18.2	4.7	0.36	67.3	8.3
Wage queries	4.2	1.4	16.8	6.8	0.87	72.4	13.5
Overtime	4.1	1.5	16.7	6.4	0.77	62.2	16.7
Training	3.1	1.8	14.5	7.2	0.73	34.6	39.1
Assessment	3.1	1.8	13.6	7.4	0.68	30.8	39.7
Work study	2.7	1.7	10.9	8.2	0.85	23.1	49.4
Recruits	1.9	1.5	8.7	7.5	0.63	12.3	73.4
Contingencies	1.8	1.6	8.9	8.0	0.59	12.9	75.5
Grading	1.7	1.3	9.2	7.2	0.44	5.8	79.4
Category average	3.1		13.5		0.66		

(a) Pearson product-moment correlations; all entries reach or exceed the five per cent level of confidence. Although the authority scale is not strictly an equal interval scale and some distributions are bimodal, comparison with the use of non-parametric statistics indicated that the same basis for interpretation is provided by parametric tests. These are used for their convenience and flexibility in order to offer a general indication of strength and direction of association.

(b) These percentages differ slightly from those given in Child *et al.*, (1980), Table 2, because answers of 'the decision does not arise in my case' type were further investigated and generally recoded as 'no authority'.

Authority coded as: 5 = supervisor has sole or full authority; 4 = supervisor shares authority with one other; 3 = supervisor shares authority with two others; 2 = supervisor shares authority with more than two others; 1 = supervisor has no authority. *Influence* coded on a scale between 1 = supervisor has no influence at all on the decision and 21 = supervisor can make the decision entirely on his own.

over design or alterations in design, purchasing materials or tools, costing and fixing or altering rates of payment. The BIM (1976) found that supervisors had some authority over safety, quality control, materials handling, allocating jobs to workers, discipline and grievance handling, but that supervisors had little authority over production scheduling, the introduction of new working methods, maintenance of plant and equipment, controlling for costs, or recruiting and promoting workers. The BIM emphasized that the supervisors' key tasks of achieving output and quality targets, meeting cost budgets and ensuring that their sections are suitably manned were those which presented supervisors with the most difficulty. They were also the very areas where the supervisor was least likely to have been consulted by management in establishing criteria and parameters. Likewise, in the present study, the decisions for which supervisors had little or no authority concern matters which determine the main parameters of operations within their sections. This is a significant comment on whether these supervisors can be said to have managerial control over their sections, and it recalls the long-term decline that has taken place in their authority.

The burden of supervisory responsibility

Many supervisors, however, also made the point that, whatever the trend with respect to their authority, the burden of responsibility they were expected to carry had increased in recent years; in particular, their range of duties had widened, for example:

> 'The pressure and responsibility is greater now than five years ago as the managers are becoming bogged down in paperwork.'

> 'The pressure is building up, the staff has got smaller, so we've got more responsibility.'

> 'The job used to be one of just disciplining the men, now there are a whole host of extra responsibilities which the supervisor carries. I don't mind this extra responsibility as it makes the job more interesting.'

So, just recently, supervisory responsibilities appear to have increased at the two Birmingham sites. Supervisors in other studies have reported similar sentiments (e.g. Nichols and Beynon, 1977). The apparent discrepancy between a historical decline in authority and a short-term increase in responsibilities indicates the need to

46

distinguish between the two concepts, with responsibility denoting duties to which accountability is attached. For example, the increased formalization of various production procedures derives from management's need for control and accountability; if as a result of increased formalization supervisors are involved in more procedures, they might perceive this as an increase in responsibility, though it would probably limit their autonomy or authority. Similarly, if the criteria for assessing supervisors were extended, this might also be viewed as an increase in the scope of their responsibilities. One can thus appreciate how the man-in-the-middle thesis argues that supervisors' responsibility exceeds their authority.

Further comment on how they saw the scope of supervision is provided by the supervisors' evaluations of statements about the supervisor's function. These are listed in Appendix 3.1. Each supervisor was asked to rate how true the statement was in respect of his own firm and also whether he thought the statement *ought* to be true. The largest discrepancy between the descriptive and normative evaluations comes with the statement that the supervisor is a line manager in every respect, which supervisors clearly wanted to see translated into reality more than it was. Taken as a whole, the supervisors tended to see their actual function as primarily involving organizing and looking after their employees, and equally co-ordinating people from different departments who affected the work in their sections. Looking after employees was also seen to involve resolving conflicts on the shopfloor. These were all functions of which supervisors approved, and indeed generally wished to perform to a fuller extent.

Managers' assessments of supervisors' authority and influence

The supervisors' authority and influence was also assessed by 41 of their immediate superiors (managers), who answered exactly the same questions as had been put to the supervisors. Their overall replies, scored in the same way as the supervisors' responses, are summarized in Appendix 3.2. The managers' replies only cover 131 of the 156 supervisors, since not every relevant manager agreed to be interviewed. It should also be borne in mind that most managers took the view that each of the supervisors under them possessed similar authority and similar influence, and they answered accordingly.

The general pattern in the managers' replies is similar to the supervisors' own responses, which were set out in Table 3.2. Managers as a whole gave a comparable rank ordering of supervisory authority within each category – out of 27 decisions, only 6 were placed in a different rank order. Managers did, however, tend to assess the authority of the supervisors under them more conservatively than did the supervisors themselves. The managers' mean scores for each category of authority and influence follow the same ordering as supervisors: highest for people decisions and least for systems decisions. Managers therefore share with supervisors a tendency to view the latter's authority primarily in terms of people management, but it is in these decisions about people that there is most disagreement between managers and supervisors over the issue of authority. In fact for eight of these ten decisions the difference between managers' and supervisors' assessments is unlikely to have occurred by chance. This indicates either that supervisory authority for people decisions is particularly ambiguous, or that these decisions are the focus of conflict between managers and supervisors over the latter's role. Traditionally, relations with the workgroup have been an area of contention for the supervisor, placed as he is between management and the shopfloor.

Boyd and Jensen (1972) conducted a questionnaire survey of 135 companies in the American midwest, which attempted to ascertain whether disagreements existed between first-line production supervisors and their immediate superiors over the extent of the supervisors' authority. This covered 39 decision situations and there was, on average, disagreement about 20 of these. Most disagreement arose over the authority that supervisors had in dealing with matters of maintenance, quality control, discipline and safety. There is some similarity here to the findings of the present study. The point of greatest disagreement between supervisors and their immediate supervisors concerns the supervisors' authority over disciplinary matters, and there are also substantial differences over maintenance (the repair of equipment), co-ordination with work study, and safety matters. Discipline and safety have been the subject of legislation which places increased constraints on the use and control of labour: the Employment Protection Act 1975 and the Health and Safety at Work Act 1974. The discussion which surrounded the implementation of this legislation has probably prompted management to reduce supervisors' authority in these areas. The two plants studied had formal procedures for discipline and safety which limited supervisory authority, although at the same time many supervisors claimed that safety was an area where their responsibilities had been increased. It is also interesting to recall (from Table 3.2) that safety and discipline are two areas where supervisors' assessments of their authority and influence were least closely related. The same pattern was found for managers' assessments of supervisory authority and influence in the areas of safety and discipline. Managers assessed supervisors as having somewhat more influence than authority over these decisions.

Managers appeared to distinguish between the concepts of authority and influence more readily than supervisors. Managers' rank ordering of decisions by supervisors' influence differs from their rank ordering by supervisors' authority, and also the degree of correlation between authority and influence is much lower for managers' scores. Managers appear more able to distinguish between the system of authority and the less formal system of influence. Whereas supervisor–manager disagreement over authority was focused on people decisions, their disagreements regarding influence are more evenly spread across all categories of decision. Some of the disagreements concerning influence reflect disagreements about authority, for example, over the repair of equipment, safety and training, but other disagreements concerning influence are not so related, as, for example, over job definition and equipment specification.

It is therefore questionable whether there is agreement between managers and supervisors over the supervisory role. A comparison of their rank orderings of decisions by supervisory authority and influence gives similar results. But this comparison is of the mean scores for each group taken as a whole. In contrast, the correspondence between the assessments for each decision made by each supervisor and his manager was very low.[1] This low degree of correspondence suggests that, taken as a whole, managers and supervisors might broadly agree about the role and functions of the supervisor, but at the level of individual manager – supervisor working relationships the extent of agreement is very limited.

Managers were also asked for their views on supervisory functions and these are summarized in Appendix 3.3. Managers see the supervisors' function primarily as that of a co-ordinator, a line manager, and a conflict resolver. They express somewhat less doubt about the supervisor being a line manager than the supervisors themselves, which must be a reflection of managerial ideology on this issue when one takes account of their low assessment of supervisors' managerial authority. The only major difference of opinion about actual functions concerns the role of a specialist organizing and looking after workers in his section, to which managers give less emphasis. This is also reflected in what supervisors and managers think the supervisors' job ought to be. Managers are less likely than supervisors to think that the latter should be specialists whose main concern is organizing and looking after their workers.

The large variation in supervisors' authority and influence

It was noted earlier that for many decisions there was considerable variation in the levels of authority and influence supervisors said they enjoyed. One of the possible explanations for this variation is that it is due to differences between the two sites, which in turn might reflect differences in technology or organization. Alternatively, variations in supervisory authority and influence might reflect the distinction between production and non-production supervisors. These possibilities are now examined in broad terms, and the following chapter pursues in some depth the relevance of factors such as technology and organizational context.

There were site differences which were unlikely to have occurred by chance – details are given in Appendix 3.4. Supervisors in the engineering plant reported having more authority and influence over many of the systems decisions, whereas supervisors in the food plant tended to report more control over technical decisions. These differences between the two sites do accord with some of the variation between supervisors, but only to a certain extent. For when decisions are examined site by site, variations in supervisors' authority and influence remain. In discussion sessions following the completion of our study, supervisors and managers both agreed that the extent of supervisors' authority did vary substantially within their own site. In fact, supervisors generally expressed their dissatisfaction with the extent of this variation. The decisions where variation in supervisory authority was greatest in both plants concerned scheduling, methods, specifying employees' duties, repairing plant, accepting repairs, training and the commencement of work study.[2]

There were also some differences in authority and influence, unlikely to have occurred by chance, between production and non-production supervisors – these are given in Appendix 3.5. Non-production supervisors, who are predominantly in maintenance and services such as quality control, generally have more authority and influence over systems and technical decisions, whereas production supervisors tend to have more authority and influence over people decisions.

Our direct observations at the food site tend to support these contrasts. Production supervisors frequently took the initiative in resolving queries about pay from their operatives on individual bonus systems. The supervisors often negotiated adjustments to pay which accompanied changes of work within the section. They dealt with minor disciplinary and grievance matters. Production supervisors' authority over the initiation of work study was not directly observed, but in so far as it is similar to their authority over other staff activities, the observations indicated that most of the production supervisors themselves took the initiative in inviting staff into their sections as and when problems arose. The non-production supervisors whom we observed, particularly in maintenance, had greater specialized knowledge than their managerial superiors. They were left to organize their men and the order of work much as they saw fit, and they often dealt directly with outside suppliers of equipment. What we observed was therefore consistent with the differences between the two groups of supervisors in their assessments of authority and influence. However, as with analysis of each site, examination of authority and influence within each group indicated that variation still remained and this was echoed by the comments which supervisors made in subsequent discussion sessions.

Analyses of variance were conducted to see how much of the overall variation in supervisors' authority and influence could be accounted for by site and by production/non-production categories jointly. For most decisions the amount of variation so explained was under ten per cent. The greater part of the variation in supervisory authority and influence remains to be explained and this will be the subject of Chapter 4.

Can the assessment of supervisors' authority and influence be simplified?

The variation and general complexity in the pattern of supervisors' authority and influence does not appear propitious for any attempt to simplify the picture down to a few indicators. Simplification, which is usually achieved through aggregating the answers for specific items (in this case individual decisions), always means losing detail. This detail may actually constitute very relevant information for the manager or organizational designer who is thinking about the specification of supervisors' jobs. Nevertheless, simplification would have the attraction of permitting bolder and less complex profiles of supervisory jobs to be constructed and would ease the process of making broad comparisons.

The question therefore arises whether our findings suggest that it is possible to simplify the assessments of supervisory authority and influence through some form of aggregation. The answer to this question depends on (1) how far the content of the aggregations is valid and (2) whether they are internally consistent (have internal reliability). If aggregation were based upon the categories of systems, technical and people-management decisions, the equivalence of these categories to the findings of previous research would suggest some degree of content validity. Tests for internal consistency between the decision data entering into an aggregated measure are available, and the formula we have adopted is that for the K–R 8 coefficient (Kuder and Richardson, 1937). In the early stages of constructing aggregated measures a modest internal reliability coefficient of between 0.5 and 0.6 may be considered encouraging (Nunnally, 1978).

The K–R 8 coefficients for different aggregations of supervisors' assessments of their authority and influence are given in Appendix 3.6 – first for aggregating across all decisions, and then for aggregating decisions in the systems, technical and people-management categories respectively. The results suggest that it is possible to perform these aggregations acceptably on statistical grounds, particularly in the case of the scores for supervisors' influence.

The aggregations for each of the three decision categories would be further confirmed, and of much more practical value, if they turned out to reflect different domains or dimensions of supervisory authority and influence: that is, if they are not highly related to each other. This was examined and the results are set out in Table 3.3. The three categories of authority (systems, technical, people) are not highly correlated. The three equivalent categories of influence are only modestly correlated. The aggregated measures of authority and influence within each category are highly correlated. This patterning indicates that aggregation into the three categories of systems, technical and people-management decisions, provides reasonably discrete measures of supervisors' authority and influence. It also suggests that distinctive profiles can be constructed among the

Table 3.3 *Inter-correlations of aggregated measures of super-visors' authority and influence (N = 156 supervisors)*

	1	2	3	4	5	6	7
(1) Systems authority	–						
(2) Technical authority	0.08	–					
(3) People authority	0.10	0.19	–				
(4) Overall authority	0.57	0.66	0.70	–			
(5) Systems influence	0.79	0.06	0.13	0.48	–		
(6) Technical influence	0.17	0.71	0.15	0.53	0.26	–	
(7) People influence	0.21	0.05	0.75	0.55	0.30	0.26	–
(8) Overall influence	0.52	0.37	0.51	0.72	0.70	0.69	0.76

Pearson product-moment correlation coefficients. Coefficients greater than .18 attain the 99 per cent level of confidence.

Correlations between the three category sub-measures of influence (nos. 5, 6 and 7 above) and the supervisor's own general estimate of influence in the area covered by the category are: systems decisions ($r = 0.33$), technical decisions ($r = 0.35$), people decisions ($r = 0.49$).

supervisors we studied, since those who have relatively high authority over systems management decisions will not necessarily have high technical or people-management authority, and so on. The fact that the category measures are not negatively correlated also indicates that one area or base of authority (or influence) does not normally compensate for a lack of authority (or influence) over other areas of decision making.

Conclusion

There was considerable variation between supervisors' jobs when these were assessed by reference to authority and influence. This variation was not simply a reflection of different sites or categories of supervisor; it occurred within sites and within categories. There was also evidence of considerable disagreement between individual supervisors and their own managers over the extent of the super-visors' authority and influence, though the picture is clouded by the managers' tendency not to discriminate in their answers between individual supervisors. It was generally agreed by both parties, however, that supervisory authority did not extend to determining most of the key parameters or boundary conditions of running their sections: this was especially true for production supervisors. Serious doubts have therefore to be raised as to whether supervisors do occupy a managerial role, and indeed some organizational analysts urge that a clear distinction be made between managerial and supervisory roles (e.g. Brunel Institute of Organization and Social Studies (BIOSS), 1977).

There is always the possibility, of course, that although perceptions of the supervisor's job varied between individual supervisors, and to a lesser extent between individual managers, the actual job of the supervisor was in fact quite uniform within each site. Against this is the point that if perceptions about the job do vary so much between individuals it is very unlikely that their behaviour in the job will be similar, or indeed that the job is effectively subject to any standardized organizational definition. The so-called 'action frame of reference' in studies of industrial behaviour has in fact drawn attention to the ways in which what a person does in his job is influenced by how he personally interprets his 'objective' situation (e.g. Silverman, 1970). Moreover, reference to our direct observations of supervisors at work, in Chapters 4 and 5, will indicate considerable differences in how they carried out their jobs.

It would be difficult to conclude from our findings so far that the supervisory role has been effectively or even intentionally designed as such. In fact, in the food plant, senior management was attempting to initiate a supervisory job evaluation scheme, but was experiencing considerable difficulties in finding a method which supervisors could accept as realistic. This attempt points to the concern which both managers and supervisors felt about the variation in supervisors' jobs across the organization: management because it suggested lack of control and possible inefficiencies, supervisors because they believed it led to anomalies. Certainly, the variability in supervisory roles within each plant, even within a category such as production, poses a problem which Thurley and Wirdenius (1973) have identified: the collapse of the supervisor's role as a specific and recognizable set of functions and relationships, and the consequent decline of consciousness about the identity of, and need for, that role. They argue that the supervisor's ability to deal with contingencies and crises, which several commentators see as his main function, requires self-confidence, adequate skills and a sense of detachment from pressures, which can only be built on the basis of feeling secure about his role: 'If supervisors do not know who they are and what they are doing then it is difficult for them to deal with the unexpected.' (Thurley and Wirdenius, 1973, p. 218).

The question remains, however, whether it is realistic to attempt to provide this role security through definition in formal terms. Existing stereotypes clearly do not account for the variation in supervisors' jobs, even though they may point to certain elements which are generally present, such as an imbalance between responsibility and authority. Further understanding of the scope for designing supervisory roles requires investigation of whether it is possible to identify factors which shape these roles, and which can therefore be treated as design contingencies. This is the subject of the next chapter.

Appendix 3.1 *Supervisors' evaluations of supervisory functions (N = 155)*

| Statements about supervisory functions (in shortened form)[a] | Supervisors' evaluations[b] Mean scores | | |
	Actually is (1)	Ought to be (2)	Difference[c] (2) − (1)
A co-ordinator of people from other departments who affect the work in his section	5.6	5.8	0.2
A specialist organizing and looking after workers	5.6	5.9	0.3**
A key figure in resolving conflicts on the shopfloor	5.2	5.6	0.4**
A line manager in every respect	5.2	6.3	1.1**
A mediator between the two sides of industry	4.7	4.9	0.2
A trouble-shooter	3.6	3.5	− 0.1

(a) These six statements are from a total of twelve on 'the supervisor's role today' which are listed in Appendix B. The other statements concern the supervisor's status and position in the firm.

(b) Each supervisor was asked to indicate on a seven-point scale how true each statement was for supervisors in his firm (1 = definitely not true; 7 = absolutely true) and whether he thought each statement should be the case (1 = definitely should not be; 7 = definitely should be).

(c) The difference is what the supervisors feel their situation ought to be *less* what they perceive it actually to be. Therefore a positive difference indicates that the supervisors wish that the statement were more the case than it actually is.

** $p < 0.01$, student's t-test.

Appendix 3.2 Managers' assessments of supervisors' authority and influence (41 managers assessing 131 supervisors)

| Decisions | Managers' scores | | | | Difference: manager minus supervisor[a] | | Managers giving supervisors | |
| | Authority | | Influence | | Authority | Influence | full authority[b] | no authority[b] |
	Mean	Standard deviation	Mean	Standard deviation	Mean	Mean	%	%
Systems decisions								
Labour allocation	4.4	1.3	17.3	4.9	0.1	−1.0	74.0	11.0
Job definition	2.5	1.8	9.5	7.0	−0.3	−3.3**	26.0	58.3
Scheduling	2.7	1.7	11.8	6.8	0.1	−0.8	21.1	50.0
Methods	2.4	1.6	9.6	6.3	−0.3	−2.1*	15.7	55.1
Machine allocation	2.1	1.7	9.5	7.0	−0.3	−0.6	20.0	69.6
Manning	1.4	1.0	8.5	5.8	−0.1	−0.4	0.0	83.5
New work	1.1	0.5	5.5	5.2	−0.1	−1.1	0.0	94.9
Category average	2.4		10.2		−0.1	−1.3		
Technical decisions								
Safety	3.5	1.3	16.7	3.6	−0.7**	−2.0**	22.9	16.5
Requisition sundries	4.3	1.4	18.1	5.5	0.1	0.3	77.2	14.2
Repair equipment	3.0	1.9	12.0	9.0	−0.9**	−4.9**	40.2	46.5
Accept repairs	3.3	1.7	14.3	6.7	−0.2	−0.9	33.1	33.9
Work quality	3.1	1.7	16.2	4.8	−0.2	0.7	33.1	36.2
Repair plant	2.7	1.9	14.9	7.2	−0.1	1.2	29.7	53.2
Materials quality	2.6	1.7	13.7	7.0	0.2	2.1*	23.6	49.6

(*Contd.*)

57

Appendix 3.2 (*Contd.*)

Purchase equipment	1.4	1.0	5.1	5.4	−0.4*	−3.3**	2.4	88.2
Specify equipment	1.3	0.9	4.8	5.0	−0.2	−2.6**	0.0	89.0
Specify plant	1.2	0.6	5.6	5.4	−0.3	0.8	0.0	93.7
Category average	2.6		12.1		−0.3	−0.9		
People decisions								
Style	3.7	1.6	14.9	6.3	−0.6**	−2.4**	40.3	23.4
Discipline	3.2	1.3	17.3	4.0	−1.2**	−0.9	30.1	4.8
Wage queries	4.7	0.7	17.2	6.8	0.4***	0.5	67.1	4.1
Overtime	4.3	1.4	16.2	5.5	0.2	−0.3	67.7	14.2
Training	2.4	1.7	11.2	7.4	−0.6**	−3.2**	15.0	57.5
Assessment	2.7	1.8	12.7	7.6	−0.4	−1.4	24.4	51.2
Work study	2.1	1.5	9.6	7.2	−0.7**	−2.2**	11.9	57.8
Recruits	1.5	1.2	7.6	7.1	−0.5**	−2.0**	6.3	82.7
Contingencies	1.4	1.2	10.3	7.3	−0.4**	1.2	7.1	88.2
Grading	1.3	0.9	9.8	6.4	−0.4**	0.4	9.4	89.0
Category average	2.7		12.7		−0.4	−1.0		

(*a*) Difference = manager minus supervisor: thus a negative difference indicates where managers score supervisory authority or influence lower than do supervisors.

(*b*) These percentages differ slightly from those given in Child *et al.* (1980), Table 2 because answers of 'the decision does not arise in his [the supervisor's] case' type were further investigated and generally re-coded as 'no authority'.

* $p < 0.05$, student's t-test; ** $p < 0.01$, student's t-test

Appendix 3.3 *Managers' evaluations of supervisory functions*

Statements about[a] supervisory functions (in shortened form)	Mean scores			
	Managers' attitudes[b]		Differences between supervisors and managers[c]	
	Actually	Ought to be	Actually	Ought to be
A co-ordinator of people from other departments who affect the work in his section	5.3	5.9	− 0.16	− 0.06
A specialist organizing and looking after workers	4.6	4.8	0.98**	1.20**
A key figure in resolving conflicts on the shopfloor	5.1		− 0.19	− 0.20
A line manager in every respect	5.3	5.7	− 0.26	0.54**
A mediator between the two sides of industry	4.8	4.8	0.06	0.16
A trouble-shooter	3.6	3.3	0.26	0.26

(*a*) Statements are listed in the same order as Appendix 3.1. and are given in full in Appendix B.

(*b*) For scoring, see footnote (*b*) to Appendix 3.1.

(*c*) Difference equals supervisor minus manager (computed for 128 supervisors). A positive difference indicates that supervisors believe the statement to be actually more true than do managers, or that supervisors feel more strongly that it ought to be true than do their managers.

**$p < 0.01$, student's t-test

Appendix 3.4 *Decisions for which supervisors reported having more authority and influence in comparison with supervisors at the other site*

Engineering site	Food site
Decisions for which engineering site supervisors reported having more authority or influence than food site supervisors	Decisions for which food site supervisors reported having more authority or influence than engineering site supervisors

Authority
Machine allocation**
Job definitions**
Methods*
Safety*
Requisition sundries*
Recruits**
Contingencies**
Assessment*

Authority
Manning**
Purchase equipment**
Specify equipment**
Work quality**
Repair plant**
Materials quality*
Specify plant*
Training*
Style*

Influence
Machine allocation**
Job definitions**
Scheduling*
Methods*
Requisition sundries**
Repair equipment*
Accept repairs*
Recruits**
Assessment**
Contingencies**
Grading*

Influence
Purchase equipment**
Repair plant**
Work quality*
Discipline*
Style*

Levels of confidence for differences in mean authority scores are given only as very broad indicators, since the nature of the measure and some distributions do not satisfy the requirements for a t-test. However, application of the non-parametric Mann-Whitney U-test for differences in mean authority scores gives very similar results to the t-test. The general correspondence between authority and influence indicators may also be noted.
*$p < 0.05$ student's t-test; **$p < 0.01$, student's t-test.

Appendix 3.5 *Differences in reported authority and influence as between production and non-production supervisors*

Production supervisors	Non-production supervisors
Decisions for which production supervisors reported having more authority or influence than non-production supervisors	Decisions for which non-production supervisors reported having more authority or influence than production supervisors

Authority	*Authority*
Wage queries**	New work**
Work study**	Scheduling**
Contingencies*	Methods**
Training*	Specify equipment**
Safety*	Specify plant**
	Work quality**
	Materials quality*
	Purchase equipment*
Influence	*Influence*
Wage queries**	Scheduling**
Contingencies*	Methods**
Work study*	Purchase equipment**
	Specify equipment**
	Specify plant**
	Work quality**
	Repair of equipment*

Levels of confidence for differences in mean authority scores are given only as very broad indicators, since the nature of the measure and some distributions do not satisfy the requirements for a t-test. However, application of the non-parametric Mann-Whitney U-test for differences in mean authority scores gave very similar results to the t-tests. The general correspondence between authority and influence indicators may also be noted.
*$p < 0.05$, student's t-test; **$p < 0.01$, student's t-test.

Appendix 3.6   *Aggregated measures of supervisors' authority and influence: coefficients of internal reliability*

| | K–R 8 Coefficients | |
Aggregated measure	Authority	Influence
All decisions	0.62	0.76
All systems decisions	0.72	0.75
All technical decisions	0.59	0.71
All people-management decisions	0.63	0.70

If the decision on manning levels is omitted from the systems authority aggregation, then the K–R 8 coefficient has a value of 0.76. If omitted from the systems influence aggregation, the K–R 8 coefficient has a value of 0.77. If decisions on plant specification and safety are omitted from the technical authority aggregation, then the K–R 8 coefficient has a value of 0.63. If omitted from the technical influence aggregation, the K–R 8 coefficient's value falls to 0.69.

4

The shaping of supervisors' jobs

> The logic of the relationship between task and operating pattern seems so compelling that it is difficult to think of alternative modes of tackling it [the production task]. (Reeves and Turner, *Administrative Science Quarterly*, 17, 1972, p. 94.)

The previous chapter showed how, in certain areas of decision making, the discretionary content of supervisors' jobs varied considerably. Broad distinctions such as location in one site rather than in the other, or supervising production rather than non-production sections, accounted for some but not much of this variation. A closer analysis seemed to be required. This chapter examines in more detail how far the variation in supervisors' authority and influence can be accounted for by the technological or organizational context in which supervisors work. This recalls the reference in Chapter 1 to Edwards' (1979) analysis of how, historically, management has tended to substitute technology and formal organization, as controls over workplace behaviour, for the older mode of control which had allowed supervisory authority a relatively free rein. The relevance of personal characteristics entering into the relationship between supervisors and their managers will also be examined.

Technology, task system and supervisors' jobs

In making the strong statement which opens this chapter, Reeves and Turner were drawing upon their study of the consequences manufacturing technology had for the way in which work is organized and for individual job roles, including those of first-line supervisors. They studied two batch firms and one mass-production firm. They concluded that the complexity and uncertainty inherent in batch production, which made accurate planning impossible, shaped the role played by supervisors. The management of the batch production process had to rely on shortages programmes: production supervisors were expected to provide relevant progress information and they also had to spend a considerable amount of their time expediting work. Because of the problems of matching the load on the factory with its capacity in the batch systems, supervisors had continually to employ strategies to deal with overloads and underloads. In these situations the supervisor 'serves as a backstop, taking care of what has been left unplanned' (Reeves and Turner, 1972: 92). In the mass-production firm, supervisors did not have to engage in shopfloor re-scheduling or short-term adaptations other than those designed to improve quality.

The Reeves and Turner study draws out associations between the technology of production plants and the activities which assumed prominence in supervisors' jobs. Other studies reporting variation in supervisors' jobs and behaviour between different sites have also pointed to a corresponding variation in work contexts (NIIP, 1957; Thurley and Hamblin, 1963; Thurley and Wirdenius, 1973). Technology has generally been singled out as the major determinant of the supervisor's role within these contexts. Woodward (1958, 1965), for example, reported that the average span of control of first-line supervisors was generally highest in mass production, lower in unit production and lowest in process technologies. Child and Mansfield (1972) reported similar findings which suggested that the supervisor's role was a function of the organizational structure, which in turn was partly a function of technology. Yanouzas (1964) drew attention to technological factors when accounting for differences in supervisors' behaviour within a jobbing and a continuous-assembly plant. Hill (1976b), in a non-manufacturing context, also reported systematic differences between dockland supervisors involved in different types of dock work, whether in the sheds, on the ships or in container operations. This view of technology as a determinant of supervisory jobs and activities clearly supports the idea that the nature of supervision is fashioned by the general parameters of each work organization.

Studies of this kind adopted a broad definition of 'technology', which implied a correspondence between a whole work organization unit, such as a production plant, and a characteristic technological system. Reeves and Turner's contrast between batch and mass production, for instance, derives from Woodward's (1965) categorization of complete production systems along a scale from process, mass production, batch production, to unit production. Woodward suggested that each main type of production system will tend to involve its own distinctive relationships between marketing, development and production functions. Analysis at this level is valuable in pointing to the probable general differences in the role of supervision when comparing productive units as a whole. Chapter 9 will, in fact, develop this insight, which also serves as a reminder that the two Birmingham plants we investigated only represent one category of production system – batch production.

This broad view of technology naturally runs the risk of over-simplification. Fletcher (1969), for example, studied supervisors in a factory which would be classified as unit production in Woodward's scheme. Yet he found that there were elements of large batch and even mass production in certain sections. Within each of the two Birmingham plants there was a considerable range of technological and workflow configurations. For example, production in the engineering plant ranged from the pressing of components, where there could be batch changes every few minutes, to assembly, where some lines were hardly ever changed. In the food plant, some standard chocolate bars were mass produced, while some confectionery was made in small batches. These differences are masked by a broad plant-wide designation of technology, yet they may be relevant to understanding the variation in the jobs of those who supervise the different production sections.

The concept of 'task' is particularly useful for an exploration of the ways in which the work performed and the technology employed in different sections can contribute to variations between the jobs of the section supervisors. Abell and Mathew (1973) defined task as 'a process whereby a distribution of inputs is converted (transformed) into a constrained distribution of outputs by the application of a technology (ies)' (p. 165). The concept can be applied at various levels of organization, including that of individual sections and their supervisors. It has the further virtue of drawing attention to the fact that the work which is done, and how it is done, are not simply functions of the technology used, but are also affected by the way the work is organized and controlled. Technology at the section level refers to the plant, equipment and tools employed.

There is broad agreement among investigators who have used the concept of task that two characteristics of major significance are

(1) the variability of tasks, namely the number of exceptions en-
countered in the work, and (2) the difficulty of tasks, namely the
degree to which the work can be analysed and its outcome predicted
(cf. Mathew, 1975; Van de Ven and Ferry, 1980). These dimensions
are very similar to those contained within Perrow's (1967, 1970)
fourfold classification of what he called technology, but which would
be more appropriately called 'task systems'. This is shown in Figure
4.1. Perrow then used this classification to suggest how supervisory
situations were likely to vary according to task systems (Figure 4.2).

In the 'non-routine' situation, characterized both by the need to
deal with many exceptions and by difficulty in analysing the work,
supervisors' discretion and power are predicted to be high. Co-
ordination of activities is by means of mutual information exchange
(feedback) between supervisors and those doing the work rather than
by advance planning laid down by higher levels of management. Not
only do supervisors have a hierarchical dependence on management;
in this task system management is predicted to depend heavily upon
supervisors as well. In the 'craft' situation, characterized by few
exceptions and difficulty in analysing the work, supervision is
predicted to retain high discretion and power, to co-ordinate through
feedback, but the degree of mutual dependence with management is
now lower. In the 'engineering' situation, supervisors are predicted to
have low discretion and power, co-ordination is on the basis of
planning, and supervisors have little interdependence with management. The 'routine' situation is predicted to be similar for supervisors, though Perrow suggests that the ability of senior management

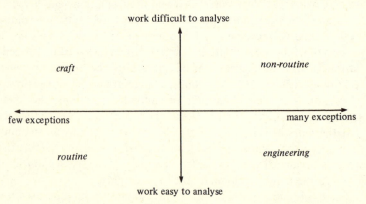

Figure 4.1 A classification of task systems. *Source*: Perrow (1970: 78).

Discretion* (authority)	Power* (influence)	Method of co-ordination	Interdependence between supervisor and management	Discretion	Power	Method of co-ordination	Interdependence between supervisor and management
High	High	Mutual feedback	Low	High	High	Mutual feedback	High
			craft	*non-routine*			
			routine	*engineering*			
Low	Low	Planning	Low	Low	Low	Planning	Low

* What Perrow called 'discretion' is reasonably equivalent to what we are calling 'authority', and his concept of 'power' is similar to our concept of 'influence'.

Figure 4.2 Possible variations of supervision in different task systems. *Source*: Perrow (1970: 81).

to control highly routine and well-understood work now reduces the discretion of middle management as well. Perrow argues that most supervisors fall into the routine situation.

We inquired about task system characteristics which we thought would be relevant to the variability and difficulty of tasks as defined above. One part of this enquiry was into relatively objective features of the task systems in supervisors' sections; the other part, which is described later, asked for supervisors' subjective perceptions of task characteristics. The task variables on which objective information was collected in both plants are listed in Table 4.1. They are indicators primarily of task variability, with only the proportion of intrinsically new work taken on over the past year having a bearing upon task difficulty. We were not, in fact, successful in finding comparative objective indicators of task difficulty and all our measures which bear directly on this facet rely upon supervisors' perceptions. It is apparent from Table 4.1 that the tendency in both plants is for little new work to be taken on and for there to be a high

Table 4.1 *Comparison of task variables in production sections of the engineering (E) and food (F) plants*

Task variable		Mean	Mode	Range
Proportion of weekly	E	61	100	5–100
work of the same type (%)	F	77	100	0–100
Proportion of monthly	E	100	100	100[a]
work of the same type (%)	F	91	100	0–100
New work over	E	6	0	0–30
past year (%)	F	12	0	0–100
Length of typical	E	1 week	3–4 hrs.	2 hrs. – several
run				years
	F	1 week	1 week	1 hr.–6 months
Length of longest	E	[b]	Several years	6 hrs.–25 years
run	F	1 month	2 weeks	1 hr.–1 year

(a) The engineering plant operated on a 4-week overall cycle.

(b) Some operations had run unchanged for many years – e.g. manufacture of porcelain insulators and some foundry work. The length of longest run for certain other operations was only a matter of hours. Calculation of a mean score would be meaningless with such extreme variations.

level of repetition in the type of work done within supervisors' sections, albeit under a regime of fairly frequent batch changes. However, the range of scores also points to very considerable variations between sections, and this reduces the meaning that can be attached to the average (mean) scores.

As part of the agreement for undertaking our investigation, our preliminary findings were reported back to all participants. In the food company this led to intensive discussions in which all supervisors and managers in production, maintenance and service areas participated. When discussing the variation in supervisors' jobs, the participants pointed to additional features in the task environment, as well as to factors such as the immediate superior's style of managing. Table 4.2 extends our previous list of task variables to include those which were suggested at the feedback sessions and which we subsequently measured in the production sections of the food plant. The list is remarkably similar to the task variables included in the lists of situational variables compiled by Lennerlöf (1968) and by Thurley and Wirdenius (1973). The variables at the bottom of the list refer more to elements of task variability caused by changes of plan and breakdowns. The variables at the top of the list introduce an extra dimension in that they refer primarily to the complexity of the task situation. The statistics given in Table 4.2 confirm that there is a wide range of variation in the production supervisor's task situation even within one plant, despite the fact that taken as a whole it could be described as a large batch production system. For example, although a majority of supervisors' sections have a high degree of repetition in their work, for one quarter of them under 50 per cent of their throughput is constant from one week to another.

The task variables contained in Table 4.2 include measures of task variability and additional characteristics which managers and supervisors in the food plant believed would also account for differences in supervisors' jobs. They suggested that the higher the variability and the greater the complexity in sections' tasks, the greater would be the authority and influence enjoyed by supervisors. This is not consistent with Perrow's reasoning, since he envisaged the difficulty in analysing tasks, rather than their variability, to be the factor according greater discretion and power to supervisors. None the less, in so far as variability and complexity generate problems which constitute exceptions to the managerial planning process, then one can

Table 4.2 *Task variables suggested by supervisors and managers to explain variations in supervisory authority and influence in the food plant*

Task variable	Mean	Mode	Range
Number of sections providing inputs	5.1	3	1–16
Number of sections receiving output	4.2	1	1–10
Number of departments making same products	1.4	0	0–5
Hours of stock held	8.8	0	0–48
Number of layouts in the section	4.1	3	1–19
Number of rooms in the section	1.8	1	1–6
Number of products made in the section	15.6	7	1–99
Size of work group	28.1	28	3–90
Grade of workers (company grading scheme)	3.9	3	2–6
Proportion of weekly work the same (%)	77	100	0–100
Proportion of monthly work the same (%)	91	100	0–100
New work (%)	12	0	0–100
Length of typical run	Weekly	Weekly	Hourly–six monthly
Length of longest run	Monthly	Fortnightly	Hourly–annually
Number of planning changes per week	6.4	2	0–40
Re-set time (hours)	4.0	4	1–9
Number of breakdowns per week	24.2	20	0–80
Normal repair time (hours)	4.2	5	2–6
Age of equipment (years)	18.5	12	1–50

appreciate the rationale behind the views which were expressed by the food plant personnel.

Appendix 4.1 gives in detail the correlations between task situation variables and measures of supervisory authority and influence. The major conclusion to be drawn is that authority and influence in different decision areas appears to be adapted differently to task complexity and variability. Authority and influence over systems decisions tends to rise in situations of complexity (e.g. number of products, higher-grade work) and of variability (shorter production runs), or in conditions such as longer equipment repair time which generate uncertainty. Influence, and to a lesser degree authority, over technical matters is greater when there are more frequent changes of work, but it is not related to the frequency of breakdowns. Supervisors' authority and influence over decisions concerning people, in contrast, tend to be lower when the task situation is more complex and variable. Thus while supervisors tend to have greater discretion in organizing work activities in situations of greater complexity, variability and uncertainty, the reverse is true for their role in handling personnel matters. Complexity and variability normally give rise to more labour problems, such as contingency adjustments of pay, and these appear to lead to intervention by managers and specialists in industrial relations and industrial engineering, much as is laid down in the food company's procedure agreement.

However, the pattern of association which emerged between variations in the task variables we measured and variation in supervisors' authority and influence was weak and patchy. It is possible that measures of task difficulty would have accounted for more variation in supervisors' discretion and power, as Perrow suggested. This is rather doubtful since the level of task difficulty appeared on the whole to be low throughout both plants, which were manufacturing relatively long-established products with well-known characteristics. It will also be seen later that subjective measures of task difficulty are not generally associated with supervisors' authority and influence.

Our conclusion, then, is that task variables (including the technological aspects) were playing some part in shaping supervisors' authority and influence, but not a large part. The design of task variables in the form of work layout and the attendant technology does not, however, exhaust the ways in which management can attempt to determine workplace activities. There are also organizational provisions it can make with a view to controlling supervisory behaviour and performance. In Chapter 1 it was suggested that the trend over the years towards 'bureaucratic' control had been manifest in organizational procedures often operated by specialists, and that these had eaten substantially into areas previously left to the discretion of supervisors. The question therefore arises whether the extent to which organizational controls were applied was associated with variations in the level of supervisors' authority and influence.

Organizational variables and supervisors' jobs

The most common managerial use of organizational design for specifying roles and instituting accountability is the bureaucratic one of formalization. This involves procedures, manuals, paperwork routines, and criteria of assessment. Table 4.3 summarizes the extent to which supervisors said that these provisions were applied to their jobs.

The most formalized aspect of supervisors' jobs in terms of procedures or manuals was working methods, with 79 per cent of the sample having these, whereas other procedures or manuals only applied to a minority of supervisors. The average number of these procedures or manuals was 2.4 with a mode of 3. Over half the sample had to deal with paperwork concerning supplies, and repairs; the average number of tasks involving paperwork was 1.8. Half the supervisors had a job description, while two-thirds had manuals covering aspects of the supervisor's role; one-third had *neither* a job description nor a job manual. Supervisors expressed some dissatisfaction with their job descriptions – that they were too brief, too meaningless and too divorced from reality. During the course of the study an exercise of supervisory job evaluation was initiated in the food plant, where job descriptions were fairly common, and senior management was aware how out-of-date and meaningless the supervisors' job descriptions had become and how difficult it was to update them.

Only one-third of the sample reported that their performance as a supervisor was formally assessed. Two-thirds of the sample reported that the performance of their section was assessed. Similar numbers reported that *both* they and their section were assessed (39) or that *neither* they nor their section were assessed (30). The most frequent

Table 4.3. *The organizational context of the supervisor*

Does the following formalization apply to supervisors' jobs?	Whole sample		Engineering plant		Food plant	
	Yes	No	Yes	No	Yes	No
Procedures or manuals for						
Work methods	122	33	29	25	93	8
Quality	64	91	15	39	49	52
Repairs	34	121	2	52	32	69
Supplies	56	100	3	51	53	49
Manning	71	84	0	54	71	30
Re-scheduling	32	123	0	54	32	69
Paperwork involved						
Quality	39	115	14	40	25	75
Repairs	77	76	47	7	30	69
Supplies	84	66	31	23	53	43
Manning	49	104	21	33	28	71
Re-scheduling	29	121	5	49	24	72
Role formalization						
Job descriptions	79	77	2	52	77	25
Job manuals	100	56	2	52	98	4
Written instructions	135	21	35	19	100	2
Organization chart	156	0	54	0	102	0
Supervisor assessed	50	106	4	50	46	56
Section assessed	115	40	35	19	80	21
Criteria of assessment						
Labour cost	53	100	2	49	51	51
Materials cost	53	100	3	48	50	52
Materials wastage	50	103	5	46	45	57
Quality	41	112	6	45	35	67
Volume of output	87	65	29	21	58	44
Stoppages/downtime	48	105	6	45	42	60
Absenteeism	31	121	8	43	23	78
Labour turnover	22	131	2	49	20	82

criterion of assessment was volume of output, followed by various cost indices. Fewer supervisors were assessed on the quality of work leaving their section.

Table 4.3 also shows that there were substantial differences between the two sites. Overall, the food site was more formalized:

when the items of role formalization were summed, engineering supervisors had an average of 2.4 compared to the food supervisors' average of 4.9. The number of procedures or manuals set out for the food supervisors was considerably greater than for engineering supervisors. Likewise, assessment both of supervisors and their section was more common in the food site than in the engineering site. This greater reliance on formalization in the much larger food plant is consistent with the generally-found association between larger organizational size and more extensive formalization (Child, 1973a). The contrast in the degree of formalization between sites was much more marked than that between production and non-production supervisors. Production supervisors were more likely to be assessed than were non-production supervisors, and to be assessed on more criteria. They were less likely, however, to have a job description.[1]

When the degree of formalization applied to supervisors' jobs was compared with the levels of authority and influence they reported, a complicated relationship emerged. This is tabulated in Appendix 4.2, which also reports correlations between authority and influence on the one hand, and, on the other, a characteristic which is likely to reflect managerial control: the frequency of supervisors' contact with their immediate supervisors over work-related (task) matters. The measures of formalization have been simplified by means of aggregation where this appeared justified.

The more formalized the supervisor's role and the more procedures which were applied to it, the less likely he was to have authority and influence over systems management – that is, over the organization of work passing through his section. Authority and influence in this area also tended to be reduced when a greater range of performance criteria was applied to the supervisor's job. These findings indicate that the attempt to define and control the supervisor's job by organizational means does have some effect on his role in managing the workflow, but has no consistent association with other areas of his authority or influence. It also became apparent that supervisors who had more frequent personal contact with their managers tended to enjoy greater authority and influence over people-management decisions. This fails to support the view that personal contact with managers reduces supervisors' discretion – rather, it appears to signify that they participate more in decision making.

Measures of organizational formalization do, then, have some association with supervisory authority and influence, which is not likely to have occurred by chance; but, like task variables, they fail to account for much of the variation between supervisors' jobs. Nor is the overall impact of formal organizational definition upon super- visors' roles a clear-cut one. The idea of supervision as an organizationally-defined role is in fact questionable when one-fifth of the supervisors studied do not perceive that their performance, or their section's, is assessed at all, and when the connection between authority and formal accountability is confused. The persistence of a high degree of autonomy from organizational (that is, managerial) definition is further indicated by the fact that half (47 per cent) the supervisors reported that they had considerable discretion in how they defined their role.

The opportunity, indeed necessity, for supervisors largely to define their own roles was illustrated repeatedly in the direct observation of 16 supervisors working in the highly-formalized food plant. Examples of such discretion included making unauthorized changes to scheduling and line speeds in order to keep employees on piece- work occupied and to maintain production levels; arranging with other supervisors to re-allocate labour between their sections as and when pressure and slack periods required; requisitioning services directly and informally from non-production departments; and bypassing managerial superiors who either lacked the specialist knowledge of the supervisor (generally in maintenance areas) or were physically located away from the supervisor. These practices ap- peared to be quite functional for the maintenance of their sections' performance, as informal practices often are (Gross, 1953). They can be understood primarily as adjustments to disturbances and other contingencies, the nature of which varied greatly between sections, even between those where operations and technology were similar. This element of variation and unpredictability without doubt constitutes a significant limitation on the ability to define and formalize a supervisor's job realistically, even in an organization like the food plant which has relatively integrated production processes and highly-developed management systems.

It may simply be that technology and organization, as elements in the supervisor's task situation, are just not as important in account- ing for how supervisors carry out their jobs as had previously been expected. In this respect, it is interesting to refer to Bellamy's (1976) study of 83 production supervisors in 17 Indiana factories, in which he found the usual curvilinear relationships between technology

75

(assessed in a manner similar to Woodward's) and the supervisory span of control (see p. 64), *but* a lack of clear-cut relationships between technology and how supervisors carried out their jobs in terms of leadership style and pattern of interaction. The problem could be methodological, in that not only is supervisory behaviour difficult to research accurately, but also it may be the demands of the work situation as the supervisor, not the observer, interprets them which have greatest significance for that behaviour. To quote Thurley and Wirdenius (1973: 75): 'Many of the job demands from the work situation. . . are also difficult to quantify and, again, they may not be apparent to anybody other than the supervisors concerned. This reminds us that it may be more important to understand the way supervisors perceive situational variables than to measure the variables themselves.'

With this in mind, we explored how supervisors perceived aspects of variability and difficulty in their task situations. Some questions on variability were derived from Child (1973b) and combined into a single measure of 'task variability'.[2] In addition, we developed questions from Lynch (1974) which were intended to provide subjective assessments of Perrow's dimensions of task variability (number of exceptions) and difficulty in analysing work. All these measures are listed in Appendix 4.3, which also shows the correlations between each measure and supervisors' reported levels of authority and influence.

The pattern of correlations bears some similarity to that which emerged when objective measures of task situation were used. Supervisors who perceive that they have high 'task variability' tend to report having greater authority and influence over the organization of work (systems management), but lower authority and influence over people management. This suggests that in more variable task situations greater reliance has to be placed on the supervisor acting as a 'backstop' for the failures in plans and procedures to cope adequately, but that in such circumstances there is now less opportunity to be involved in handling personnel matters. The remaining subjective measures of task variability and difficulty, derived from Perrow's analytical scheme, were not generally associated with supervisors' authority and influence. With the exception of a possible link between difficulty of the task and reduced supervisory authority and influence over technical decisions, there was little evidence to suggest that the level of supervisors' discretion was at all associated with the difficulty of the problems they had to deal with.

All in all, the attempt to account for variations in supervisors' authority and influence by reference to technology, task and formalization has not led to particularly convincing results. These are all organizational attributes which represent a direct or indirect attempt to structure the supervisor's work situation, but the amount of variation in supervisors' jobs for which they actually account remains very limited. It is appropriate here to note Hill's (1976b) criticism of the view that task characteristics will be determinants of the supervisor's role. In his study of dockland supervisors, Hill found that their jobs varied, but he could not uncover any direct link between this variation and task characteristics; indeed he concluded that it was not really possible to distinguish routine from non-routine tasks in a situation where a degree of variation was normal (p. 82).

Personal variables and supervisors' jobs

Supervisors and managers, in their discussions of our preliminary findings, expressed the view that differences in task situations only partially accounted for variations in supervisory authority and influence. The personalities involved could be equally, if not more important, because the supervisor's immediate superior has some discretion in his dealings with supervisors, particularly over how much authority he delegates to them and how much influence he allows their views to have. It is possible that the manager's experience is relevant here, the argument being that less experienced managers will generally have less understanding of shopfloor conditions and so be more inclined to delegate to supervisors. Several writers have also assumed that supervisors' own personal characteristics, such as age and experience, influence how they carry out their jobs (see Thurley and Wirdenius, 1973: Chapter 4).

The basic characteristics of both supervisors' and managers' age and experience were therefore analysed in relation to supervisory authority and influence. One other characteristic of supervisors was also included in the analysis – their 'personal flexibility'. We have emphasized the need which most supervisors face to handle what Thurley and Wirdenius call 'disturbances' – unforeseen and un-planned contingencies such as shortages, breakdowns and employee grievances. The more willing a supervisor is to accept changing and unusual circumstances – which is what we mean by his 'personal flexibility' – the greater is likely to be his capability for handling disturbances, and therefore the amount of authority and influence he can 'safely' be left with. This concept of personal flexibility was developed from Ellis and Child's (1973) study of managers, and the specific questions put to supervisors in order to measure the concept are listed in Appendix C.[3]

The supervisors' degree of personal flexibility emerged very clearly as the major factor associated with their authority and influence in both the systems and technical areas (Appendix 4.4 lists the correlation coefficients). Supervisors who expressed themselves willing to face uncertainty were given, by their own reckoning, greater scope for dealing with problems in the areas where much of the uncertainty occurs (e.g. changes of work plans, shortages, and breakdowns). There was also some tendency for supervisors who had a longer work experience outside the present company to enjoy greater authority and influence in these areas, especially over technical matters. Those supervisors who had been in post longer had somewhat greater authority over people decisions. Supervisors also tended to enjoy greater authority and influence over systems decisions when they were managed by a relative newcomer to the company. The more seniority in age they had over their managers, the greater tended to be their authority and influence, though again the area of people decisions did not form part of this pattern. Greater seniority over managers in terms of years spent in the company was also associated with higher influence in the systems and technical areas.

These findings indicate that the scope of the supervisor's job in terms of authority and influence is not shaped solely, or even predominantly, by technological or organizational factors. The supervisor's own expressed ease about uncertain and changing work conditions has emerged as the strongest of an admittedly weak bunch of predictors. There are also signs that the experience possessed by both supervisors and managers, and the extent to which the two parties match in this respect, may have some bearing upon the way the supervisor's job is actually defined. In other words, there is an important informal element in the way supervisory authority and influence is distributed which is based upon the supervisor's own personal coping abilities and also upon his relationship to the manager. If we had had the opportunity to explore the personal characteristics of supervisors and their managers further, their contribution to shaping the supervisor's job might have emerged as even more significant.

The selection of 16 supervisors for direct observation was designed to afford some comparisons of supervisors working in similar task situations as well as some comparisons of supervisors reporting to the same manager. The intention here was to see whether any further light could be thrown on the two processes which, we have suggested, define supervisors' jobs: their formally-structured definition through the technology and design of the work situation and their informal definition through the manager's style and relationship with the supervisor.

Comparisons through direct observation

It was possible to observe four groups of supervisors whose sections were similarly located within the production system of the food factory. The first group was a pair of supervisors in charge of cutting and wrapping assorted confectionery. The second group was a pair supervising the packing of assortments. The third group consisted of three supervisors in charge of sections wrapping moulded chocolate. The fourth group was a pair of supervisors concerned with cutting card for packaging and boxing confectionery. These groups were selected because their sections appeared to employ similar equipment and because, on initial enquiry, their task systems appeared to be comparable. A close comparison of our observations on how these supervisors carried out their jobs and the assessments of their authority and influence which they and their managers gave, however, only revealed any degree of correspondence with technology in the case of the two card-cutting supervisors. Even in this case it was not so much technology in any limited sense of plant and equipment but rather the systems of planning and control over work which appeared, through their erratic nature, to play a large part in shaping the supervisors' jobs. The fact that both supervisors were in charge of a highly-unionized, relatively militant labour force of printing workers also had to be taken into account as a common factor when explaining the decisions they took in an attempt to reconcile changes of plan and shortages with the men's pressure to maintain piecework earnings.

The other three groups of supervisors' jobs turned out to be more marked by their differences than by their similarities. It soon became clear that (1) similar technology can be located within dissimilar task situations and (2) that even the technology itself, when examined in detail, may be less similar than at first appeared. These points are illustrated by the two assortment-packing sections where the layout and mix of equipment were different, though most measures of technology employed in organizational studies would classify the sections as identical. Partly because of the age of its equipment, one section experienced more frequent breakdowns than the other. The latter section, however, was more prone to shortages of units to be packed. The supervisor in the first section took authority upon herself to initiate repairs when breakdowns occurred and to re-allocate labour to alternative equipment; the second supervisor took initiatives in re-scheduling work when shortages of units occurred. This helps to explain why the first supervisor saw herself having greatest influence over technical decisions, while the second reported having greatest influence over systems ᴧrk organization) decisions. Similar technology *per se* does not tell us very much about these variations in the supervisors' jobs. Rather, it is the uncertainties contained within the supervisor's task system, associated with variabilities such as breakdowns or shortages, which emerge as the critical factor.

Another important qualification to the broad-brush analysis of technology as a predictor of variation in supervisors' jobs also soon became evident on close observation. If a section has within its technology an experimental piece of equipment, or one that is experiencing teething troubles, attention to this machine and to its impact upon the organization of the rest of the section's activities can take up a large part of the supervisor's time and affect his decision-making behaviour. When such equipment was present, the uncertainties it caused seemed to increase the scope management allowed to the supervisor to handle the ensuing problems. Only a very detailed analysis of technology would be sensitive to this kind of phenomenon.

These illustrations indicate both that technology alone may be of limited significance for understanding supervisors' jobs without examination of other factors which comprise the socio-technical system of the workplace – such as the planning of workflow and the interaction between workflow and payment to employees – and that a quite detailed analysis of technology is in any case required in order to understand any specific effects it may have. The very modest correlations we have been able to report between technological or task variables and supervisors' authority and influence is probably due in part to a failure to pursue this examination far enough – indeed the interviewing on which much of our investigation depended is not a wholly adequate method for assessing task systems in detail. It is worth recalling here how even Hill (1976b), who combined observation with interviewing, concluded that he could not clearly distinguish different levels of task variability confronting supervisors. We have, however, also mentioned the further possibility that, in addition to the more formal structuring of the work situation through the design of technology and systems, a less formal process also operates whereby the supervisor's job is shaped by factors such as the manager's style and his relationship with the supervisor.

Again, the picture which emerged from observations is extremely complex, and we are only able to suggest certain of its outlines. It was possible to make comparisons of four pairs of supervisors, where each pair had respectively the same manager. Two factors emerged from the supervisor–manager relationship which appeared to have an effect on the supervisor's authority and influence. The first is the physical proximity between manager and supervisor. In the case of two pairs, the manager's office was located next to that of one supervisor but several minutes' walk away from the office of the other supervisor. The supervisors located in close proximity to their managers had considerably more frequent contact with them. They also claimed to have somewhat greater authority and influence than did the supervisors located at a distance. This is consistent with the statistical association reported in Appendix 4.2. In the cases observed, a close *rapport* had developed between the proximate managers and supervisors, which appeared to give the manager confidence to delegate more to the supervisor. Proximity to the supervisor's section also offered the manager more ready feedback and the potential for swift intervention should things go wrong. This must add to his confidence about delegating authority to the supervisor.

The second factor concerns the levels of specialist knowledge relevant to the section's work held by supervisor and manager respectively. One pair of supervisors with the same manager was in charge of craft sections; their specialized knowledge of problems under their charge, such as lift maintenance and plant removal, could not be matched by their more generalist manager. This meant that the supervisors had to take decisions on many matters, especially technical ones, without reference to the manager, and they also frequently dealt directly with 'client' managers, sometimes two levels up in the hierarchy. The other case was rather different in that the manager was bypassed and ignored because the supervisors felt that he was not willing to face up to difficulties. This is not so much an example of knowledge differences, but it still has to do with the respective competence of manager and supervisor. When the supervisor has the advantage he may be left with a larger part in decision making.

Other idiosyncratic factors also intervened in the relationships between managers and supervisors which we observed. For example, two supervisors expressed considerable frustration at having been passed over for better jobs – in one case promotion to manager. They both avoided their managers whenever possible, though one cannot definitely say that this had a bearing on the authority and influence they enjoyed, because other factors also intervened. Nevertheless, it becomes apparent through specific comparisons of the type we have just outlined that both formally-structured and informal factors may shape the supervisor's role. The possible combinations of such influences are very many, and the present study has certainly not taken every relevant one into account. The variety of supervisory jobs is therefore not something to regard with surprise, though it presents a significant challenge to the designers of job definitions, job evaluations and training programmes.

Conclusion

One approach to identifying the scope of supervisors' jobs is by reference to the degree of discretion and influence they enjoy. Employing this criterion, we found that only a small amount of variation in supervisors' jobs could be attributed to the technological and organizational context designed by management, which has been given prominence in writings on organization theory. In so far as these factors did shape supervisors' jobs, the nature of the relationship was consistent with the predictions of organizational theory. The less variable and uncertain the work situation, the more scope there appeared for taking systems and technical decisions out of supervisors' hands, and for leaving them to concentrate on purely 'supervisory' duties to do with managing people. It was also found that when management formalizes supervisors' jobs through job definitions, procedures and performance assessment, the supervisors concerned report that they enjoy diminished levels of authority and influence over the organization of work passing through their sections. These two sets of findings are compatible, and they suggest that management can to a degree create a structured role for supervisors in task system conditions which make this practical. Nevertheless, the technological and organizational attributes of formal structuring only accounted for a small proportion of the variation among supervisors' perceptions of their authority and influence in the batch plants we investigated.

Informal factors also play a part in shaping supervisors' jobs, and these cannot so readily be incorporated into a planned design of the supervisor's role. The supervisor's own ability and willingness to cope with variety is important here, while there is some evidence to suggest that the supervisor's job is also shaped importantly by a process of accommodation between the supervisor and his manager. These informal factors will set limits to the extent that management can design the supervisor's job. For instance, the intention to have certain decisions delegated to supervisors may well be frustrated by the immediate superior's unwillingness to accede to such a policy and/or by the supervisor's poor ability to cope with the additional responsibilities entailed.

The opportunity of observing a small number of supervisors at work served to confirm the complexity of the process by which supervisors' jobs are shaped. The role of technology and task systems has to be examined in quite specific detail. The parts played by the supervisor himself, and by his relations with the manager, are also very specific, though certain relevant factors of a more general nature became apparent, such as physical proximity between the manager and the supervisor.

One of the reasons for unplanned and apparently idiosyncratic differences between supervisors' jobs lies in their inability to satisfy equally all the conflicting requirements that are placed upon them. As will be seen in the following chapter, the majority of the supervisors we studied feel under pressure and this is associated partly with receiving conflicting instructions from different parts of management and partly with a conflict between workload and the resources of time and energy to cope with it. If supervisors cannot satisfy all the requirements placed upon them, they will have to select their own priorities from among these, a process which is likely to generate further variations among supervisors in how they conduct their jobs.

Appendix 4.1 *The relationship between supervisory authority and influence and the task context at the food site (N = 58 production supervisors)[a]*

Task variables	Authority and influence[b]							
	Systems authority	Systems influence	Technical authority	Technical influence	People authority	People influence	Overall authority	Overall influence
Number of inputs	00	09	−22*	−09	10	03	−06	01
Number of outputs	21	22**	−10	−19	−07	01	00	01
Number of substitute departments	−13	−11	03	−05	−03	−08	−06	−12
Hours of stock	13	30**	14	12	05	08	16	23*
Number of layouts	06	14	−04	03	−22*	−18	−11	−02
Number of rooms	00	10	−11	01	−09	−03	−11	03
Number of products	27*	28*	−12	−04	−26*	−28*	−09	−05
Size of workgroup	−07	−08	−04	−13	−02	−12	−07	−17
Grade of workers	28*	35**	−10	09	−28*	−17	−09	11
Weekly repetition[c]	15	14	−19	−12	−23*	−33**	−17	−19
Monthly repetition[c]	−12	−06	−05	02	−17	−27*	−16	−17
New work	03	−01	09	12	01	−11	08	−01
Length of typical run[c]	17	26*	18	40***	−04	−10	14	24*
Length of longest run[c]	24*	39**	22	36**	08	04	26*	35**
Number of planning changes	08	18	31**	32**	09	10	25*	29**
Re-set time	−09	−14	16	21	−11	−17	00	−06

Number of breakdowns	− 18	− 17	05	12	− 21	− 34**	− 17	− 21
Repair time	22*	26*	− 01	07	14	17	17	25*
Age of equipment	− 05	00	13	12	− 04	01	08	07

(a) Pearson product-moment correlations, decimal points omitted; * p < 0.05; ** p < 0.01; *** p < 0.001.

(b) Authority and influence as assessed by the supervisor. These are aggregations of scores for individual decisions, as described in Chapter 3.

(c) These scores have been reversed so that their direction is consistent with the other task variables in terms of complexity and variability: a positive correlation indicates that greater authority/influence is associated with higher complexity or variability.

Appendix 4.2 *The relationship between supervisory authority and influence and selected organizational variables (N = 156 supervisors)[a]*

Organizational variables bearing upon the supervisory role	Authority and influence[b]							
	Systems authority	Systems influence	Technical authority	Technical influence	People authority	People influence	Overall authority	Overall influence
Development of procedures[c]	−28**	−23**	16*	03	10	−04	00	−11
Degree of role formalization[c]	−23**	−28**	24**	03	03	−18*	03	−20**
Number of criteria supervisors assessed on[c]	−22**	−17*	10	01	13	05	02	−05
Frequency of task contacts with managers (assessed by supervisors)	10	03	07	17*	25**	30**	15*	23**
Ditto (assessed by managers)	00	−07	−18*	18*	15*	18*	00	01

(*a*) Pearson product-moment correlations, decimal points omitted; *p < 0.05; **p < 0.01; ***p < 0.001.
(*b*) See note (*b*) to Appendix 4.1.
(*c*) Sum of variables listed in Table 4.3, Chapter 4.

Appendix 4.3 *The relationship between supervisory authority and influence and supervisors' subjective assessments of their task situation (N = 156 supervisors)*[a]

Task situation variables	Authority and influence[b]							
	Systems authority	Systems influence	Technical authority	Technical influence	People authority	People influence	Overall authority	Overall influence
Task variability								
Task variability[c]	19*	16*	09	15*	−22**	−21**	02	03
Events cannot be anticipated	11	00	06	−13	−05	−14*	06	−14*
Some problems do not recur	09	12	10	−08	−11	−20*	04	−09
Differences in problem solving and search	−02	−02	−03	−09	02	−02	−01	−06
Decisions are difficult	−04	−06	10	04	−02	−05	02	−03
Task difficulty								
Problems not readily analysable	09	07	−19**	−17**	−10	−07	−11	−08

(*Contd.*)

Appendix 4.3 (*Contd.*)

Task situation variables	Authority and influence[b]							
	Systems authority	Systems influence	Technical authority	Technical influence	People authority	People influence	Overall authority	Overall influence
Technical problems are difficult	08	10	01	−01	06	08	08	08
Human problems are difficult	01	00	−16*	−16*	11	04	−01	−05

(*a*) Pearson product-moment correlations, decimal points omitted; * p < 0.05; ** p < 0.01.
(*b*) See note (*b*) to Appendix 4.1.
(*c*) Composite variable, described in note 2 to Chapter 4.

Authority and influence[b]

Personal variables	Systems authority	Systems influence	Technical authority	Technical influence	People authority	People influence	Overall authority	Overall influence
(1) Supervisor's:								
Age	12	08	17*	16*	−01	−02	13*	09
Years in company	03	04	02	06	10	07	08	08
Years as supervisor	02	03	11	11	22**	12	19*	12
Years outside experience	14*	13	15*	23**	−15*	−12	03	09
Personal flexibility	34***	37***	22**	27**	08	11	32***	33***
(2) Manager's:								
Age	−07	−15*	−04	−01	−14	−10	−13	−12
Years in company	−17*	−23**	−15*	−12	08	08	−10	−11
Years as manager	−03	−06	−02	07	02	04	−01	03
(3) Difference in:[c]								
Ages	12	16*	19*	19*	08	01	19*	15*
Years in company	14	20**	15*	16*	−01	−04	13	13
Years in post	00	05	12	09	19*	10	16*	11

(a) Pearson product-moment correlations, decimal points omitted; * p < 0.05; ** p < 0.01; *** p < 0.001.

(b) See note (b), Appendix 4.1.

(c) Differences = supervisor's score *minus* manager's, so that a positive correlation indicates that greater supervisory authority/influence is associated with the supervisor being more experienced than his manager.

5

Coping and surviving

'Some days I could scream.' (Birmingham supervisor)

It has often been said that the supervisor's job is a stressful one. He has, of course, been characterized as 'caught in the middle', between the opposing forces of management and labour, as well as facing the conflicting or unco-ordinated requirements of different managerial functions bearing upon the point of production. Other portraits of the supervisor show him to be weighed down by continual pressures to keep work moving, without sufficient authority to carry out the responsibilities allocated to him, and subject to ambiguities about the proper scope of his job.

Some studies have attempted to assess the extent to which supervisors are caught in the middle. They have generally found this to be less of a problem than was expected. For example, Mann and Dent (1954) found that under half (47 per cent) of the supervisors in one American company thought of themselves as standing in the middle between management and workers. Yanouzas (1964) reported that foremen in an American jobbing plant adjusted to their position as a buffer between higher management and shopfloor employees by accepting it as an integral part of their job. Hill (1976b) found that while 67 per cent of the British dockyard supervisors he studied said they were in the middle, only 17 per cent could give instances of role conflict where they had been faced with two sets of opposed expectations which both related to the same issue. Findings such as these lead one to question whether supervisors should necessarily be characterized as caught in the middle. Hill's conclusion (1976b: 156) is that the 'marginal men' stereotype more readily fitted the supervisors he studied, though he prefers the description of the 'man outside' – outside, or irrelevant to, the main chain of command and occupying only a minor role in the lines of communication between management and workers.

The supervisors in the Birmingham batch production plants we investigated reported rather higher levels of role conflict and pressure. For many of them, being caught in the middle, and other problems in their role, constituted a reality which could be quite stressful.

Conditions of the job: conflict, pressure and ambiguity

Ninety-seven supervisors (65 per cent) in our sample said they were subject to what social scientists call 'inter-sender role conflict': that is, where the supervisor is caught in the middle between other parties who disagree over a particular issue. An even larger number (128) gave one or more examples of having been affected by conflict of this kind.

The most frequently mentioned form of inter-sender role conflict was that in which the supervisor was caught in the middle between management and shopfloor. An example frequently cited in the food plant concerned labour mobility. When there was insufficient work for employees within one section, perhaps due to machine breakdown, the formal management policy was for the spare employees to be moved temporarily to other sections which were short of labour. Employees resented this policy, however, and as a result supervisors would often attempt to 'find' work in order to avoid having people moved out of their section.[1] Many comments made by supervisors showed that they were clearly aware of being caught in the middle. For example:

> 'the supervisor is the shock absorber between the shopfloor and management';

> 'the company give the shopfloor a free hand. If you're not careful you can become the yo-yo in the middle';

> 'you've got to keep both sides happy';

> 'he [the supervisor] is often in trouble from all sides, getting blamed for everything';

> 'you can be pulled in all sorts of directions'.

Some supervisors went on to comment, however, that being in the middle was an inevitable part of the job; something they had to put up with. For example, one said:

> 'I think it's part of my job to have pressure from the top and also from the bottom';

and another commented:

> 'It's obvious you've got to be used to a certain extent because of what the job entails. Somebody's got to be in the middle.'

Two of the twelve statements on 'the supervisor's role today', which supervisors were asked to evaluate, were about being placed in the middle between management and workers.[2] Fifty-six per cent of them perceived that supervisors in their firm were 'pushed about from above and from below at the same time'. Seventy-five per cent saw the supervisor acting as 'a mediator between the two sides of industry'. The great majority (88 per cent) disapproved of the situation described by the first statement which clearly expresses the pressures of being in the middle and subjected to role conflict. By contrast, a majority (75 per cent) approved of the other 'in the middle' role, that of mediator between management and workers, in which, however, there are not necessarily any strong pressures bearing upon the supervisor personally.

While being pressured by management and shopfloor was the most frequently mentioned form of inter-sender role conflict, it was not the only kind that supervisors experienced. Management itself is not a unitary body, and 40 per cent of the supervisors reported receiving conflicting instructions from different sections of management. Production issues figured most prominently in this kind of conflict. For example, conflicting instructions could be issued by different planners, particularly in the food plant. In both plants, production planning instructions could be at variance with the type or quantity of materials that storekeepers were able to release. Different customer departments might demand priority of output, especially if there was a shortage of labour or a breakdown in equipment. There were also the perennial problems of balancing output versus quality, maintenance and safety.

Overall, more supervisors (49 per cent) gave examples of production situations in which they were caught between different sections of management than gave examples of labour problems in this category (32 per cent). Labour problems did, nevertheless, generate particularly intense conflict or emotion. The intensity which supervisors experienced when they were involved in conflict over labour issues was heightened by the personal element often present and by the threat to what little authority they still possessed over employees. For example, one supervisor followed management policy as officially defined by the Personnel Department in reporting two employees for smoking in the toilets, but his line production management superiors declined to set the relevant disciplinary procedure into motion. The supervisor felt particularly bitter about this inconsistency in managerial policies which left him in an invidious position *vis-à-vis* the employees concerned.

More than half (68 per cent) of the supervisors experienced another form of role conflict, in which they became involved in disagreement with just one other party over an issue. This could also be a source of strain. Supervisors frequently mentioned tensions with shop-stewards in this category, particularly in the engineering site, from which the following fairly routine example involving lost production is taken:

> 'One morning I found that a press operator had been sitting
> down for half-an-hour because the guard on his machine
> was too hard to push down and the shop-steward had
> told him to stop. He hadn't been to see the tool-setter. I
> said that he should have come to me. I made him start
> work, sent for the tool-setter, and told the shop-steward.'

Though role conflict can pose problems for supervisors, they may also be subject to pressures which do not involve interpersonal conflict. A sense of being under general pressure was in fact a common feature of the supervisors' jobs. Seventy-three (49 per cent) reported being under 'quite a lot' of pressure and a further 27 (18 per cent) reported 'a great deal'. Twice as many supervisors said that most of the pressure on them came from management as said that most came from the shopfloor. Pressure was most frequently defined in terms of the workload bearing upon the supervisor (63 per cent said this was a considerable pressure), followed by labour problems (37 per cent), and having to cope with an uneven flow of work or changes of plan (35 per cent). Just over half the supervisors were 'bothered' by having too heavy a workload, and because the amount of work they had to do interfered with how well they did it. This contrasts with the fact that only about one-third (36 per cent) reported being 'bothered' by role conflict: 'not being able to satisfy the conflicting demands of various people over you'.

In some cases, pressure of workload was due to supervisors being called upon to undertake extra duties, such as paperwork duties during the manager's illness, or compensating for a reduction in staff. In the food company, the introduction of a new costing system had increased supervisors' workloads. In both plants, producing as they were on a batch basis, the inability of planning systems to cope with the complexity and uncertainty of production could result in considerable pressure on production supervisors, who had to make compensating adjustments to scheduling. They often blamed planning for what may be a problem inherent in this type of production system (Reeves and Turner, 1972), as the following quotations illustrate. First, from the engineering plant:

> 'We have such a variety of jobs . . . Unless they plan it properly they find that they have to get me to drop the line I'm doing and put on an urgent one. And I say "Why didn't you tell me this before?" because I've then got to reset a job up which means taking out a couple of tons of tools. They don't think about the amount of tonnage which has to be moved around . . . Because each operation isn't independent of the others, a change on any one line means taking a whole line apart and then we're not producing.'

Second, from the food plant:

> 'Most of the pressure on me comes from the cock-up in planning. The industrial engineering system is inadequate – the men are not able to earn their money. The planners have no sense of urgency and no training.'

Table 5.1 illustrates in summary form how far conclusions drawn from observations of 16 food plant supervisors tie in with the main pressures they mentioned in their interviews. The comparison suggests that when supervisors mention 'pressures of workload' this constitutes a general category which masks certain contributory processes. Thus technical breakdowns or shortages can give rise to pressures bearing on the supervisor due to his having to re-schedule work, re-allocate labour and mollify employees who stand to lose piecework earnings. Piecework was the general method of payment

Table 5.1 *Summary comparison of pressures in the supervisor's job drawn from (1) interviews and (2) direct observation involving 16 supervisors in the food plant (supervisors 1 to 12 inclusive are in production areas)*

Supervisor code	Interview[a]	Direct observation
(1)	WORKLOAD	Has four 'departments' under his supervision, but is a newly promoted and inexperienced man, facing teething troubles with new plant, and different problems virtually every day.
(2)	WORKLOAD; quality, labour problems	Main problem is absenteeism: evening shift. Also difficulties in maintaining discipline. Re-allocation of labour leads to quality problems; supervisor often does manual work to fill gaps.
(3)	WORKLOAD; costs, quality	This supervisor undertakes an unusually wide range of activities as well as being active in ASTMS. Duties include budgeting. High incidence of quality and malfunction problems.
(4)	TECHNICAL PROBLEMS; workload, change of plans, shortages	Antiquated equipment: great deal of his time is spent dealing with machine breakdowns and consequent disruptions to plans.
(5)	KEEPING COSTS DOWN	Works out efficiency figures daily for each of three lines. Assistant relieves supervisor of much direct supervision, so he spends most time on technical problems and dealing with labour shortage.
(6)	TECHNICAL PROBLEMS; quality	Breakdowns and shortages of materials (especially wrapping) are prominent. Much time spent dealing with machine adjustments and checking on quality.
(7)	WORKLOAD	Experiencing teething problems on new machine. Frequent checking and trouble-shooting: constant stream of incidents. Frequent, direct contact with other departments (mainly maintenance and services).

(*Contd.*)

Table 5.1 (*Contd.*)

Supervisor code	Interview[a]	Direct observation
(8)	LABOUR PROBLEMS; technical problems	Breakdowns frequent, which lead to need for re-allocating labour, which gives rise to tension over payment with operators on piecework.
(9)	All (except keeping costs down)	Major problem concerns teething troubles with experimental caramel processing drum. Also with temperamental wrapping machines.
(10)	CHANGE OF PLANS; workload, shortages	Main disturbance is due to a shortage of containers. This creates a need to re-schedule throughputs frequently.
(11)	LABOUR PROBLEMS; workload, change of plans, shortages	Planning deficiencies lead to uncertainties about new work and to frequent re-allocation of jobs. Operatives are resentful. Sustained disturbance-handling.
(12)	WORKLOAD; costs, quality, labour problems	Similar problems to no. 11 (same department). Planning let-downs, inaccurate recording of material identifications, etc. Supervisor's job has been extended to encompass monitoring of efficiency rates, stocktaking.
(13)	WORKLOAD; labour problems	In charge of millwrights. Continually on the move through the factory. Supervision difficult because men are strongly unionized and resent discipline. This supervisor now does work of two. Covers whole plant.
(14)	CHANGE OF PLANS; workload, shortages	In charge of electricians. Failings in the planning system co-ordinating electrical jobs with others cause supervisor to do great deal of chasing around. Shortages break up continuity of work and cause dissatisfaction among men.
(15)	WORKLOAD; labour problems	In charge of lifts and internal transport maintenance. During observation most work involved contact with outside suppliers and contractors and co-

(*Contd.*)

Table 5.1 (*Contd.*)

Supervisor code	Interview[a]	Direct observation
		ordination with other supervisors. No labour problems observed.
(16)	SHORTAGES; workload	In charge of a service section. Pressure from client departments for jobs to be expedited. No examples of problems due to shortages were observed.

(*a*) Main pressure experienced (capitals); other pressures described as 'considerable'.

for production workers in both plants. It is also worth noting from Table 5.1, apropos of the validity of the interview data, that there is a fair degree of matching with conclusions drawn from the observations.

Almost two-thirds of the supervisors reported experiencing ambiguity about what they were expected to do in their jobs, though only a few (13 per cent) claimed that this happened often. About half of them complained that they did not have sufficient information to do their job adequately. Problems of ambiguity and uncertainty mostly arose over production problems, closely followed by technical and labour problems. For example, in production:

> 'If a job comes through which I've not done before, then I'm not quite sure what's to be done with it. Normally you get no instructions with a new job . . . For instance, you don't know where it's got to go after this section';

and on a labour problem:

> 'A chap refused some alternative work, and I thought I should send him home. But I don't know if I can. Do I just let him sit down and pay him?'

These complaints concern problems of how to perform the job, but there is a more personal side to ambiguity about the supervisor's role. For example, 43 per cent of the supervisors complained about not knowing how their superior evaluated them and 50 per cent were bothered about the lack of clarity in criteria for further promotion.

The incidence of different types of pressure varied between the two plants and between production and non-production supervisors. For example, supervisors in the food plant, where much of the equipment was elderly, reported greater pressures from quality and technical problems, unevenness in work and changes of plan, and workload generally. Engineering supervisors reported greater pressures from labour problems, since they were not always confident of receiving management's backing in their handling of them. Production supervisors reported greater pressures over the quality of their section's work, and over labour, technical and breakdown problems, than did their non-production counterparts. There was no appreciable difference in the distributions of role conflict and ambiguity reported either by site or type or supervisor. None the less, the differences in type of pressure experienced between sites and categories of supervisor again urges caution against an uncritical adoption of any one stereotype to characterize supervisors or their jobs.

Stress, tension and job satisfaction

Nearly half (46 per cent) the supervisors said that the conditions of their job placed them under stress on frequent occasions, in contrast to only 18 per cent who said that their job was never stressful. Many supervisors pointed to the frequent recurrence of crises as a particular source of stress. Nearly all (91 per cent) thought that their job was more stressful than that of shopfloor workers, but their opinions were evenly divided as to whether they experienced more stress than their immediate superiors.

We endeavoured to obtain a systematic assessment of what aspects of their jobs gave rise to stress for supervisors by asking a series of 16 questions adapted from Kahn *et al.*'s (1964) 'Job-Related Tension Index'. In each question, supervisors were asked how much the feature in their job 'bothered' them. The method of scoring and the results are summarized in Table 5.2.

The problems which created least tension in supervisors' minds concerned their personal acceptability, their level of training and ambiguity about the scope of their responsibilities. Their attitude to training, given that a majority had not received any training for the job, suggests that they consider personal qualities and experience to be of greater importance in carrying out their work. This contrasts

Table 5.2 *Job tension: problems which bothered supervisors in their jobs[a]*

	Problem	Mean score[b]
(1)	Pay not determined on a fair basis relative to other groups	3.3
(2)	Too few opportunities for promotion	2.6
(3)	Having too heavy a workload	2.5
(4)	Not having enough information to do the job	2.5
(5)	Volume of work interferes with performance of job	2.5
(6)	Having to do things against one's better judgement	2.5
(7)	Having too little authority to carry out one's responsibilities	2.4
(8)	Having to decide things that affect lives of people one knows	2.4
(9)	Not being able to satisfy conflicting demands of different people	2.3
(10)	Not knowing how superior evaluates one's performance	2.3
(11)	Feeling unable to influence superior's decisions	2.2
(12)	Not knowing what is expected of one	2.1
(13)	Having too much responsibility	2.0
(14)	Being unclear as to scope and responsibilities of the job	1.8
(15)	Feeling that one is not fully trained to handle the job	1.7
(16)	Feeling not liked or accepted by people one works with	1.6

(*a*) Responses to the 16 statements can be aggregated. Conceptually they all refer to potential tension about the job, and statistically the internal consistency of an aggregated measure is high: the K–R 8 Coefficient is 0.86. This measure is labelled 'job tension'.

(*b*) The above 16 statements are abbreviated and ordered according to their mean score, not as in the original interview. Each problem was scored on a five-point scale where 1 = the problem never bothers me; 2 = not often; 3 = sometimes; 4 = rather often; and 5 = nearly all the time.

with the concern voiced for supervisory training in management publications (e.g. BIM, 1976; Bates and Hosking, 1977). Ambiguity in the form of insufficient information (problem 4) did bother supervisors to some extent, but ambiguity about definitions of the job (problems 12 and 14) were not serious sources of tension for most of them. A lack of clear formal definition can, of course, provide an opportunity for exercising discretion in the conduct of a job, which is probably more compatible with the variable nature of most of the supervisors' jobs than a high degree of formal definition would have been.

Two kinds of problems bothered supervisors more. The first concerned their status, notably the feeling that their pay was unfairly determined relative to other groups, and their lack of promotion prospects.[3] The reaction of supervisors to statements on 'the supervisor's role today' concerning their status also clearly indicated that they felt they had not been accepted into management as much as they should be and that they did not enjoy adequate promotion prospects. Only 42 per cent of the supervisors believed that they had been accepted into management, compared with 81 per cent who said this should have happened. Ninety-five per cent said that able supervisors should be given promotion opportunities, but only 60 per cent perceived that these were available.

The second kind of problem which bothered supervisors was related to pressures in the job: having too heavy a workload, not having enough information to do the job, and the volume of work interfering with performance. These sources of tension reflect the main pressure supervisors identified, the burden of their workloads, for the insufficiency of information was partly caused by their lack of time to go and obtain it.

'Job tension', the aggregation of the 16 job-related tension scores described in Table 5.2 note (*a*), was closely associated with the level of overall job satisfaction among the supervisors, in that greater job tension was accompanied by lower job satisfaction ($r = -0.52$, $p < 0.001$). Overall job satisfaction was computed by summing supervisors' responses on their degree of satisfaction with 20 specific aspects of their jobs. These specific aspects are listed in Table 5.3. The aggregation of satisfaction scores for different aspects of the supervisor's job is conceptually acceptable in terms of the notion of 'general' job satisfaction, and it has a statistical basis, too, in that the composite measure has a high internal reliability coefficient.[4]

Having said that, one has to be mindful of the fact that a job is not simply an entity but also a complex amalgam of different aspects (tasks, responsibilities, roles, relationships, rewards) and that each aspect is an interesting phenomenon in its own right. In order to gain a more refined appreciation of supervisors' job satisfaction, attention must therefore be given to the individual job aspects. Satisfaction with these in fact varied in a way that is obscured by the fairly high level of overall job satisfaction. Table 5.3 summarizes these findings and also the levels of importance which supervisors, on average, attached to each of the 20 job aspects.

Table 5.3 *Supervisors' satisfaction with 20 aspects of their jobs, and the importance they attached to each aspect*

Aspects of the job	Satisfaction mean score[a]	Importance mean score[b]
The work itself	1.8	1.5
Relations with the workgroup	1.8	1.5
Relations with immediate manager	1.9	1.6
Job security	1.9	1.6
Relations with other supervisors	1.9	1.7
Opportunities for achievement	2.1	1.6
Amount of responsibility	2.1	2.0
Physical working conditions	2.1	2.2
Hours of work	2.1	2.5
Company policy and administration	2.2	1.6
Backing from management	2.3	2.2
Style of management	2.3	2.2
Procedures for settling one's grievances	2.4	1.8
Opportunities for developing one's abilities	2.4	2.2
Recognition by management	2.6	2.1
Amount of authority	2.6	2.2
Relations with higher management	2.7	2.0
Benefits and privileges	2.7	2.1
Pay	2.9	1.8
Opportunities for promotion	2.9	3.0
Total of above 20 aspects	46.0	

(*a*) Satisfaction was scored on a five-point scale: 1 = completely satisfied, 2 = fairly satisfied, 3 = neither satisfied nor dissatisfied, 4 = fairly dissatisfied, 5 = completely dissatisfied.
(*b*) Importance was similarly scored on a five-point scale: 1 = extremely important, 2 = important, 3 = fairly important, 4 = not of too much importance, 5 = not particularly important.

Supervisors were most satisfied with the work itself, the relationships they enjoyed with workers, managers and other supervisors, and with their job security. These were also the aspects of the job to which they tended to attach most importance. Other very important aspects in their eyes were opportunities for achievement, general company policy, grievance procedures and pay. The degree of satisfaction derived from their work and working relationships is remarkable, considering the pressures which supervisors experienced. Their work brings pressures but also satisfaction. While there may be less satisfaction nowadays in occupying a role which historically has declined in status and differential reward, pride and satisfaction can still be had in performing a supervisor's job. Perhaps keeping things going, despite the problems and conflicts involved, represents a visible achievement.[5]

The aspects of the job with which supervisors were least satisfied were pay, promotion prospects, benefits and privileges, relations with higher management, recognition and the authority they enjoyed. These refer not to their work but to their status. With the exception of promotion, which most supervisors did not expect to achieve, these aspects were regarded as at least moderately important, and pay quite highly so. The relative dissatisfaction with status, recognition and authority reflects the concern which was shown by reactions to statements on 'the supervisor's role today'. For satisfaction with all these aspects of the job declined the more the supervisors' perceptions of their line management status and acceptance into management fell short of what they felt they should be. This was reflected in overall job satisfaction (sum of all 20 aspects) which declined the greater was the perceived shortfall in (1) line management status and in (2) acceptance into management.[6]

The fact that supervisors tended at one and the same time to be satisfied with their work and working relationships and yet to experience conflict and pressure suggests that most of them were located rather more in the middle of hierarchical and communication flows than on the outside. Their status position was, however, a different matter. Supervisors by and large felt that they had not been accepted into management, that their status left much to be desired, and that they were not always appreciated or recognized. In these respects, they were 'on the margin', certainly in their position *vis-à-vis* management. Different characterizations are therefore required for the supervisor's work role and for his status position.

Conditions of the job and how supervisors feel about it

Appendix 5.1 lists the correlations between the conditions of their jobs reported by supervisors (role conflict, pressure, and ambiguity) and the stress, job tension and job satisfaction they felt.

The two forms of inter-sender role conflict were liable to be reported together: these were (1) being caught between management's and workers' demands and (2) receiving conflicting instructions from within management. Both these forms of being caught in the middle were rather more strongly associated with supervisors experiencing pressure than was conflict with only one other party. Pressure on supervisors tends to be greatest when they are subject to conflicting expectations from above and below, and when they receive conflicting orders from management. The experience of ambiguity stands out as a separate phenomenon, which is not generally linked to role conflict or to pressure.

The above indicators of job conditions are each associated with job tension: this is increased by role conflict, pressure and ambiguity. Receiving conflicting orders from within management is the most strongly related to job tension. The experience of stress, on the other hand, is most closely linked to conflict with one other person and to pressure, in such a way that the greater the interpersonal conflict and the pressure, the higher the stress a supervisor tends to experience. Levels of job satisfaction do not vary markedly with job conditions. Lower job satisfaction, however, does accompany higher stress and, particularly, greater job tension.

Although the cross-sectional data we collected at one point in time cannot demonstrate cause and effect, they do suggest that job conditions may influence levels of job satisfaction through a two-stage process. In the first stage, unfavourable job conditions involving conflict, pressure and ambiguity generate stress and job tension for many, though not all, supervisors. Supervisors, being individuals with their own temperaments, personalities and experience, do not all react to job conditions in the same way; but nevertheless there is a trend.[7] In the second stage, stress and job tension contribute to a lowering of job satisfaction – again a trend which will be true for many but not for all supervisors. The use of partial correlation analysis supports this suggestion of a two-stage relationship: the strength of associations between stress and job tension, respectively, with unfavourable job conditions is to some degree independent of the connection between stress, job tension and job satisfaction. The latter connection is also partly independent of the link that job conditions have with stress and job tension.

Coping with the job

Up to this point, we have given attention to the incidence of conflicts and pressures experienced by the supervisors, without considering how they adjusted the balance of their activities to meet these problems. Supervisors' descriptions of how they coped with conflicts and pressures suggested that a number of alternative strategies are adopted. One is to attempt to supervise in a way that particularly closely reflects managerial concerns for output, quality, cost effectiveness and discipline, and to depend heavily upon the superior manager's authority by referring to him rather than taking the initiative. A second coping strategy appears to place greater emphasis upon maintaining a high quality of morale and effectiveness among the workgroup, coupled with a desire on the supervisor's part to settle problems arising in his section on his own initiative. Supervisors adopting this approach tended to say, for example, that 'my policy is to keep problems away from my manager' and 'I try to sort it out at my level'. Other supervisors, thirdly, tended to withdraw from role conflicts and pressures, sometimes by spending more time on paperwork or looking over equipment and sometimes by meeting crises not through confrontation but through doing manual work as a stop-gap measure. This approach was exemplified by remarks such as 'if there's no work for the men, management expect you to find them other work – but the men won't do it so I just turn a blind eye.'[8]

These indications that supervisors might be adopting somewhat different strategies for coping with conflicts and pressure encouraged us to try and examine the possibility more systematically, with reference to the priority ratings which supervisors had given to a set of 18 tasks and activities on which we questioned them. The supposition here was that conflicts and pressures would oblige supervisors to make a choice of priority activities, and that examination of these priorities might therefore throw more light on coping strategies. Our method of ascertaining priorities is described first, followed by what we found, and then by an attempt to explore coping strategies on the basis of these findings.

1. Ascertaining priorities

We focused on the priority attached to each activity by the supervisor himself. This is not to suggest that any of the activities would not be important at some time, but rather that when more than one task is being urgently demanded by other parties a question of priority arises. This methodology contrasts with the more traditional activity analysis of supervisory tasks where importance is assessed by reference to the time allocation between tasks, the assumption being that time reflects importance. Whilst one American study of supervisory activities did conclude that the importance and the perceived frequency of supervisory activities were very similar (Dowell and Wexley, 1978), most studies have failed to test the assertion that time reflects importance. Supervisors we talked to emphasized the irregularity of certain key tasks: sometimes these would take up a great amount of time, but on other occasions they were dealt with in a shorter amount of time.

Various studies of supervisory and managerial behaviour have pointed to a constant switching between tasks; that is, supervisors and managers rarely have time to complete a task before being called away to tackle something else. Activity analysis has difficulty in handling this constant switching between tasks (e.g. Guest, 1956; Mintzberg, 1973). Because activity analysis is limited to what can be observed, it is difficult to explore the interrelation between activities or even the same activity fragmented over a longer period of time. An analogy can be drawn between the supervisor's job and a multi-stranded rope of fibres of different lengths where each fibre comes to the surface one or more times in observable episodes (Marples, 1967). The fibres represent the supervisory tasks. The observer only sees the episodes/activities and misses the nature of the task. The present approach, by focusing on the significance attached to the activity by the supervisor himself, attempts to cope with the problem of interrelating fragmented behaviour over a period of time.

The activities/tasks which the supervisors had to rate are shown in Table 5.4. The development of this list of activities started from a consideration of the supervisory functions discussed in Thurley and Hamblin (1963) and Thurley and Wirdenius (1973). Supervisors were encouraged to add other supervisory tasks or activities to the list, but few supervisors made use of this facility, which suggests that the list includes most if not all their more important activities.

Table 5.4   *List of tasks and activities to which supervisors were asked to attach priority*

Title	Description
Subordinates	Communicating with members of supervisor's own workgroup
Supervisors	Communicating with other supervisors
Superiors	Communicating with superiors
Pace	Maintaining the pace of work
Quality	Ensuring the quality of work
Discipline	Maintaining discipline
Safety	Handling safety problems
Records	Keeping records
Costs	Keeping costs down
Materials	Ensuring the supply of materials
Tools	Ensuring the supply of tools
Recruits	Getting the right recruits
Equipment	Keeping an eye on the equipment
Workload	Planning and allocating the workload
Labour	Matching men to jobs and allocating labour
Queries	Dealing with workers' queries
Training	Training members of the workgroup
Direct work	Personally doing direct or operative work

2. Supervisors' priorities

Table 5.5 shows how supervisors scored the activities in terms of their priorities. The priorities are listed in descending order of importance by their mean average score. The priorities were scored on a twenty-one point scale with 1 = top priority and 21 = low priority. The lower the score, the higher the priority.

The highest priority overall was maintaining quality, closely followed by planning and allocating the workload, although more supervisors gave this as their top priority (n = 44). The spread of responses as measured by the standard deviation was much lower for maintaining quality, which indicates that supervisors who did not rate quality as their highest priority were still likely to rate it very highly. Communication with superiors was rated as top priority by 37 supervisors.

It has generally been accepted that the primary function of the

Table 5.5 Supervisory priorities

Sample	Priorities																	
	Quality	Workload	Communicating with superiors	Materials	Communicating with subordinates	Discipline	Safety	Pace	Costs	Communicating with supervisors	Queries	Labour	Equipment	Training	Recruits	Records	Tools	Direct work
All supervisors																		
Mean scores	5.1	5.6	6.5	7.0	7.4	7.4	7.5	7.5	8.5	9.0	9.0	9.5	11.2	11.6	11.6	11.7	11.7	16.2
Standard deviation	3.5	5.4	4.8	5.0	4.9	4.0	4.2	4.9	4.8	5.1	4.5	6.0	4.8	5.7	6.6	5.5	5.7	4.8
Nos. highest priority[a]	22	44	37	14	17	8	11	14	2	9	5	10	4	5	17	7	3	2
Engineering supervisors																		
Mean scores	5.7	7.2*	8.0*	9.2*	8.7*	6.3*	6.7	8.3	10.9*	9.8*	7.6	8.8	10.5	9.6*	8.5*	12.7	11.5	16.6
Standard deviation	3.9	5.6	5.4	5.6	5.1	3.7	4.4	4.8	4.7	5.2	4.5	5.7	4.6	5.9	6.0	5.3	5.7	4.2
Nos. highest priority[a]	6	9	8	4	3	4	7	3	0	1	2	3	1	2	12	3	0	1
Food supervisors																		
Mean scores	4.8	4.8*	5.7*	5.8*	6.6*	8.0*	7.8	7.1	7.3*	8.5	9.7	9.9	11.5	12.5*	13.3*	11.2	11.9	16.1
Standard deviation	3.3	5.2	4.3	4.3	4.6	4.0	4.0	4.9	4.3	5.1	4.3	6.1	4.9	5.4	6.3	5.5	5.7	5.1
Nos. highest priority[a]	16	35	29	10	14	4	4	11	2	8	3	7	3	3	5	4	3	1
Production supervisors																		
Mean scores	5.2	6.3	7.3+	6.1+	7.9	7.3	7.6	7.5	8.4	9.8+	9.4	9.7	11.3	11.3	11.3	12.8+	11.8	16.4
Standard deviation	3.5	5.9	5.0	4.5	5.1	3.9	4.2	4.8	4.6	5.2	4.6	5.9	4.9	5.9	6.6	5.0	5.9	4.4
Nos. highest priority[a]	17	28	23	12	12	5	7	9	1	4	4	8	2	4	13	2	3	1

(Contd.)

Table 5.5 (*Contd.*)

	Priorities																	
Sample	Quality	Workload	Communicating with superiors	Materials	Communicating with subordinates	Discipline	Safety	Pace	Costs	Communicating with supervisors	Queries	Labour	Equipment	Training	Recruits	Records	Tools	Direct work
Non-production supervisors																		
Mean scores	4.9	4.2	4.9[+]	9.1[+]	6.1	7.8	7.0	7.5	8.9	7.0[+]	8.1	9.1	10.8	11.9	12.4	9.1[+]	11.5	16.0
Standard deviation	3.7	4.1	3.8	5.5	4.0	4.2	4.0	5.2	5.0	4.6	4.0	6.1	4.7	5.3	6.4	5.6	5.1	5.8
Nos. highest priority[a]	5	16	14	2	5	3	4	5	1	5	1	2	2	1	4	.5	0	1

(a) Numbers of supervisors giving that activity/task the highest priority score; numbers sum to more than 156, as some supervisors gave more than one equal highest priority.

* t-test, p < 0.01, for mean difference between sites.   [+] t-test, p < 0.01, for mean differences between production and non-production supervisors.

supervisor is the achievement of production targets within established efficiency and quality standards (BIM, 1976). Hill (1976b), similarly, reported that the most important supervisory function was to ensure the adequate flow of work. One activity analysis of American jobbing supervisors found that progressing the work was the most important supervisory activity and that 'quality' accounted for a higher percentage of supervisors' time than any other activity (Guest, 1956). A further American study, of a pipe-line construction company, found that supervisors rated 'quality' as their most important responsibility, even above their responsibility for production (Cummings, 1972).

The present findings about 'quality' and 'planning and allocating the workload' are broadly comparable with these other studies despite the differences in the respective methodologies, with the emphasis here being on priorities as opposed to time allocation. One difference in the present study is the relatively middling priority attached to 'maintaining the pace of work', with only 14 supervisors placing it as their top priority. This relatively low ranking is probably explained by the fact that many of the jobs in the workgroups were machine paced, and that piecework payment systems in production relieved supervisors of the need to motivate employees towards high output. The lowest priority by far was for doing direct or operative work of a non-supervisory nature. This contrasts significantly with the activity analysis studies mentioned above, where direct or operative work took up substantial percentages of the supervisors' time. The contrast here is primarily due to the fact that interviews can record that supervisors give low priority to doing direct/operative work, while observational methods can record how much of their time it takes up. Thus our own observations showed that some supervisors who gave doing direct/operative work a low priority nevertheless spent a portion of their time doing it in order to cover for an absentee or because there were no competing demands on them.

Supervisors tended to give higher priority to communications with superiors than to communications with subordinates. Communications with other supervisors came much lower down the list still. There is a contrast here between supervisors' priorities in communications and the importance they attached to having good relationships with the same groups as a factor contributing to job satisfaction (cf. Table 5.3). In the context of job satisfaction, having satisfactory relationships with other supervisors is virtually as important as having good relations with the workgroup and the immediate superior. In the context of performing the job, often under pressure from above and below, vertical communications assume greater priority for most supervisors than do lateral ones with other supervisors. It is noted later, in Chapter 8 (page 184), how a similar contrast emerges in supervisors' views on social identification within the firm. They tend to see themselves as most similar to other supervisors so far as attitudes and modes of behaviour are concerned. This similarity makes for congenial social relationships and will presumably contribute to job satisfaction. However, they attached greater priority to the links they had with management and shopfloor workers (in that order), than to their links with other supervisors.

There is no evidence from their ratings of priorities to suggest that the supervisors as a whole did not accept management's objective of efficient shopfloor operations, with emphasis on quality, output and cost reduction. Supervisors attached greater importance in pursuit of their work to communication with management than to communication with other groups. We have earlier seen that supervisors approved of their job being considered as part of line management (Chapter 3). Our later examination of supervisory unionism will point to a continued identification on the part of most supervisors with their immediate managerial superiors, though not necessarily with the 'company' as a whole. This evidence is noted here, because it implies that the pressures and strains supervisors experience arise by and large in the process of carrying out a role aligned towards managerial production objectives which they accept, rather than arising because they reject such objectives. Other studies also suggest that supervisors generally identify positively with management's production objectives (e.g. Woodward, 1970; Beynon, 1973).

Table 5.5 also points to some variations in the priority values which supervisors attached to particular activities; that is, while the majority experienced conflicts and pressures in the course of doing their job, they responded in different ways. A small part of the variation can be accounted for by differences between the sites. Although the rank ordering of priorities is similar for the two plants there are significant differences in the mean priority scores for eight of the eighteen activities. There are also significant differences between production and non-production supervisors for four activities. However, analysis of variance indicated that site and production/non-production differences can together only account for seven per cent of the variation in individual supervisors' priorities. This suggests that supervisors were exercising choice in the priorities they attached to activities and that these may represent different coping strategies.

When the supervisors' immediate superiors were asked to give priority ratings to the same activities in those supervisors' jobs, they generally discriminated between activities far less than supervisors themselves. The managers also tended to rate every activity as having higher priority than did supervisors. While managers and supervisors as a whole ranked the 18 activities in a similar order, there were many cases of disagreement between individual supervisors and their managers. This could mean that some managers at least had little idea of what their supervisors did, a conclusion which other investigators have also reached (e.g. Hill, 1976b; Smith, 1978). It is a situation which could exacerbate conflict between manager and supervisor over how the latter's job is to be carried out, if the manager attempts to intervene in shopfloor management. In practice, however, it often seems to provide the supervisor with some freedom to choose his own approach to coping with the demands of the job.

3. *Alternative coping strategies*

We earlier recorded our impression that supervisors tended to adopt one of three main strategies for coping with conflicts and pressures. One was a 'management-oriented' strategy, in the sense that it reflected management concerns particularly closely and involved referral of many problems to the manager. The second was 'workgroup-oriented' in the sense that it relied on maintaining high workgroup morale, coupled with a preference by the supervisor for settling problems himself with his section. The third strategy was 'neutral', in the sense of favouring withdrawal from conflicts between management and labour by giving more attention to less contentious issues such as technology or paper work.

The supervisory behaviour associated with each strategy may not be so drastically different since there was also a general tendency to give the 'management-oriented' activities high priority. Rather, a difference of emphasis is involved. Indeed, the three strategies cannot be mutually exclusive. Workgroup-oriented supervisors cannot resolve everything without reference to management, or be seen to identify completely with the workgroup. Similarly, a supervisor inclined towards a neutral strategy cannot completely opt out of conflict-prone areas, such as controlling the work and exercising positive shopfloor leadership, although he may attempt to minimize his engagement in them.

Examples of each strategy have been highlighted in previous studies. Beynon (1973) has described the behaviour of management-oriented supervisors on the assembly line. Nichols and Beynon (1977) have described management-oriented supervisors in a chemical company who emphasized their technical ability, even though they lacked technical qualifications, and adopted a managerialist ideology pushing for improved productivity and lower costs: they ignored workgroup norms and were highly critical of management for not living up to their managerial ideal.

Examples of workgroup-oriented supervisory behaviour are forthcoming from studies of piecework payment systems. Brown (1973) has shown how supervisors in this situation used their discretion to bend management rules: where a worker was paid less when waiting for a machine to be repaired than when he was assisting the fitter to repair it, the supervisor would give the worker a spanner to hold. These actions are not simply a question of fiddling the company but should rather be seen as colluding with the workgroup to get the work done. In some cases supervisory involvement may be more than collusion, as the supervisor may well initiate the practice (Roy, 1954). Apart from this tendency to strain the limits of their discretion, such supervisors tend to go beyond this limit if they stand little chance of being detected. Kuhn (1961) showed that as long as the work left the supervisor's section on schedule the supervisor could afford to ignore problems of labour costs and awkward precedents. A workgroup-oriented strategy may also result in some reciprocity: in some stable workgroups supervisors have been found to carry out some of the representative functions of shop-stewards (National Board for Prices and Incomes (NBPI), 1968), whilst some supervisors use shop-stewards as they might use chargehands (Brown, 1973).

Hill (1976b) has provided an example of neutrally-oriented supervisors who did not identify either with management or with the workgroup. This is not an example of dual identification but rather one demonstrating the use of bureaucratic techniques by supervisors to shelter themselves from pressure and conflict.

In the present study it was possible to classify supervisors into one or other of the three orientations just described in terms of their priorities. Priorities have a discretionary element: the supervisor is forced to choose between competing legitimate but incompatible demands; that is, any of the choices he makes in such a situation is legitimate. Therefore the discretionary choice of priorities implies a strategy for coping with the role conflicts of the job. Management-oriented supervisors could be expected to give higher priority to the task-related activities of planning and allocating workload, maintaining the pace of work, ensuring quality, keeping costs down, maintaining discipline and communicating with superiors. Similarly, workgroup-oriented supervisors could be expected to give higher priority to the employee-related activities of training, recruitment, labour allocation, ensuring the supply of tools for workers, progressing materials, and communication with subordinates. In contrast, neutrally-oriented supervisors could be expected to give higher priority to the remaining activities not allocated under the other strategies; that is, keeping an eye on the equipment, maintaining records, dealing with workers' queries, handling safety problems, communicating with other supervisors and doing direct/operative work. The higher priority given to these neutral activities reflects the lower priority given to the management-oriented and workgroup-oriented activities.

Supervisors were grouped into these three categories of coping strategy on the basis of their patterns of priorities. Appendix 5.2 provides statistical details about the categories, internal consistencies, and also the method by which supervisors were allocated to each one. The validity of the classification was further tested by a discriminant analysis, shown in Appendix 5.3. This supported the method of categorization which was employed by discriminating fairly clearly between the two strongest categories: 'workgroup-oriented' and 'neutral'.

All three coping strategies – workgroup-oriented, neutral and management-oriented – were found in both sites and among production as well as non-production supervisors. It seemed possible, nevertheless, that the supervisors' choice of coping strategies would be influenced by their location in particular task situations rather than by their personal preference or orientation. This was not borne out in practice. An analysis employing the detailed information we had collected on task variables from the food plant (see Chapter 4), indicated only that a higher priority tended to be given to planning and allocating the workload (a component of the management-oriented strategy) where the work of the supervisor's section was less repetitious and where production runs were shorte·. The choice of coping strategies as a whole was not found to be associated with the task variables we measured.

Some indication of the qualitative differences in coping strategies to which the statistical analysis points can be provided by extracts from our observation study notebooks. In the following three sections necessarily brief half-hour extracts are given, with comments, for three supervisors whom the discriminant analysis labelled as pursuing respectively a 'workgroup-oriented', 'management-oriented' and 'neutral' strategy.

(1) Supervisor number 7, workgroup-oriented strategy

This supervisor is in very frequent contact with operatives (every few minutes) – he supervises a relatively small group of 14 people. He has far less frequent contact with his manager, who is located in another part of the factory. He directs employees without much reference to the manager. Employees come to him freely, but he is very much in command and employs a rather directive style. His responses to questions on style also indicate that he believes in combining the consulting of employees with a rigid approach to discipline plus a moderate degree of pressure and close supervision. He rates his influence as highest in the area of people management. He spends little time in his office. He cites workload as his main pressure. The following half-hour sequence seemed to be reasonably typical of the mode in which this supervisor coped with the demands of his job:

1.20 Collects replacement for absentee and brings her back into the section.

1.25 Meets one of the operatives who informs him about a breakdown: the wire conveyor belt on the enrober has broken.

1.26 Back in office – makes a telephone call for technician.

1.27 Leaves office to go down to enrober, meets room cleaner on the way. He tells supervisor that he has refused to clean the bagging area because of the clutter of boxes, etc. Supervisor tells him that he will have to see the bagging machine supervisor.

1.30 Down by the Solformat enrober the operatives have already got the section maintenance man in, but he says that he can't do anything.

Coping and surviving

1.31 Phones up maintenance to get a fitter.
1.32 Another replacement worker who was expected has still not turned up. Supervisor phones manager to find out what has happened; the woman has had to go home. Manager says she will send a replacement.
1.37 Gives out pay slips to employees.
1.38 A fitter is repairing the Solformat; supervisor has a word with him.
1.40 Walking back up the room, notices a leak from the steam cupboard – phones up pipe fitters.
1.45 Back in office, starts to plan the night work. The replacement woman turns up and the supervisor shows her where to work.
1.51 Back in office, pay query from one of the workers. Supervisor phones up the industrial engineers about the rates of pay for the job.

(2) Supervisor number 3, management-oriented strategy

This supervisor enjoys as frequent a contact with his manager as with his workers. His manager's office is next door to his own. He supervises a relatively large group of 40 people, though their supervision is shared with one other supervisor. He refers to his manager more often than does the previous supervisor (number 7), but since he is a supervisor of some twenty years' experience his manager often relies on him for detailed knowledge of what is happening. This supervisor believes in a consultative style of supervision and in being flexible about discipline. He does not believe in close supervision. He reckons that he carries the same influence in all the main areas of his job. He spends a moderate amount of his time off the section, in his office or in meetings, and he appears to give more attention to stock records, costs and budgeting requirements than does supervisor number 7. He cites his main pressures as workload, keeping costs down and maintaining quality. This balance of activities is partly due to sharing supervision: the other supervisor in the section gives more attention to labour matters. The following summarized half-hour sequence illustrates this more office-based, administratively-oriented approach:

10.40 Back in his office, a temporary stand-in comes in. Maintenance manager then comes in to ask about padlocks for the safety locking system.
10.50 Services supervisor and the trainee manager from the fourth

115

floor come into the office. Trainee manager reports breakdown on wrapper is repaired – can supervisor's section (no. 27 plant) start feeding more output? Services supervisor passes on message about breakdown upstream which may affect the section later on.

11.00 Operative of no. 27 plant comes in – it will take until after lunch to increase output.

11.03 Telephone call – supervisor takes message. Maintenance manager comes in with latest news on the safety locking system.

11.05 Fourth floor trainee manager comes into office again to find out about no. 27's output.

11.07 Telephone call – supervisor takes message.

11.10 Supervisor passes on telephone message to services supervisor.

(3) Supervisor number 6, neutral strategy

This supervisor is in more frequent contact with his workgroup of 18 people than he is with his manager. He relies quite a lot on the informal network he has built up with other supervisors which helps by exchanging labour and services to suit contingencies. He consciously adopts a low profile style – 'don't make too much fuss', and spends a good deal of his time checking the equipment. He describes an appropriate style as task-centred but also consultative. He does not take an extreme view either way on discipline or sticking to the book on working methods, and is not strongly inclined to close supervision or putting pressure on employees. He rates his influence as higher on organization and technical matters than on managing people. He spends a large proportion of his time walking and looking around, and not much in his office. The following is a half-hour sequence which illustrates this approach:

9.30 New load of caramel arrives – in fact done as a favour by the blackcurrant boilers. Visual watch on loading. Checks with trolley man how things are in U4 (the section which feeds into his own) – still having problems with vanilla kettles. Asks him to pass on news about no overtime this Saturday morning to one operator in U4 who boils up caramel for the supervisor.

9.36 Returns to office – collects mail: details of Christmas sale arrangements. Takes it to leading woman – she will make a copy of it. Comments to observer that 'if you just put it on the notice board somebody will pinch it; then people will keep pestering me for the information which I won't know'.

9.39 Service man comes in for keys – returns them within five minutes.

9.45 Goes for a walk around the section: 'to see what's happening'. Cut and wrap still not working at full speed. Fitter is still there – in the meantime the two wrapping machines which broke down yesterday are still waiting to be repaired. No real change; has few words with anyone. Visual check 'let people see me: I rely on them to raise any problems with me'.

9.57 Operator on blackcurrant extruder comes up to supervisor and complains about an overflow of nougat from his hopper . . . which is rapidly hardening.

10.01 Go and see fitter: 'That operator is a perpetual moaner, but I have to be seen to do something'.

Conclusion

The supervisors we studied in two Birmingham batch production plants were centrally and actively involved in maintaining the operations of their sections. It would be more correct to conclude that they were in the middle of things rather than outside the main vertical hierarchy and the main lines of communication. Many of them felt under pressure from problems arising in keeping the work of their sections going, and a majority were liable to face various forms of role conflict. Pressures in the job appeared, on the whole, to create more strain for supervisors than did conflict or ambiguities in their role. For many, though certainly not all, the job was stressful, appreciably more so than the shopfloor life from which they had been promoted. This comparison with the shopfloor helps one to appreciate why the problem which bothered supervisors most was the inequity, as they saw it, of their pay levels compared with those for other groups. As will be seen in Chapter 7, shopfloor pay levels in both plants could overlap with those for supervisors.

A combination of evidence from listening to supervisors, observing a small number of them and analysing their pattern of priorities suggests that different supervisors tend to adopt different strategies to cope with pressures and conflicts in the job. These strategies represent differences of emphasis rather than discrete approaches to the job. The distinctions drawn here are still only tentative; we are still investigating them further both from a qualitative angle and also to see whether they can be understood in the context of the supervisor's own characteristics and those of the immediate work context.

It appears very unlikely, judging both by our findings and those of other investigators, that many of the supervisors' own managers fully understand the pressures and conflict that those supervisors may have to cope with. They probably have even less appreciation of the rationales behind the coping strategies which supervisors adopt. Our observations showed clearly that managers were not in close contact with shopfloor or maintenance operations, or with the stream of contingencies to be handled which in some cases seemed virtually continuous. Nor could managers have been closely aware of the conflicting demands which supervisors can face, both in production and non-production sections, and which are heightened as a result of the disturbances to other people's expectations when work is not accomplished because of unreliable equipment, the 'knock-on' effects of short-term planning changes, shortages, and other problems which are primarily inabilities or inadequacies in the *management* system.

The likelihood that managerial superiors have only a distant understanding of what their supervisors do or of supervisors' policies for coping with what is expected of them, raises the question of on what basis they assess supervisors' levels of performance. This is the subject of the following chapter.

Appendix 5.1 *Correlations between conditions of their jobs reported by supervisors and their feelings about these jobs (range of Ns = 145 to 148 supervisors)*

	1	2	3	4	5	6	7
(1) Inter-sender role conflict: men in the middle[a]	—						
(2) Inter-sender role conflict: conflicting orders from management[b]	38***	—					
(3) Conflict with one other party/person[a]	10	17*	—				
(4) Amount of pressure[b]	20**	32***	16*	—			
(5) Role ambiguity[a]	02	10	14*	03	—		
(6) Stress[a]	05	17*	23**	30***	13	—	
(7) Job tension[c]	23**	38***	24**	15*	27***	26***	—
(8) Overall job satisfaction[c]	−12	−08	−12	−19*	−19*	−29***	−52***

Pearson product-moment correlation coefficients, decimal points omitted. $*p < 0.05$; $**p < 0.01$; $***p < 0.001$.
(a) Measured by 3-point scale (b) Measured by 5-point scale. (c) Measure described in text (Tables 5.2 and 5.3).

Appendix 5.2   *Supervisors' coping strategies: internal reliability coefficients and method of allocating supervisors to the three categories*

Coping strategy	Internal reliability (K–R 8)
'Neutral'	0.70
'Workgroup-oriented'	0.77
'Management-oriented'	0.51

The *'neutral'coping strategy* contained the following priority items: keeping an eye on equipment, keeping records, dealing with workers' queries, handling safety problems, communicating with other supervisors, and doing direct/operative work. The *'workgroup-oriented' strategy* initially contained six priority items: recruits, training, labour allocation, progressing tools for workers, progressing materials and communicating with subordinates. Omitting the last two items improved the internal reliability coefficient of the category to 0.77. There is some justification for treating these two activities as task-related and they were therefore added to the management-oriented activities which then attained the marginally acceptable reliability of 0.51. Priorities included in the *'management-oriented' category* are: planning and allocating the workload, maintaining the pace of work, ensuring quality, keeping costs down, maintaining discipline, communicating with superiors, progressing materials, and communicating with subordinates.

It was possible to allocate all but three supervisors to one of these coping strategy categories. Where supervisors had given above average priority scores to either neutral or workgroup-oriented categories, they were classified as adopting that particular strategy. Where supervisors gave below average priority scores to both sets of activities, they were classified as management-oriented on the grounds that they entered into neither of the other two stronger categories. If a supervisor scored above average on both neutral and workgroup-oriented categories, he was left unclassified. The justification for identifying management-oriented supervisors by means of a residual category when its reliability coefficient is not very satisfactory is that the set of activities so identified included eight of the nine activities to which supervisors overall gave highest priority, and that these activities are all task-oriented.

Appendix 5.3   *Discriminant analysis of supervisory priorities*

| Priorities[a] | Standardized discriminant function coefficients[b] | |
	Function 1 (workgroup strategy)	Function 2 (neutral strategy)
Recruits	0.72	0.14
Training	0.61	− 0.40
Labour allocation	0.53	0.11
Tools	0.49	0.00
Subordinates	− 0.12	− 0.34
Quality	0.06	− 0.32
Workload	− 0.05	− 0.22
Materials	− 0.13	0.04
Pace	− 0.38	0.06
Costs	0.05	0.15
Safety	− 0.12	0.18
Superiors	− 0.19	0.21
Discipline	− 0.20	0.23
Supervisors	− 0.07	0.46
Equipment	0.25	0.47
Direct work	0.15	0.49
Queries	0.28	0.51
Records	0.11	0.63

(a) See Chapter 5, Table 5.4 for a description of these priorities.
(b) These coefficients indicate the relative contribution of each priority to the strategy (function). As with factor analysis these coefficients can be used to label the strategies (functions) by identifying the dominant characteristic they measure. Conventionally, coefficients of over 0.50 are taken to define a function while those over 0.30 can be used to add detail (Youngman, 1979). The tests of significance for the two discriminant functions are respectively: Wilks' Lambda 0.08 and 0.33; Chi-square 185 and 82 ($p < 0.001$)

6

Assessing supervisory performance

There is grave doubt as to whether there is any real purpose in designing studies which purport to measure supervisory effectiveness as a single and discrete problem. (Thurley and Wirdenius, *Supervision: A Reappraisal* (1973: 55))

Supervisors do not normally produce any tangible output which can be measured. Their roles appear to be ill-defined and variable, and so do not offer a secure foundation upon which to erect standardized criteria of performance. It is therefore not possible to assess supervisory performance straightforwardly by reference to 'objective' and standard measurements. The problem is compounded by the difficulty of isolating a unique supervisory contribution, as Thurley and Wirdenius point out above, for supervisors typically work as part of a wider social system. Their performance depends upon co-operation from others and upon the quality of those management policies and procedures within which the supervisors carry out their jobs (Bates and Hosking, 1977: 52).

Subjective assessment of supervisory performance also runs into problems. Those who search for a valid subjectively-based measurement of supervisory or managerial performance have to admit to making little progress despite many studies since the Second World War (cf. Smith, 1976). The very notion of 'good' supervisory performance as something upon which all parties can agree is open to serious question. The discontinuities in expectations and understandings of the supervisory role between managers, specialists, supervisors and employees, which give rise to role conflict and pressures for supervisors, indicate that one should not expect to find high agreement between different assessments of a supervisor's performance. Such assessments have to be understood with reference not only to the supervisor, but also to characteristics of the assessor, to how the assessor's experience and expectations differ from the supervisor's and to the quality of the relationship which prevails between the two people.[1]

When supervisory performance is assessed in practice, rating scales are the most common measuring instruments, usually being completed by immediate superiors. Although we have pointed to disagreements between supervisors and their managers over supervisory priorities and authority, the prevailing definition of appropriate supervisory behaviour will probably be influenced primarily by the immediately superior manager (Pfeffer and Salancik, 1975). For the manager can usually exert a substantial influence over the supervisor's psychological working environment in terms of pressure, praise and so forth. He may also exert some influence over the supervisor's level of reward and over whatever opportunities there are for upgrading or promotion.

With this in mind, the present chapter reports on the ways in which managers rated supervisors' performance, and compares these with the supervisors' self-ratings. It then examines the proposition that subjective ratings tell one about the rater as well as about the person being rated, and it concludes by discussing the implications of evidence in support of the proposition.

Ratings of supervisors' performance

Managers were asked to give ratings for each of their subordinate supervisors along six dimensions. These dimensions were rated in the following order:

(1) planning and organizing work in the supervisor's section;
(2) following-up policy, procedures and regulations;
(3) relations with superiors and colleagues;
(4) relations with subordinates (employees);
(5) dealing with technical matters, including technical problems in his subordinates' work;
(6) general performance.

Each supervisor was also asked to rate himself, but only in terms of the last dimension: 'general performance'. The six dimensions were rated along percentage scales marked by 10 per cent intervals which effectively permitted discrimination down to 5 per cent differences. The scales were not 'anchored' by behavioural descriptions; the numerical scale was simply labelled 'least effective 10%', 'average' (at the half-way point), and 'most effective 10%'. It was thought to be too difficult and complicating to provide behavioural anchors for the scales because of the potentially wide differences in the work of supervisors' sections; it was also recognized that behavioural anchoring may not provide significantly improved results compared with simpler rating scales (De Cotiis, 1977).

The distributional characteristics for each performance rating scale are shown in Table 6.1 and their intercorrelations are given in Table 6.2. Some managers declined to be interviewed and a few were reluctant to give ratings or to discriminate between supervisors. This accounts for the lower number of managers' ratings. In common with many previous analyses of performance ratings, the present results all demonstrate a skew towards the higher ends of the scales. Also fairly typical are the modest positive correlations between ratings by superiors and self-ratings (cf. Brief *et al.*, 1977). Over the whole sample, there was at most only nine per cent of common agreement between managers' ratings of their supervisors' performance and the supervisors' ratings of their own performance.

The managers' ratings along the five specific dimensions of supervisory performance were all highly intercorrelated, though there was a degree of independence between rating for relations with employees and for dealing with technical matters. Their aggregation appears to be statistically acceptable and also conceptually justified as an alternative rating of supervisors' overall performance.[2] This aggregated measure will be used in the following analysis, together with the other overall managerial rating – that of supervisors' 'general performance'.

Interpreting managers' and supervisors' ratings

The limited amount of agreement between managers and supervisors in their ratings of supervisory performance creates problems of interpretation. Could the variability and lack of clarity in supervisory roles introduce an element of haphazardness into both sets of performance ratings? Are the supervisors likely to have responded frankly on their own performance in a face-to-face interview? Do their managers have a sufficiently close appreciation of what supervisors do to provide an assessment of their performance that is valid even by managerial criteria? It may be recalled from Chapter 4 that only a minority of supervisors were subject to any formal assessment.

Table 6.1 *Distributional characteristics of ratings of supervisory performance*

Ratings by manager of the supervisor's performance	Number of ratings	Maximum possible range	Actual range	Mean	Standard deviation	Median	Skewness[a]
(1) Planning and organizing work in his section	116	0–100	20–95	69.66	16.18	71.75	−0.639
(2) Following up of policy, procedures, regulations	117	0–100	20–90	67.86	14.86	69.66	− 0.475
(3) Relations with superiors and colleagues	117	0–100	30–100	71.81	15.88	78.15	− 0.754
(4) Relations with employees	117	0–100	20–95	69.49	16.14	71.63	− 0.763
(5) Dealing with technical matters	116	0–100	30–100	68.11	17.43	70.29	− 0.335
(6) General performance	117	0–100	20–100	70.23	16.18	70.86	− 0.713
(7) Sum of items 1–5 inclusive[b]	115	0–500	130–460	346.94	68.06	359.63	− 0.752
Rating by supervisor of his own general performance	147	0–100	50–100	78.22	13.44	79.77	− 0.441

(a) Skewness computed as per Statistical Package for the Social Sciences (SPSS) formula (Nie *et al.*, 1975: 185). A negative value indicates clustering above the mean.

(b) Coefficient of internal reliability (K–R 8) = 0.93.

Table 6.2 *Intercorrelations between ratings of supervisory performance*

		Ratings						
		2	3	4	5	6	7	8
Ratings by manager of the supervisor's performance								
(1) Planning and organizing work in his section	N = 116	78	60	59	67	79	86	27**
(2) Follow-up of policy, procedures, regulations	N = 117	–	63	58	65	79	86	21*
(3) Relations with superiors and col- leagues	N = 117		–	72	63	72	85	30**
(4) Relations with employees	N = 117			–	48	71	80	19*
(5) Dealing with technical matters	N = 116				–	63	82	24*
(6) General performance	N = 117					–	87	29**
(7) Sum of items 1–5 inclusive	N = 115						–	30**
(8) Rating by supervisor of his own general performance	N = 147							–

Pearson product-moment correlations; decimal points omitted.
For all coefficients $p < 0.001$ (two-tail test) except those marked: * $p < 0.05$, ** $p < 0.01$.

Such questions are difficult to answer since we have no other standards of supervisory performance against which to compare managers' and supervisors' ratings, or indeed any sure basis for agreement as to what such standards should be. Some clue as to their status may perhaps be afforded by examining how closely each set of ratings is associated with other variables which one would expect to accompany supervisory effectiveness in the rather general sense of coping with the demands of the job. Two such variables are supervisors' 'personal flexibility' and their levels of influence.

Previous chapters have drawn attention to the need to cope with the uncertainties and pressures which many supervisors face. What Thurley and Wirdenius (1973) call 'disturbance handling' – dealing with unforeseen contingencies such as shortages, breakdowns and employee grievances – often comprises a substantial portion of supervisory work. Therefore, supervisors who can handle such disturbances well should rate themselves as good performers and be recognized as such by their managers, since poor handling will deposit the problem very visibly into these managers' laps and add to the pressures they experience. The personal characteristics which are expected to enhance a supervisor's capability for handling disturbances include a willingness to accept changing and unusual conditions: what we have called 'personal flexibility'. Our method of measuring this concept is described in Chapter 4 and Appendix C.

The correlations between supervisors' personal flexibility and ratings of their performance by their managers are modest but positive, as expected, and not very likely to have occurred by chance. The correlation between personal flexibility and the supervisors' ratings of their own performance is very low and is much more likely to have occurred by chance. The correlations are shown in Table 6.3. If it is accepted that personal flexibility is necessary for supervisors to cope with the demands of their jobs, these results suggest that their managers' ratings may provide a better guide to their success than their own self-ratings.

Having influence in decision making is probably a good guide to a supervisor's performance. Greater influence implies greater respect for a supervisor's capabilities and past achievement. It represents a willingness to trust his judgement and to impose less constraint upon his initiative. Influence may, of course, be accorded more readily to those who tend to see matters the way management does, but, even in such cases, one would expect higher influence to reflect an established

Table 6.3

Ratings of supervisor's performance	Correlations with the supervisor's 'personal flexibility'.	Level of confidence (P)
Ratings by the manager:		
Supervisor's general performance	0.26	0.003
Sum of five specific ratings	0.20	0.019
Supervisor's ratings of his own performance	0.11	0.102

Numbers of ratings are as per Table 6.1.

track record. We therefore attempted to interpret managers' and supervisors' ratings of supervisory performance further by comparing their correlations with assessments of supervisors' influence. One complication in so doing is that, as may be recalled from Chapter 3, individual managers and supervisors did not agree much about the latter's influence.

The correlations between performance ratings and assessments of the supervisors' level of influence over systems, technical and people management decisions are tabulated in Appendix 6.1. There is some tendency for supervisors' ratings of their own performance to be associated positively with their self-assessed levels of influence, and also for managers' ratings and assessments to go together. The overall picture is not clear-cut, however. Examination of the five specific performance ratings given by managers actually shows that when the managers said their supervisors exercised influence over technical decisions, they were more likely than not to down-rate these supervisors' performance in dealing with technical matters! In the area of systems management and managing people, the managers' assessments of supervisors' influence were more closely connected with their ratings of supervisors' performance especially along the most relevant performance dimensions. When managers reported that their supervisors had high influence over acceptance of new work, discretion given to employees, maintaining discipline and co-ordination with work study, they were particularly likely to give those supervisors high performance ratings as well.

Reference to supervisory influence therefore leaves the interpretation of managers' and supervisors' ratings of supervisory performance somewhat clouded. Neither managers nor supervisors' ratings are clearly superior if one uses influence as an indicator of supervisory competence. The fact that, on the whole, managers' performance ratings are more closely linked with managers' influence assessments, and supervisors' responses likewise, suggests that managers inhabit a perceptual world *vis-à-vis* supervisory performance that is at least partly divorced from the supervisors' own perceptual world. The nature of this managerial world is now explored further.

Factors associated with managerial ratings

It was implied earlier that ratings of supervisory performance have to be understood not only by referring (1) to the supervisor, but also to (2) the person doing the rating, (3) the extent to which he perceives his expectations of the supervisor to be satisfied, (4) differences between rater and supervisor in expectations of the latter's role and in their backgrounds, and (5) the relationships between the two parties. A full analysis and statement of hypotheses about the influence of these factors on managerial ratings of supervisory performance is set out in Child (1980a). These are considered more briefly for present purposes.

Previous studies of managerial success, often assessed in terms of career or salary progression, have suggested certain personal attributes as correlates (e.g. Campbell *et al.,* 1970; Ghiselli, 1971). Progression criteria are not generally applicable to supervisors, for whom few promotion opportunities are available and whose salaries are now, in Britain, often determined on a collective basis. Nevertheless, it seems highly likely that supervisors' personal attributes – abilities, personality, experience – will influence their level of performance, and we have already noted personal flexibility to be one example. We also examined length of supervisory experience, possession of relevant training and youthfulness, each as potential contributors to good performance; but none of these variables was related to managerial ratings of supervisors' performance, or for that matter to supervisors' self-ratings.

Secondly, some investigators have found an association between managers' own levels of effectiveness and the criteria they applied to their assessments of subordinates' performance. It is possible that a manager's sense of competence, even security, within his job can have a bearing on the level of credit he is prepared to grant his subordinates. Competence may be indicated by qualifications, and a manager's sense of competence and security is likely to increase with his length of experience as a manager. Landy and Farr (1980) show that this argument receives some, albeit patchy, support from previous research. It implies that the longer-serving and better-qualified manager will be more likely to give greater credit to his subordinates, since he will feel less threatened by them.

We found some support for this argument. Although managers' levels of education and training were not associated with their ratings of supervisors' performance, their length of experience was. The number of years they had been a manager was correlated positively both with their rating of supervisors' general performance ($r = 0.27$, $p < 0.01$) and with the sum of their five specific ratings ($r = 0.35$, $p < 0.001$). There was also a link with managers' age, since managers in their fifties tended to give their supervisors lower performance ratings than did other managers. A possible explanation could be that a manager who is still working at this level at 50 plus cannot be regarded as highly successful in career terms and, according to our previous argument, this reflects on the credit he is prepared to accord his subordinates. By the time he is in his 60s he may be reconciled to his career position and more concerned with looking ahead to retirement. A two-way analysis of variance, with managers' age and length of experience in a managerial position treated as independent variables, indicated that both had independent discriminatory effects on performance ratings when split at their median levels (51 years in the case of managers' age). Interaction effects were negligible. These findings suggest that knowledge of the rater's personal characteristics is very relevant for predicting the level of ratings he tends to give to supervisors.

There is, thirdly, the proposition that managers' ratings of supervisory performance will be higher when they perceive that supervisors carry out their jobs in a manner which the managers think is appropriate. We examined this possibility by referring to how closely managers saw reality in their firm agreeing with what they thought should prevail, with reference to the twelve statements about 'the supervisor's role today' (listed in Appendix B). No support was offered for the proposition. The twelve statements do, however, refer rather generally to supervisors in the firm, not to particular supervisors. The fact that when managers allow their supervisors high influence on systems and people-management decisions they tend to rate their performance higher, may caution outright rejection of the proposition, in so far as higher supervisory influence can be said to betoken managerial approval.

Fourthly, one would expect managers' ratings of supervisory performance to be lower when there are differences between manager and supervisor.[3] These could be differences in opinion about how the supervisor's job should be carried out. They might also be differences in personal characteristics, such as age and experience, which lead to a divergence in views, mode of approach, energies and so on.

We examined differences of *opinion* between managers and supervisors with regard to (1) normative views on 'the supervisor's role today' statements; (2) supervisory priorities; and (3) appropriate supervisory style. There were no systematic links between differences of opinion (neither the absolute level nor the direction of difference) over the supervisor's role today and managers' ratings of supervisory performance. Differences between managers' and supervisors' views about priorities in the supervisor's job did link with performance ratings, though these were rather weak and concerned the direction of difference more often than the absolute level of disagreement.

The tasks for which the direction of difference in managers' and supervisors' priority scores was associated with both managerial ratings of performance were: (1) communicating with other supervisors and departments, (2) communicating with superiors, (3) personally doing direct or manual work, and (4) keeping costs down. The supervisors who attached higher priority to these tasks compared to their managers tended to be rated as lower performers. There were three other tasks for which a higher priority rating by supervisors compared to their managers was associated with receiving a lower score on just one of the two main performance ratings. These were recruitment of employees, ensuring the supply of tools and training employees. Supervisors also tended to receive lower scores on one of the performance ratings when they attached less priority to the task of labour allocation than did their managers. A common element in these findings would seem to be that those supervisors who attach higher priority than do their managers to tasks which fall *outside* the core activities of organizing and supervising the work in their sections, tend to obtain lower performance ratings.

Supervisors and their managers expressed their views on what was an appropriate style of supervision by rating six dimensions of style along seven-point scales. The ends of each scale were anchored by statements of opposite behaviours. Appendix 6.2 lists the six dimensions and presents the correlations found between (1) absolute and relative differences in managers' and supervisors' views on style and (2) managers' ratings of supervisory performance. Absolute levels of disagreement between managers and supervisors about appropriate supervisory style did not have a bearing on performance ratings, but differences in a certain direction did. When a supervisor gave less approval than did his manager to (1) adopting an employee-centred style, (2) enforcing discipline flexibly, and (3) supervising without keeping employees under pressure, he tended to receive a lower performance rating. The complement is that when a supervisor placed greater emphasis on these elements of style relative to his manager's view, he tended to receive a higher performance rating.

All in all, the proposition that absolute levels of difference in opinion between supervisors and their managers will lower those managers' ratings of the supervisors' performance does not receive any significant support. Some differences in a certain direction do, however, appear to contribute to variations in managerial ratings.

Another possibility is that differences in the *personal profiles* of supervisors and managers affect the performance ratings which managers give. Our preliminary investigations in the metal plants indicated that higher ratings were given by managers whose age, experience and qualifications matched those of supervisors than when there were marked contrasts, expecially younger managers rating older supervisors. However, when age, experience and qualifications were compared for the present sample of managers and supervisors, the only 'effect' on performance ratings which secured a high level of statistical confidence was that of the manager's length of experience. The degree of *matching* in personal profiles between supervisors and managers did not influence managerial ratings of supervisory performance.

The last of the factors we listed as potential influences on managerial ratings is the quality of relationship between manager and supervisor. It has been found that a manager's rating of a subordinate's performance is influenced by the degree of friendship between the two persons (Campbell *et al.*, 1970). Friendship tends to enhance the level of ratings given. This is compatible with Kipnis's

(1976a, b) findings that the more people perceive that they hold power over others, the more they tend to devalue the other person(s) *and* to express a preference for maintaining social distance from them. Good performance ratings presumably denote high evaluation of supervisors and, according to Kipnis, should therefore be accompanied by managerial raters reporting closer social contact with more highly-rated supervisory subordinates. The causality implied here is from performance ratings to social contact rather than vice versa, but it leads to the same proposition that the two factors should be related. It is also possible that a high frequency of interaction in the work situation between the supervisor and his manager will raise the level of managerial ratings because the chance of misunderstanding between the two parties is thereby reduced and, following Homans (1950), because interaction may foster personal friendship.

Managers and supervisors were asked independently to provide information on task-related and social contacts between themselves. The question on task-related contacts referred to frequency of personal or telephone contact on the subject of work and responses were categorized into eleven time frequencies. The question on social relations referred simultaneously to two varieties: 'having a chat, sharing lunch or teabreaks at work' and 'friendships outside work'. This was subsequently dichotomized into the presence or absence of such social relations.

The results of correlating task and social relations with the managers' ratings of supervisors' performance are complicated. Managers tended to give higher ratings to supervisors with whom they reported having social relations,[4] and also to supervisors who reported more frequent contact with those managers on matters to do with work.[5] Supervisors' reports on social relations and managers' estimates of task contact frequency were not associated with the level of performance ratings. The reporting by supervisors on task contact frequency was more accurate than their managers' estimates in cases we observed directly, and it is also likely to be more accurate than managers' reports, since many managers gave the same estimate for different supervisors. We have no means of assessing the accuracy of replies on social relations.

These findings suggest that managers are more likely to conclude that supervisors are performing their jobs well when the supervisors keep them informed through frequent contact, but in a manner which the managers see as unobtrusive and partly social, rather than bringing up task-related issues which would probably constitute additional problems for the manager to deal with.

Prediction of managerial ratings from a combination of factors

Guided by a number of propositions about managerial ratings of supervisory performance, we found evidence to suggest that the following factors are predictors of *higher* ratings. They are listed in the five categories employed previously:

(1) *The supervisor* — greater personal flexibility.

(2) *The managerial rater* — longer experience in a managerial position; age below 50 years or above 60 years.

(3) *Satisfaction of the rater's expectations* — higher assessment of the supervisor's influence over systems and people management.

(4) *Differences between rater and supervisor* — the higher the supervisor's rating (compared to his manager's) of employee-centredness, flexible enforcement of discipline, and supervising without constant pressure as components of an appropriate supervisory style.

the supervisor does *not* assign higher priority to non-core elements in his job than does his manager.

(5) *Relationships between rater and supervisor* — the recognition by the manager that he has social (non-task) contacts with the supervisor;

greater frequency of task contacts between supervisor and manager (though perceived by the supervisor, not by the manager).

Multiple regression analysis was used to calculate the proportion of variance in managers' ratings of supervisory performance that is accounted for by combinations of these factors. Performance ratings were treated as 'dependent' variables for the purposes of this analysis. It was found that approaching half the variation in managerial ratings could be accounted for by equations which only included variables one could be highly confident were having independent pred ctive effects.[6] The components of the equation for predicting managers' ratings of supervisors' 'general performance' are set out in Appendix 6.3 as an illustration. Five factors are seen to account for 44 per cent of the variance in these ratings: (1) the supervisor's personal flexibility; (2) the manager's assessment of the supervisor's influence over systems decisions; (3) his assessment of the supervisor's influence over people decisions; (4) differences between the manager's and supervisor's view over discipline, where the supervisor favours a flexible approach to discipline; and (5) the length of the manager's experience as a manager. The same combination of factors predicts 39 per cent of variation in the sum of the five specific managerial ratings, and when account is also taken of managers' endorsements of social contacts with their supervisors, this proportion rises to 47 per cent.

Conclusion

There was only modest agreement between the ratings of supervisory performance given by managers and by the supervisors themselves. The two sets of ratings appear to belong to different perceptual worlds, and this is consistent with the presence of other differences between the perceptions held by managers and supervisors which have been noted in previous chapters.

Nevertheless, the way their immediate superior rates their performance is important for supervisors. It was possible to predict over 40 per cent of the variation in superiors' ratings and in so doing to obtain some idea of the factors which may influence these. It is remarkable that only one predictor was a supervisory attribute independent of the rater – personal flexibility – though of course there are probably others we did not examine. However, another consistent predictor of more favourable ratings, namely the length of the rater's managerial experience, was *in no way* an attribute of the supervisors being rated or of how they carried out their jobs. Quite clearly, the ratings of supervisory performance by managers tell one at least as much about the rater as they do about the supervisor. Their subjectivity is thereby heavily underlined, and their value as ratings of supervisors' performance must be considered suspect.

This is not a novel conclusion within the literature on performance ratings. It serves to remind us, none the less, that it is important to remain aware of their subjectivity and the factors concerning the rater which they incorporate. This is important both from the point of view of preserving equity in the eyes of the supervisor, and from that of avoiding distorted reports on supervisors' capabilities. These considerations speak for a procedure whereby both manager and supervisor are led to discuss the latter's performance and then to prepare a set of ratings to which each can add his formal acceptance. This might move their two perceptual worlds into closer alignment, though the difficulty of identifying mutually acceptable and adequate criteria should not be underestimated, for the reasons mentioned at the beginning of this chapter.

When managers give a high performance rating to their supervisors, they are in effect approving a particular conception of the supervisory role. It is possible to extrapolate from the factors associated with higher ratings, in order to hazard an outline of the supervisory role that managers tend to rate as 'effective'. The 'effective' supervisor is flexible enough to cope with the everyday disturbances in the work and relationships within his section. He actually approaches questions of shopfloor discipline more flexibly, and is also more employee-centred, than his manager believes to be appropriate. This supervisor is able to take a lead in decision making that is sufficient to handle the people in his charge, including their discipline and discretion, and to organize the workflow within his section. His initiative also extends to managing everyday relationships between his section and staff personnel, such as work study, who affect its activities. (However, as Chapter 3 records, this does not mean that even highly-rated supervisors can normally decide on the basic parameters affecting their sections.) As a result of the 'effective' supervisor keeping things going and coping with disturbances to the flow of work in this way, his manager can emphasize the social aspect of their relationship and, as Kipnis (1976a,b) suggests, is perhaps more inclined to cultivate social interaction with the highly regarded supervisor. The supervisor may see his manager over matters of work quite frequently, but he is adjudged to be effective when he does not present the manager with too many unresolved problems which 'intrude' upon the manager's own work.

This interpretation suggests that one of the contingencies which the highly-rated supervisor has to handle is the protection of his superior from the disturbance of having to resolve too many problems on the shopfloor. He has to do this by providing a flexible 'buffer' between shopfloor vicissitudes and the calmer realm of management. The observation studies in the food plant tend to reinforce this interpretation: the supervisors in production who took more initiative upon themselves to rearrange work, change jobs, alter line speeds and rectify problems received high performance ratings, as did the three maintenance supervisors observed whose specialist expertise meant that they were able to deal with problems without referring to their managers.

There is some affinity between this view of the supervisor's role and what in Chapter 5 was called a 'workgroup-oriented' strategy. Supervisors adopting such a strategy would be thought less likely to pass problems to their managers than those following what we called a 'management-oriented' strategy. It is interesting to note that managers tended to rate supervisors adopting the first strategy more highly than those following the second on the performance dimension of relations with subordinates ($p < 0.05$). The supervisors adopting a workgroup-oriented strategy also tended to rate their own performance more highly than did those adopting the management-oriented approach ($p < 0.01$).

Mant (1979) has concluded that, in Britain, managers 'manage', but in a way that often involves little contact with, or understanding of, the productive work of their organization. The 'approved' role of supervision which seems to emerge from performance ratings is consistent with this conclusion and also with an observation that the major break in the vertical structure of British companies today comes between shopfloor supervision and management proper, rather than between supervision and shopfloor. The two following chapters examine this possibility from a more sociological perspective, addressing the question of whether the distance between managers and supervisors is reflected in supervisors' class position and in their recent unionization.

Appendix 6.1 *Correlations between assessments of supervisors' influence and ratings of supervisors' performance*

Ratings of supervisors' performance (number of ratings as per Table 6.1)	Assessment of supervisors' influence (S = by supervisor; M = by his manager)					
	Overall influence with regard to systems management		Overall influence with regard to technical management		Overall influence with regard to people management	
	S	M	S	M	S	M
1. By supervisors themselves	28***	− 02	13	− 07	23**	18*
2. By managers:						
2.1. Supervisors' general performance	16*	17*	14	− 04	15	37***
2.2. Sum of 5 specific ratings	20*	17*	20*	− 08	19*	31***
2.3. Planning and organizing work	18*	23**	19*	08	15	26**
2.4. Follow-up of policy etc.	19*	13	17*	− 07	12	31***
2.5. Relations with superiors and colleagues	18*	12	18*	− 19*	27**	25**
2.6. Relations with employees	10	32***	11	01	10	31***
2.7. Dealing with technical matters	18*	− 07	18*	− 18*	16*	18*

Pearson product-moment correlations; decimal points omitted. ***$p < 0.001$; **$p < 0.01$; *$p < 0.05$.

Note. This table presents supervisors' and managers' responses to the single-item questions on supervisors' overall influence, rather than to the composite measures described in Chapter 3, because the internal-item structures of the composite measures are not identical for both the supervisor and manager samples.

Appendix 6.2 *Correlations between (1) differences in super-visors' and managers' opinions on appropriate supervisory style, and (2) ratings of supervisory performance by managers*

Dimensions of supervisory style (the first row of correlations are for *absolute* differences between managers' and supervisors' scores. The second row are for managers' scores *subtracted* from supervisors')	Correlations with ratings by manager of the supervisor's performance	
	General performance	Sum of five specific ratings
	N = 117 ratings	N = 115 ratings
Close supervision	10 − 06	02 − 10
Pressure on employees	− 02 − 09	− 02 − 17*
Employee-centredness (not confining relations with employees to matters of work)	− 12 18*	− 12 23**
Consultation with employees	08 07	− 01 11
Rigidity over work methods	− 12 − 03	− 09 − 01
Flexible enforcement of discipline (as opposed to a strict and rigid approach)	12 27**	04 18*

Pearson product-moment correlations; decimal points omitted. *p < 0.05; **p < 0.01.

Appendix 6.3 *Prediction of variation in managers' ratings of supervisors' 'general performance'*

Independent variables (in order of entry into equation)	Beta coefficient	F	Level of confidence (p)	Simple R	Cumulative multiple R^2
(1) Manager's perception of supervisor's influence over people management	0.321	14.36	$\simeq 0.000$	0.45	0.21
(2) Differences between manager and supervisor on maintaining discipline (positive score denotes higher emphasis by supervisor on flexible discipline	0.225	8.61	0.004	0.31	0.29
(3) Supervisor's personal flexibility	0.290	14.31	$\simeq 0.000$	0.28	0.36
(4) Length of manager's experience as a manager	0.299	12.39	0.001	0.29	0.39
(5) Manager's perception of supervisor's influence over systems management	0.241	7.01	0.009	0.22	0.44

$R^2 = 0.435$; N = 105; F = 15.244; p < 0.001.

Inter-correlations between independent variables (numbered as above)

Variable	2	3	4	5
1	05	00	11	37
2	–	07	13	03
3		–	03	–14
4			–	–35
5				–

PART III

Social identification

In Part II of this book, we examined the workplace situation of supervisors. We gave particular attention to how far supervisors' jobs contain a managerial component, assessing this by reference to the authority and influence that supervisors enjoy over workplace decisions. It became evident that one of the influences upon the scope of a supervisor's decision-making discretion is his own immediate managerial superior. The relationship which supervisors have with management also needs to be taken into account for understanding the conflicts and pressures which supervisors can experience, and for predicting the evaluations which are made of their performance.

The supervisors accepted management's workplace objectives. They generally believed that it was appropriate for supervisors to form part of the line of managerial command and to enjoy managerial authority. In the work setting, they accorded high priority to their communications and relationship with management, especially with their immediate superiors. Yet, at the same time, many supervisors were distanced from management in the performance of their work. They were held at arm's length by management in the making of many decisions which affected the running of their sections in important ways. The little authority that supervisors retained over shopfloor employees was not always upheld by management when conflicts arose. Managers did not appear to have a close understanding of their supervisors' problems and they were generally less discriminating than were supervisors in the priority they gave to different components of the supervisor's job. The gap between the perspectives which managers and supervisors applied to the latter's jobs was manifested in their very modest levels of agreement over the level of individual supervisors' performance.

Where does this distancing from management leave the supervisor? What does he conclude about his present position in industry and within an industrial society? Does the supervisor's attenuation from the role and standing of workshop manager, which Chapter 1 traced historically and which our investigation has illustrated for the present day, mean that he is now lost to management in a more general social sense? Does he still regard himself as the employer's man or does he now take the view that his lot is essentially that of the manual workers he supervises? While supervisors accept management's workplace objectives and value their working relationship with management, this may perhaps have more to do with the requirements for carrying out and retaining their jobs than with a more deep-seated personal social identification. Supervisors have joined unions in large numbers over the past twenty years, and this could perhaps indicate a major shift in their allegiances. Was this so among the highly-unionized Birmingham supervisors we studied, or was joining a union much more a matter of reluctant necessity to protect and enhance conditions of employment?

Chapters 7 and 8, forming Part III of this book, consider these questions concerning the supervisor's wider social identification. The dichotomy between management and workers has for a long time been regarded as a major divide between social classes in Britain. Chapter 7 examines the class to which supervisors can be said to belong and that with which they personally identified. Chapter 8 examines the process which has led a majority of the supervisors to join a trade union, the meaning that union membership has for them, and the implications such membership carries for their identity within industry and society. As was the case in Part II, a prime interest of our enquiry is the position which supervisors today occupy in relation to management.

7

Supervisors at the class divide

The working class can lick my arse,
I've got the foreman's job at last. (Traditional)

As the verse suggests, promotion to a supervisory position used to be regarded as a step up in the social world. Even though it has been argued that supervisors were in an anomalous position, 'exercising authority over members of the subordinate class without actually being part of the dominant class' (Parkin, 1972: 87), they enjoyed a clearly superior standing to the general run of manual workers. Today, with a great many supervisors playing a substantially diminished role in control of the workplace, it is questionable whether promotion to their job represents any real advancement out of the working class.

On the other hand, managerial thinking continues to claim the supervisor as part of management (e.g. BIM, 1976). The supervisor who accepts this claim as valid may perhaps perceive his class position to be superior to that of manual workers, and possibly a middle-class one. Similarly, those supervisors who have experienced a non-manual social environment either in previous jobs or in their family life might be more inclined to regard themselves as being in a position superior to that of the working class.

This chapter examines the class position supervisors can be deemed to occupy as well as their perceptions on the matter. Such an examination may help to throw more light on a facet of the great class divide in British industry.

Supervisors' class position

Lockwood (1958) in his study of clerical workers, identified three factors which together comprise a person's 'class position':

> First, 'market situation', that is to say the economic position narrowly conceived, consisting of source and size of income, degree of job-security, and opportunity for upward occupational mobility. Secondly, 'work situation', the set of social relationships in which the individual is involved at work by virtue of his position in the division of labour. And finally, 'status situation', or the position of the individual in the hierarchy of prestige in the society at large (p.15).

Market position and work situation, as defined by Lockwood, are reasonably tangible phenomena which can be assessed and are also likely to be quite apparent to the individuals concerned. Status situation is a much more ambiguous concept, and while public opinion surveys demonstrate some consistency in rankings of occupational status, it is not clear just what meaning people attach to such rankings.

Although we shall comment upon the market position and work situation of supervisors, and also report on supervisors' own assessments of their general status, some sociologists working in a Marxist tradition would regard Lockwood's scheme as insufficient. They would classify Lockwood's three factors as surface manifestations or corollaries of a more fundamental position that a person occupies in the structure of productive relationships in a capitalist society. However, rather than persist with the older crude distinction between capital and labour, contemporary Marxists such as Carchedi (1975) recognize that managers, administrators and supervisors comprise a third group which, in varying proportions, carries out both capital and labour functions. Thus, according to Crompton (1976: 419), the supervisor 'both co-ordinates the supply of raw materials and tools [which is labour necessary to any complex production process] . . . and acts as the front line of managerial authority [which is a capital function exercising control and surveillance on behalf of the owner]'. This combination of functions is said to make for ambiguity in the real class position of the occupations concerned. For present purposes this form of analysis suggests that the degree to which a supervisor has authority over others provides a significant criterion of his or her class position. The lower this is, the closer can the supervisor's class position be said to approximate to that of ordinary workers. (See also Wright, 1976: 32–4.)

With these considerations in mind, we now look more closely at the class position of the Birmingham supervisors by reference to the criteria of authority, social relationships in the work situation and market position.

1 Authority and work situation

In Chapter 3, we examined the authority and influence which the supervisors enjoyed. All the decisions we asked about affect the conduct and performance of the section for which the supervisor is, at least nominally, held accountable. In the two plants studied, however, supervisors on the whole appeared to have no authority over matters which determine the parameters or boundary conditions of their section's work – such as the acceptance of new types of work, choice of plant and equipment, manning levels, appointment of new workers, and adjustments to pay and grading. Quite a large proportion of supervisors also stated that they had no authority over matters of shorter term adjustment within their sections, such as the scheduling of work, work methods and machines to be used, specification of workers' duties and whether repairs were to be made to plant. Their managers' responses generally confirmed, indeed reinforced, this pattern of greatly-restricted supervisory authority.

Supervisors cannot be said to occupy a managerial position, when assessed by these findings. Even if the definition of managerial authority is confined to control and discipline over the labour force (as Crompton suggests it should be, p. 419), this conclusion still stands. The supervisors were at most very minor managerial 'agents of capital' and, judged by this criterion, members of a subordinate class.

The pattern of social relationships described by the supervisors also suggests a somewhat closer attachment to manual workers than to management. They were asked who, from a list of 21 categories of people in the plant, they chose to interact with socially at work (have a chat, share lunch or tea breaks) and outside work. Out of 155 supervisors, 75 per cent indicated that they had some sort of social contact with other plant supervisors both inside and outside work; 70 per cent spent time with shopfloor workers, 58 per cent with their immediate superiors, and 30 per cent with managers at higher levels. It could be argued, however, that some interaction arises within the plant in the normal course of doing work and that non-work-directed friendship relations outside the factory are a more discriminating criterion. The patterning for relations outside the workplace is similar, with shopfloor workers now assuming the highest ranking. Thus 37 per cent of the 155 supervisors said that they spent social time outside work with shopfloor workers from their plant; 36 per cent mentioned spending such time with other supervisors, 28 per cent with their immediate superiors and 19 per cent with managers at higher levels. This seems to be consistent with the conclusion reached by Fores *et al.* (1978: 87) that 'the foreman (in Britain) has a life style closer to that of those whom he supervises than to that of people higher up in the company. He is in the position of the corporal who reports to senior non-commissioned officers, but still "messes with the men"'.

2 Market situation

As Dunkerley has noted (1975: 159) it is likely that the traditional payment differential between supervisors and shopfloor workers has been eroded in many British plants during recent years. Data from the annual New Earnings Survey indicate that this erosion continued during the period of Labour's incomes policy. A detailed survey of about 3,000 supervisors carried out in 1978 confirms the erosion in differentials and shows that in some companies supervisors could earn less than those they are supervising (Incomes Data Services (IDS), 1979). This was also the situation in the two plants studied. In the engineering plant, production workers on high piecework bonuses could earn some 5 to 6 per cent more than their supervisors over a 40-hour week. In the food plant, the working of a typical 45-hour week early in 1977 provided a range of earnings for production workers of between £53.45 and £62.95 per week. The earnings of production supervisors for the same length of working week ranged from £59.25 to £70.25 per week. There could therefore be some degree of overlap in earnings between production supervisors and the workers they supervised, though workers would not, of course, always expect to achieve high bonuses and substantial overtime. In both the plants studied, the differential in fringe benefits, eating facilities and other 'perks' was on the whole greater between supervisors and management than it was between supervisors and shopfloor workers. This was also shown to be the case for a national sample (Wedderburn and Craig, 1974).[1]

So far as could be ascertained, avenues for upward mobility were largely absent for supervisors in the two plants. In the food processing plant, only 21 supervisors had been promoted during the period 1971 to 1976, out of an average annual total which had been somewhat larger than the 232 supervisors in post in 1976. It was not possible to secure accurate figures from the electrical engineering plant, but one informant stated that only two supervisors had been promoted during the past 15 years. It was increasingly the case in both plants that applicants for managerial positions immediately above the supervisor had to possess formal qualifications. It may be recalled that 84 per cent of the supervisors sampled had no formal qualifications whatsoever. Information from two other surveys suggests that an absence of upward mobility for largely unqualified supervisors is now a widespread characteristic of British industry (BIM, 1976; Institute of Personnel Management (IPM), 1975).

Lockwood identified job security as a further component of market situation. It is only possible to assess what degree of security the supervisors studied enjoyed by reference to circumstantial evidence. In other parts of the company to which the electrical engineering plant belonged, supervisors had been declared redundant along with shopfloor workers. At the time of writing, a few supervisors in the food plant have been retired early. The job security of the supervisors was certainly not guaranteed. That they felt insecure is possibly indicated by the top priority which the Birmingham supervisors, taken as a whole, gave to job security out of the six job attributes which they were asked, through pairs of forced choices, to rate in importance. These six factors were good pay, security, quality of relationships, responsibility, interesting work and promotion prospects. Whereas the supervisor's job security has probably declined from a situation in which it could be virtually taken for granted, the manual worker is far better protected and compensated than before through legislation on unfair dismissal, contracts of employment and redundancy payments.

3 Assessment of class position

Whichever criteria are applied, the class position of these supervisors was not sharply differentiated from that of the manual workers they supervised. In Marxist terms, the control exercised over a subordinate class by the supervisor is now so diluted as to be of little more than symbolic significance. Applying Lockwood's criteria of work and market situation, the Birmingham supervisors did not enjoy markedly superior conditions to those of manual employees and this appears to be typical of supervisors in Britain today. These supervisors also tended to form closer social relationships with their employees than with managers. While the Marxist analyst might point out that this means that the manifest indicators of the supervisor's class position are now more closely aligned with his basic structural position, another perspective would suggest that supervisors are today likely to find their situation disturbingly ambiguous. That is, their class position is now more or less proletarian, but their status position, especially as defined by managerially derived norms, remains distinctive from that of manual workers. This raises the question of how supervisors actually perceive their class position.

Supervisors' perceptions of class

People in most ages and places appear to have held some everyday conception of class (Ossowski, 1963). Generally these perceptions have been of a hierarchical structure, whether divided in terms of rich and poor, status gradations, or capital and labour. We therefore expected that most supervisors would have some view of class which meant something in their everyday lives and which, however ill-formed or internally inconsistent, could be conveyed to us. We set out to find whether this was true, and if so, what these perceptions were: what structure of classes existed in their view, what was the nature of such classes, and where did they see themselves fitting into the total picture. We looked for a subjective definition of 'classes' of a kind that Roberts *et al.* have described as 'the collectivities with which individuals identify themselves in making the hierarchical environments they inhabit meaningful' (1977: 18).

There are many serious methodological problems with attempts to capture people's perceptions of class. It is a sensitive subject in Britain, and there are many difficulties in interpreting what people say on the matter especially if it appears to be ill-formed or inconsistent. These and other problems are discussed in Child *et al.* (1980), which also presents the full results of our investigation into supervisors' class perceptions. Basically, the approach we adopted, after some learning experience in our preliminary studies, was to rely primarily upon open-ended questioning towards the end of our second interview, by which time the supervisors had received some feedback on the first interview results, had come to know us quite well, and for these reasons probably trusted our intentions. We also tried to avoid suggesting any particular model or meaning of class in our questioning. For example, we did not proceed with, let alone suggest in the interviews, the simple two-class (middle and working) model which has been given wide currency by some sociologists (e.g. Mackenzie, 1975) and even by some writers on supervisors (e.g. Dunkerley, 1975).

We employed six indicators of supervisors' class perceptions. These are:

(1) the overall structure they envisaged for British society;
(2) the number of classes they perceived in this structure;
(3) the level in the class structure at which they saw their own class to be located;
(4) their self-description through selection from a randomly-ordered list of 12 'class' labels;
(5) the kind of people they saw comprising their own class;
(6) the criteria which they employed for differentiating between classes.

1 The overall structure envisaged

Each supervisor was presented with a ladder graded from 0 (top) to 100 per cent (bottom) in five per cent rungs. The rungs had no description attached to them. The supervisor was then invited to divide the ladder into whatever classes made up 'the total population of this country'. He could respond with up to 20 divisions, or as few as he wished, though the invitation to divide up the ladder biased responses away from the option of denying that there was a stratified hierarchy at all. Six supervisors did, in fact, answer that they perceived no vertical distinction in British society. When each supervisor had decided on his division of the class hierarchy, allocating upper and lower limits to each category, he was then asked in which category he would place himself, what kinds of people he would place in each class, and what he thought distinguished one class from another.

This general line of questioning derives from Mackenzie's study (1973) of class perceptions held by skilled craftsmen in America. Mackenzie imposed a fourfold division upon his respondents when inviting them to apportion the hierarchical ladder, a procedure which he himself recognized to be arbitrary. In the present study, the ladder presented to supervisors was an open one, except that it did impose a vertical structure which future investigation may show to be an over-simplifying constraint upon people's expression of their perception. For instance, the method we adopted does not readily permit respondents to portray simultaneous lateral divisions or class structures of a branching type.

The class structures visualized by the supervisors were categorized according to their overall shape and to self-allocated position within that shape. Eight distinct structures were portrayed by 129 supervisors; another 13 gave miscellaneous or unclassified structures; 6 did not draw any class distinctions, and one supervisor did not answer this part of the interview. The five structures most often described are shown in Table 7.1 and they account for 110 supervisors, or 77 per cent of those distinguishing a structure. In drawing these five structures we have discarded the purely rectangular format used in the interview (a box containing parallel rungs at 5 per cent intervals) in order to highlight inherent differences. The number of class levels drawn is the most typical response for each structure.

The two most frequently-mentioned class structures may be called the traditional pyramid (N = 33 supervisors) and the traditional diamond (N = 25). The term 'traditional' is employed since these structures correspond to the ideal type constructs of working and middle class imagery respectively which Mackenzie (1975) has conceptualized. The traditional pyramid is a structure in which the respondent sees himself belonging to the largest class which occupies the base of a pyramid of increasingly smaller higher classes. Only 9 out of the 33 supervisors perceived this larger bottom class to be the lower half of a simple two-class model. The traditional diamond is a structure in which the respondent sees himself belonging to the largest class which occupies the middle ground in a diamond-like (or thick sandwich) hierarchy.

The upwardly-skewed diamond structure portrayed by 21 supervisors is similar to the traditional pyramid, except that a relatively small class (usually 5 to 10 per cent of the total structure) is

Table 7.1 *Supervisors' perceptions of class structure*

	Class structure[a]	Number	Percentage
Traditional pyramid		33	30
Traditional diamond[b]		25	23
Upwardly-skewed diamond		21	19
Non-traditional pyramid		18	16
Downwardly-skewed diamond		13	12

(a) ▨ Denotes class in which respondent placed himself.

(b) Replies were categorized as traditional diamond when the middle class identified was the largest, and when there was no greater than 5 per cent difference in size between the classes on either side of this middle one. Every respondent falling into this category identified three classes (an alternative would have been five classes).

identified below the large lower class in which the respondent locates himself. This small bottom class was usually described as comprising the unemployed and low-wage earners. While the upwardly-skewed diamond comes close to the supposedly traditional working-class image of society, the two remaining major categories represent a self-assignment of supervisors at a relatively higher level in the hierarchy.

The non-traditional pyramid described by 18 supervisors is a structure in which the respondent sees himself belonging not to the largest bottom class but to one which is a middle-level tier within an overall pyramid shape. The downwardly-skewed diamond described by 13 supervisors is a structure in which the respondent sees himself belonging to the largest single class, which has a higher proportion of the population in classes placed below it than in classes placed above it.

Three other class structures were envisaged by smaller groups of supervisors. Ten supervisors saw themselves as a minority class sandwiched between two larger ones. This is a perception that matches with the 'men-in-the-middle' stereotype which has been accorded to supervisors (e.g. Gardner and Whyte, 1945; also cf. Fletcher, 1969). It is interesting to note that so few supervisors held this view of their social position. Six supervisors perceived a diamond structure in which they placed themselves above the bulk of the population and above the largest, middle-level class. Three supervisors envisaged a diamond structure in which they were placed below the bulk of the population and below the largest, middle-level class.

On the basis that the traditional pyramid and upwardly-skewed diamond are the two perceived class structures which (1) approximate to Mackenzie's working-class stereotype and (2) clearly incorporate supervisors into a relatively large lower class, 38 per cent of the supervisors describing a class structure could be said to have a working class identification (or 42 per cent if purely miscellaneous structures are excluded). This distribution was not the same in the two sites. In the engineering plant, 48 per cent of supervisors describing a class structure portrayed a traditional pyramid or an upwardly-skewed diamond. In the food plant, the proportion was only 33 per cent. While only a very general comparison is possible, this proportion of supervisors adhering to 'working-class' models of class structure is considerably lower than the equivalent proportion which has been found among samples of Luton 'affluent workers' and Tyneside shipbuilding workers. Thus 74 per cent of the Luton workers placed themselves in the bottom class of the hierarchy (Goldthorpe, 1970: Table 3), while 80 per cent of the shipbuilding workers held an image of class structure which would be classified in our scheme as traditional pyramid (Cousins and Brown, 1975: 68). These comparisons suggest that while a sizeable proportion of the

Birmingham supervisors perceived themselves to be in a working-class position within a working-class image of class structure, it is an appreciably smaller proportion than is likely to be found among manual workers, even relatively affluent ones.

2 The number of classes envisaged

In describing how they saw British society to be divided, the supervisors indicated how many classes they envisaged. While replies ranged from one to seven classes, the largest single group (44 per cent) saw British society as comprising three classes. This compares closely with the 48 per cent of Luton 'affluent' workers who also identified three classes (Goldthorpe, 1970). However, only 9 per cent of the supervisors envisaged the two-class structure traditionally associated with a working class 'them and us' outlook. This compares with the 33 per cent among both the Luton workers and the shipyard workers investigated by Cousins and Brown (1975) who envisaged a two-class model. Forty-two per cent of the supervisors perceived a more finely-graded structure of four to seven classes, which it has been claimed is consistent with a typical middle-class outlook.

3 Level in the class structure

In the same exercise, supervisors had indicated the upper and lower percentage limits for the position of their own class within the overall British class hierarchy. The mid-point between these limits provides an indicator of the level they saw their class occupying. The average of these mid-points came just below the halfway mark (52.6) as did the median (52.0). Despite this slight downward bias, only a quarter of the sample portrayed the class to which they belonged as the very bottom one, while almost half (49 per cent) placed the upper boundary of their class in the top quartile of the population.

4 Selection of class labels for self-description

This indicator is the only one deriving from 'forced choice' questioning, and was included partly to assess the validity of such an approach. The supervisors were presented with a list of 12 class labels and asked to say to which group they thought they belonged. Some archaic and seemingly inappropriate labels (for instance: aristocracy, merchant class) were included in the list to make less obvious a deliberate re-arrangement in the normal hierarchical order of the conventional labels, and also to 'shock' respondents into some reflection. In the event, all 146 supervisors to whom this question was put chose one of five conventional labels with the distribution shown in Table 7.2.

The sample split approximately equally between those selecting middle-class designations (47 per cent) and working-class desig-nations (53 per cent). These proportions are very similar to those reported by Hill (1976b: 189) for London dock foremen, 55 per cent of whom saw themselves as working class. However, some 36 per cent selected labels which imply a position in the middle ground, very close to the boundary between middle and working class (that is, lower middle class, upper working class). With this in mind, the sample could also be said to have divided roughly equally into those who indicated they were fully middle class, those on the boundary, and those indicating a fully working-class position. At the extremes, only 4.8 per cent chose to describe themselves as 'upper middle class' and no-one selected the label 'lower working class'.

5 Composition of supervisors' own class

The findings which have been described suggest that a greater proportion of the Birmingham supervisors see themselves occupying a middle-class position than is true of manual workers, even relatively affluent ones. This picture does not appear to be greatly at variance with that reported for London dock foremen, the only other group of supervisors known to us for which a comparison can be made. A

Table 7.2 *Supervisors' selection of class labels for themselves*

Label	Number	Percentage	
Upper middle class	7	4.8	
Middle class	37	25.3	47.2
Lower middle class	25	17.1	
Upper working class	28	19.2	52.8
Working class	49	33.6	
TOTAL	146	100.0	

substantial proportion of our supervisors appear to see themselves occupying a middle ground which, if anything, straddles the working/middle-class divide.

This interpretation is strengthened by the results of asking the supervisors to describe 'the sort of people' they saw as coming into the class category they had distinguished as their own. They were free to use any description they wished. The majority described people in terms of industrial occupations. In 114 cases the answers given permitted us to apply the broad classification which is used in Table 7.3.

The table draws attention to the fact that, when permitted to express their social identity without significant predetermined restrictions, a large proportion of supervisors (46 per cent) described themselves as belonging to an apparently middle-ground class which included some workers and managers as well. An alternative interpretation would point out that 78 per cent of supervisors placed themselves in a class which they saw as including some levels of management. Whichever interpretation is preferred, it is apparent that supervisors tended to see themselves as belonging to major social classes rather than to a small separate grouping of their own. This is consistent with the fact that 71 per cent of the sample describing classifiable class structures placed themselves in the largest single class (whatever its level) they distinguished within the overall stratification hierarchy. Whether or not supervisors experience marginality within the work situation, they do not generally appear to see themselves as a marginal group within society as a whole.

Table 7.3 *Supervisors' perceived composition of their own class*

	Number	Percentage
In the same class as shopfloor workers, but not managers	25	21.9
In the same class as workers, managers and (sometimes mentioned) professional employees	52	45.6
In the same class as managers, but not shopfloor workers	37	32.4
TOTAL	114	99.9

6 Criteria for differentiating between classes

The supervisors were asked what features they saw dividing the classes they had distinguished from one another. A content analysis of their replies provided a set of eleven categories (Child *et al.*, 1980: Table 7). Wealth and income were the two most frequently mentioned criteria of class differentiation. One hundred and three supervisors (or 73 per cent of the 142 supervisors responding to this question) mentioned one or more of the monetary criteria: wealth, income and standard of living. There is a similarity here to the large majority of Tyneside shipbuilding workers who also selected monetary criteria for distinguishing between social classes (Cousins and Brown, 1975: 70). However, as with the shipbuilding workers, a wide range of other criteria were also identified: each supervisor on average identified 2.3 criteria.

Some of the criteria selected by the supervisors imply that they perceived a relatively rigid class structure, since they are features which it is difficult to acquire if one does not already possess them. Ownership of wealth, education, power in the wider society, and whether people have an economic need to work, fall into this 'fixed' category. Other criteria imply somewhat less difficulty of movement between classes, and so portray a more fluid structure. People may, for example, be able to change their attitudes. Further criteria of this kind are income, standard of living and characteristics of people's jobs. Indeed, income and living standards will, for the great majority of people, derive from their jobs. In so far as some movement between jobs is possible, and this is to some extent under the individual's own control, these, together with attitudes, may be regarded as indicators of fluidity in the perceived class structure. Fluid criteria of class differentiation were mentioned 165 times and fixed criteria 139 times.

7 Associations between indicators of class perception

Six indicators of supervisors' class perceptions have been employed. If they are found to link together, this could signify a degree of cohesion and consistency in supervisors' views of class. There has been some debate among students of manual workers as to how internally consistent one can expect their images of society to be and also how far this consistency is a product of the research methodology and situation (cf. Bulmer, 1975: 164).

A crude summary of the presence or absence of association

between the six class-perception indicators is given in Table 7.4 (full tables are presented in Child *et al.*, 1980: Appendices 1 to 8). It is immediately evident from the table that the overall structure envisaged is a central indicator, partly because several other measures were derived from the same set of responses. The patterns of association between the indicators are all in a direction to be expected – for example, choice of a middle-class label is associated with: (1) perception of a class structure in which the supervisor's class is not a large, lower one; (2) the mid-point of his own class coming in the upper half of the class hierarchy; and (3) membership of the same class as managers.

There is a clustering between supervisors' replies on class structure, perceived level in the structure, selection of descriptive class labels and perceived composition of their own class, which has as a common factor the *level* at which supervisors see themselves located at the present time within society. Another, weaker cluster connects the perceived shape of the total class structure with criteria of class differentiation and number of classes. In this second cluster, those supervisors who portrayed class structure in pyramidal terms mentioned 'fixed' criteria of class differentiation (as defined in section 6 above) more often than did those supervisors portraying diamond structures ($\chi^2 = 18.26, p < 0.01$). A pyramid image of society implies a steadily diminishing opportunity for upward mobility as a person rises from the base of the hierarchy, while a diamond image implies that such opportunities only begin to diminish at a point nearer the top of the hierarchy. Supervisors employing a diamond image also tended to identify a greater number of classes in society ($t = 2.15$, $p = 0.03$), which implies the availability of more steps for possible

Table 7.4 *Supervisors: presence ($\sqrt{}$) or absence ($\times$)*
of association between indicators of class perception

	2	3	4	5	6
(1) Overall class structure	$\sqrt{}$	$\sqrt{}$	$\sqrt{}$	$\sqrt{}$	$\sqrt{}$
(2) Number of classes	–	$\times$	$\times$	$\times$	$\times$
(3) Level in class structure		–	$\sqrt{}$	$\sqrt{}$	$\times$
(4) Selection of class labels			–	$\sqrt{}$	$\times$
(5) Composition of own class				–	$\times$
(6) Criteria of class differentiation					–

upward mobility. These connections with the class structure image suggest that another aspect of the supervisors' class perceptions concerns the *shape of the overall structure and mobility opportunities within it.*

The remainder of this chapter concentrates on the main cluster of indicators which refer to the level at which supervisors see themselves placed within society.

Class perceptions, social background and previous work experience

We expected to find that those supervisors who had experienced a non-manual social environment would be more likely than others to regard themselves as a 'cut above' the working class. This non-manual experience might either take a relational form, such as an upbringing in a home where the father was in white-collar employment, or having one or more children in white-collar jobs. It might also take the form of occupational membership as, for example, experience of white-collar employment. We examined these possibilities together with a wide range of other aspects of supervisors' background, including type of schooling, level of qualification and previous career history.

The only aspect of white-collar social contact which proved relevant for present perceptions of class was experience in a white-collar job, which 35 of the supervisors had. These supervisors tended more often to ascribe middle-class status to themselves in their choice of labels ($\chi^2 = 4.36$, p = 0.04), and they more often saw the mid-point of their own class coming in the upper half of society than did the other supervisors ($\chi^2 = 7.07$, p = 0.01). There was also a weak tendency for supervisors with white-collar job experience to avoid viewing the class structure in 'working-class' terms – either as a traditional pyramid or an upwardly-skewed diamond (p = 0.11). Exposure to white-collar employment does therefore appear to encourage self-description as a middle-class person, at least in the case of this sample of supervisors. There was, however, no connection at all between having white-collar relations in the family and the manner in which supervisors viewed the class structure or their place within it. No other aspects of the supervisors' background were significantly or consistently related to our indicators of their class perception.

The main conclusion this suggests, therefore, is that it is previous working experience in an *occupational role* which has relevance for supervisors' class perceptions, rather than their immediate family relationships. In this connection, it may be noted that Hill's more extensive questioning about dock foremen's family and social relationships led him to conclude that these on the whole were only slightly and not consistently related to the foremen's class and other social perspectives (1976b, pp. 193–4). If their previous work experience has some connection with how supervisors view their class position, it seems likely that the way in which they perceive their present work situation will also be relevant, particularly whether or not they see themselves as part of management. This is now examined.

Class perceptions and identification within the work situation

The class position (level) of the Birmingham supervisors appears to be only marginally superior to that of the manual workers whom they supervise. A sizeable proportion do, however, perceive that they belong to a higher social class than manual workers, and some describe this specifically as a managerial class. We suggested earlier that the supervisors who see themselves occupying a high class position might be those who accept the view, contained in some management statements, that supervisors should and do have a managerial role, standing and allegiance.

In Chapter 3, we described how supervisors were asked for their views on twelve statements concerning 'the supervisor's role today'. Four of these statements referred specifically to the managerial orientation of the supervisor's job and economic interests. Every supervisor was asked how true he thought the statement was of the supervisor's position in his firm (descriptive) and how much the condition described in the statement should in his opinion prevail (normative). Seven-point scales were used for rating purposes. The four statements are set out in Table 7.5.

There was no relationship between the degree of normative approval which supervisors gave to the four statements and their class perceptions. Their ratings of the statements as valid descriptions of the situations within their firms were only associated with perceived level of their class position, and in a very limited manner. Supervisors who placed the mid-point of their class within the upper half of British society tended to record more agreement with statements depicting them as line managers ($t = 3.40$, $p = 0.001$) and

Table 7.5 *Four statements concerning the managerial nature of the supervisor's role*

═══

(1) *Acceptance into management*
'The supervisor is really a breed of his own; he has left the ranks of labour without being accepted into management.'

(2) *Economic interests*
'In industrial conditions today, the economic interests of the supervisor are much the same as those of his workers.'

(3) *Line manager*
'The supervisor is the first line of management and a line manager in every respect.'

(4) *Promotion opportunities*
'There are still plenty of opportunities for an able supervisor to be promoted into management.'

═══

as having been accepted into management ($t = 2.15$, $p = 0.03$). What appears to be much more germane to supervisors' perceptions of class is the extent to which their assessment of their place within management *falls short* of what they think it should be.

Virtually every one believed that the managerial nature of the supervisor's role should be greater than it was. Many articulated their awareness of this discrepancy, and the following are a few examples. First, from the engineering plant:

> 'Management should realize that we are the first-line of management, they're always telling us that we are, but when something crops up such as a strike, then they equate us with the shopfloor.'

> 'The supervisor here is like the NCO in wartime. Although he is supposed to be on the same level as a commissioned officer, they always let him know that they don't regard him as the same. Even where supervisors are doing something more than their job of supervision, management refuses to pay or recognize that this is so. He should be bringing the authority of the Board of Directors to his section. His statements should be automatically accepted and not questioned in front of the operators and shop stewards.'

And from the food plant:

> 'Supervisors are left out on a limb. We've been given more responsibility but have been left out on our own as far as being accepted into management.'

> 'The men on the shopfloor don't accept the supervisor as part of management unless he can make really important decisions.'

> 'In my opinion, I am still a manual worker. The managers have a club of their own: there is nothing like that for supervisors.'

Appendix 7.1 presents a full statistical analysis of how far supervisors' perceptions of such discrepancies were linked to how they saw their class position. Although their strength varies considerably, the associations between (1) supervisors' assessments of how far their place in management falls short of what it ought to be and (2) their perceived class position are all in a consistent direction, with the notable exception of promotion. This could be because promotion into management portrays a potential, rather than a current affiliation with management of the kind captured by the other three statements. The main relationships are:

(1) supervisors perceiving a low divergence between what should be and what is, with respect to acceptance into management, are more likely to portray a class structure in which they belong to a middle-level or superior class;

(2) similarly, supervisors perceiving a low divergence between normative and descriptive with respect to their recognition as line managers are more likely to perceive a structure in which they belong to a superior class;

(3) supervisors perceiving a low divergence between normative and descriptive with respect to the two aspects of managerialism just mentioned are more likely to perceive that their class is located primarily in the upper part of the stratification hierarchy (as assessed by mid-point between upper and lower limits);

(4) somewhat marginally in terms of statistical confidence, supervisors perceiving a low divergence between normative and descriptive with respect to (1) acceptance into management and (2) economic interests, tended to describe themselves in terms of middle-class rather than working-class labels;

163

(5) also marginally, supervisors perceiving a low divergence between normative and descriptive with respect to recognition as line managers tend to see their class as an exclusively managerial one.

In short, it is not primarily whether or not a supervisor perceives that he and his colleagues occupy a managerial position which is associated with how he tends to view his class position. It is rather the extent to which that perception accords with the level of managerialism the supervisor thinks he *should* enjoy. Supervisors are given no encouragement to regard themselves as anything but working-class if they are led by managerial ideology to expect treatment as managers but find that management practice keeps them at arm's length from the authority, status and condition pertaining to a managerial role. The poignancy of such a contrast between normative and actual may even encourage class consciousness among supervisors.

As with the findings on social background and previous experience, examination of supervisors in their current work situation suggests that it is their *occupational role* (as they see it), rather than the *social relationships* into which they enter, which is associated with how they view their class position. As mentioned towards the beginning of this chapter, we asked supervisors about their social relationships with other groups including senior managers and their immediate superiors. There was no evidence whatsoever to indicate that the nature of these social relationships had any association with class identification (though, as Child *et al.*, 1980, report, supervisors claiming to *identify* more closely with senior managers generally placed themselves higher up in the class hierarchy). The way in which supervisors regard the job itself, and the conditions attaching to it, seems to be a more potent factor in the assessment of their class position (and class perception might also contribute to how they view their jobs) than the social relationships in which they are involved.

Conclusion

When assessed in terms of authority, market position and work situation, the supervisors we studied appeared to share a similar class position, which was only marginally superior to that of manual workers. The perceptions they had of class did not, however, reveal an equivalent degree of homogeneity nor a dominant tendency towards a working-class outlook and identification.

While a sizeable proportion of the supervisors placed themselves in a subordinate-class category, shared with manual workers, this proportion did not appreciably exceed half the sample on any of the indicators which were applied. This is a far lower proportion than has been found among samples of British manual workers by other investigators. In fact, when given an opportunity to describe the upper limits of the class to which they belonged, a large minority of supervisors (46 per cent) stated that some managerial groups were members, as well as shopfloor workers, and a similar proportion (49 per cent) placed the upper boundary of their class in the top quartile of the population. In other words, many supervisors saw themselves belonging to a class which spanned the traditional manual/non-manual (or working/middle-class) divide, and which incorporated some groups from either side of that 'boundary'. Another, smaller group of supervisors, judging by several indicators, perceived themselves to be in a position more distinctly superior to that of shopfloor workers and/or the 'lower' class. Most of this group adopted middle-class labels.

There was, then, substantial variation in the class perceptions held by supervisors. In considering the possible sources of this variation, it is relevant to note not only the present class position of supervisors but also the fact that they have been promoted from the ranks of manual labour. Of itself, being a supervisor, with the conditions attaching to the job, would perhaps not strongly dispose a person to consider himself removed from the working class. But having been formally promoted out of the manual working population into a position to which the expectation of 'acceptance into management' is still attached, the supervisor might now come to see himself as having at least one foot in the non-manual, non-working-class camp. Or rather he might now think that he *ought* to be differentiated in this way from the working class, as his predecessors were some 50 years or more ago. It is in this light that one can understand the finding that supervisors' perceived class levels tended to be higher the less they saw their place in the firm falling short of the degree of acceptance into management that they believed to be appropriate. The fact that it was how they saw their role *relative* to what was believed appropriate which predicted variations in class perception suggests that the way people perceive their class position may be more a consequence of their standing relative to their own norm rather than of their position in absolute terms.

It would be an oversimplification to conclude that the industrial supervisors we studied belong in a straightforward manner either to a proletarianized middle class (in the terms set out by Roberts *et al.*, 1977) or to a sector of the working class that had adopted middle-class characteristics. They are people of predominantly working-class origins who fill an occupational role which is no longer sharply distinguished from that of manual workers, but which is at the same time claimed ideologically to be managerial. Historically, supervision may have been a lower-middle-class occupation which has become eroded and 'proletarianized' over time, though recruitment to it has probably always come primarily from the working class. Currently, it would be more accurate to conclude that the supervisors in this study are people of largely working-class origins who have not completely left that class, even though they are ideologically encouraged in that aspiration and in some cases perceive that they have advanced to a higher level in society.

Our study leaves open the question how far variations in managerial policy towards supervisors can generate differences in their class perceptions and how far, in contrast, these are shaped at an earlier stage of primary and occupational socialization and have become impervious to managerial actions. We found evidence that both previous work experience and how supervisors see their present position at work are related to their general social identification. This suggests that management policies may influence the ways in which supervisors regard their position in society. Management certainly controls some of the features which contribute to the supervisor's class position, notably his authority, conditions of employment, opportunities for career advancement and status within the system of in-plant relationships. If such features were improved for supervisors, this would reduce the gap between the objective reality of their position and its normative definition, a definition which the great majority of both managers and supervisors in the two Birmingham plants claim to share. It is not apparent, however, that this would expand a middle-class identification among *all* supervisors since it is clear from our findings that their perceptions of a largely shared reality do differ. Nor does it follow any more in Britain that employees who consider themselves to be middle-class will not take overt and organized action against management. The growth of union membership among white-collar employees over the past 20 years, and their increased involvement in industrial disputes, are developments which now extend to many supervisors as well. They are considered in the following chapter.

Appendix 7.1 *Comparison of supervisors' class perceptions with differences between normative and descriptive ratings of the managerial nature of their role*

Indicators of class perception		Mean differences between ratings given to statements (1) on normative grounds and (2) as descriptions of reality, scored so that a positive indicates that supervisors assess their role as less managerial than they think it should be[a]			
	Number of supervisors	1 Acceptance into management	2 Economic interests	3 Line manager	4 Promotion opportunities
(1) Selection of class labels					
1.1 Middle-class labels	69	1.32	0.43	0.86	1.99
1.2 Working-class labels	77	2.03	1.04	1.24	1.75
		($t = 1.81$, $p = 0.07$)	($t = 1.70$, $p = 0.09$)	($t = 1.43$, $p = 0.15$)	($t = 0.64$, $p = 0.52$)
(2) Class structure envisaged					
2.1 Traditional diamond	25	0.88	0.44	0.52	1.96
2.2 Non-traditional pyramid	18	1.17	0.78	0.50	1.88
2.3 Downwardly-skewed diamond	13	1.92	0.54	0.85	1.77
2.4 Upwardly-skewed diamond	21	1.86	1.00	2.33	1.81
2.5 Traditional pyramid	33	2.66	1.33	1.50	2.18
		($F = 2.43$, $p = 0.05$)	($F = 0.66$, $p = 0.62$)	($F = 5.64$, $p < 0.001$)	($F = 0.14$, $p = 0.97$)

(*Contd.*)

Appendix 7.1 (Contd.)

Indicators of class perception		Mean differences between ratings given to statements (1) on normative grounds and (2) as descriptions of reality, scored so that a positive indicates that supervisors assess their role as less managerial than they think it should be			
(3) Perceived composition of own class					
3.1 Same as managers only	37	1.36	0.89	0.68	2.14
3.2 Same as managers plus shopfloor workers	52	2.15	0.83	1.29	1.92
3.3 Same as shopfloor workers only	25	2.28	1.16	1.58	1.56
		$(F = 1.53, p = 0.22)$	$(F = 0.18, p = 0.83)$	$(F = 2.60, p = 0.08)$	$(F = 0.44, p = 0.64)$
(4) Perceived level in class structure					
4.1 Own class in top part (50 per cent and above)	70	1.23	0.71	0.62	1.71
4.2 Own class in bottom part (below 50 per cent)	72	2.20	0.82	1.57	1.99
		$(t = 2.45, p = 0.02)$	$(t = 0.29, p = 0.78)$	$(t = 23.24, p < 0.001)$	$(t = 0.73, p = 0.47)$

Levels of statistical confidence are given in parentheses

8

Looking to management or to union?

> They [foremen] want a union but they don't want strikes, and they don't want to be 'lumped in with the workers'. What they want is protection. (Nichols and Beynon, *Living with Capitalism* (1977: 64))

Since the mid-1960s supervisors have joined unions in large numbers. This has been part of the general growth in white-collar unionization, which must be considered as one of the major post-war social developments in Britain (Jenkins and Sherman, 1979). Despite their normally manual-working backgrounds, supervisors fall into the white-collar category, at least according to the criterion suggested by Bain and Price (1972) of possessing or being in proximity to authority.

There has been a great deal of debate about the nature and process of white-collar unionism.[1] This chapter considers the union membership of the Birmingham supervisors and adopts as its main framework several key issues in the debate. These are:

(1) the process whereby large numbers of supervisors in a place of work decide to join a union;
(2) the meaning which union membership has for supervisors;
(3) whether, for supervisors, looking to a union for assistance is compatible with looking to management as a source of identity in the workplace, and how attitudes towards unionism may relate to their social identity and background in general.

Union membership and participation in union activities

Ninety-eight per cent (146) of the supervisors we interviewed about trade unionism were union members. Membership was 100 per cent in the food manufacturing plant and 94 per cent in the engineering

169

plant. A different union represented the majority of supervisors in each plant. In the food plant, membership in our sample was:

ASTMS   70 supervisors (59 in charge of pro-
                               duction sections, 11 non-production)
AUEW   15 supervisors (all non-production)
ACTSS, SOGAT, NGA   each 2 supervisors
other unions   8 supervisors

In the engineering plant, union membership in our sample was:

ACTSS   46 supervisors (37 production, 9 non-
                               production)
AUEW   1 non-production supervisor

Of the unionized supervisors whom we interviewed, 81 per cent belonged to a specifically white-collar union (ASTMS, ACTSS). The largest segment in the remaining membership comprised maintenance supervisors who had chosen to remain in the AUEW. Just over 40 per cent of the food supervisors and half the engineering ones had not belonged to any other union before. Of those supervisors who had belonged to another union, normally before their promotion to supervisor, the majority had been members of the TGWU, which was the main shopfloor union in both plants. Over a quarter of the supervisors (28 per cent) stated that they did not mind which union they belonged to, though we shall note later that most of the supervisors regarded white-collar, indeed managerial, unions as being the more appropriate.

When questioned about attendance at branch meetings, voting in local and national union elections, and willingness to hold local union office, supervisors were divided between those who claimed to participate highly in union affairs and those who were inactive, with relatively few people coming in between (full details are given in Child, 1980b). Compared with figures reported by Hill (1976b: 130n.) for London dock foremen, the overall participation in union affairs by the Birmingham foremen was quite high. The supervisors in charge of non-production sections were less localized in their pattern of union activity. They attended local branch meetings less frequently but voted in national union elections more often than did most production supervisors. This was particularly marked among the 15 AUEW members in the food plant where the branch was not based on the place of work and where the union's particularly democratic constitution lends national elections a special significance.

These different aspects of participation in union affairs were generally found to vary in common, though some supervisors were exceptions. Up to a point, it is therefore possible to refer to these variables together as a basis for distinguishing the more active union member from the less active.

The process of unionization

The interviews with supervisors were conducted during the first half of 1976. In the engineering plant, 51 per cent of the supervisors interviewed who were union members had joined since the beginning of 1971; in the food plant 63 per cent had joined their union since that date. Taking the two plants together, supervisors had on average joined their present union some two and a half years after appointment to the job of supervisor and at an average age of 40.4 years. While these averages were fairly comparable for each site, they mask very considerable differences between production and non-production supervisors. Non-production supervisors, in the main, had been members of a union before becoming supervisors – on average for 7.9 years before and at a joining age of 31.2 years – whereas production supervisors joined on average 7.3 years after becoming a supervisor and at age 44.5 years (for both differences, $p < 0.001$).

The increase in membership during the first half of the 1970s in both plants had largely been confined to production supervisors, and our subsequent detailed questioning on the process of unionization therefore focused on the production area. The process had intensified at certain points in time. This was very noticeable in the food plant, where one-half of all the supervisors interviewed had joined in the period 1971 to 1973. In the engineering plant, 28 per cent had joined in late 1973 and 1974, with a lesser surge apparent between late 1968 and early 1969 (17 per cent had joined then).

Events in both plants were consistent with the conclusion drawn by Roberts *et al.* (1972) for the unionization of technicians: namely that a nucleus of union card-carriers was an essential prerequisite of organization. The process was, however, much more clear-cut, immediate and dramatic in the food plant, in which the threat of redundancy provided the main spur to unionization among supervisors and represented, both in itself and in the way it was handled by

171

management, a sharp break with the company's previous traditions of labour relations. This case will be discussed first.

The food company (Company F) had merged with another company in the late 1960s. Company F had been family-owned and controlled. It had for many years pursued a highly welfare-oriented policy towards employees, and redundancies had been unheard of. The secretary of the ASTMS factory branch which organized production and some non-production supervisors had worked for the company since leaving school, and this was not unusual. As he put it: 'F was a family business: you were looked after from the cradle to the grave. Once you came to F you were there for life'. The company it merged with brought in a strong financial management expertise, and a greater financial orientation. In 1970, the new joint company launched its 'Operation Profitability' which led to a reduction of about one-fifth in production supervisors and about half in their immediate superiors (section managers), chiefly in 1970 and 1971. It is significant that the supervisors and managers we talked to recalled the reduction being as high as one-half for both groups. There was no consultation by senior management about redundancies or about how they might be handled.

This event was a dramatic culture shock for supervisors and their immediate superiors, who subsequently joined ASTMS *en masse*. In describing unionization to us, the view that supervisors were forced and driven into unionism by the new development was repeatedly put, as in the following quotations:

> 'It took something pretty dramatic to force F's supervisors and managers into a union.'

> 'If you'd have thought about F's supervisors in 1960 or 1965, you wouldn't have got a chance of any of them ever joining a union because things were there to protect them. Then [the newly merged company] became an empire – the hard face of capitalism came in.'

> 'It was fear in the first place that drove F's supervisors into a union.'

The present secretary of the ASTMS branch at Company F played a key role in mobilizing union membership once the events of 1970–71 had changed the perspectives of supervisors. He had always worked for F and had always been a union member: first joining the

TGWU on the shopfloor and then ASTMS when he became a supervisor. He belonged to ASTMS before supervisory redundancies took place. When these were occurring, and production supervisors developed an interest in possible assistance from a union, he took the initiative of inviting officers from the TGWU, Association of Professional, Executive, Clerical and Computer Staff (APEX), and ASTMS to address the supervisors and section managers on the site. Only the ASTMS district officer responded. Although this officer is well known for holding left-wing and militant views, he did not express these at the meeting, and at the time there was no evidence of militancy in the supervisors' attitude towards the company. Supervisors across all the production sections then decided to join ASTMS in large numbers. Subsequently, the same branch secretary, together with the branch chairman, was invited to address supervisors in other plants and depots on the benefit of union membership. As a result, ASTMS membership spread widely throughout the company's supervisors and section managers, and some staff-grade clerical employees, with many of them joining the original Birmingham factory branch.

In Company F, then, the threat to security and the shock of an abrupt change in management philosophy provided the immediate reason for supervisory unionization, while the process was considerably facilitated, and perhaps only made possible, by the activities of one or two key actors who were already card-carrying members of the union concerned.

The nature of supervisory unionism within Company F subsequently changed between the period of initial mobilization among production supervisors and the time of our interviews in 1976. It was put to us by local officials and by a personnel officer that, while the full-time ASTMS organization had, when invited, played an active role in assisting initial mobilization, the local supervisors' and managers' ASTMS branch in Company F had now come to operate with a greater degree of autonomy from the main union organization. Thus, whatever policy might be laid down within ASTMS as a whole, the decision whether to accept its provisions was put to members of the local branch for approval. As was said: 'we believe that we pay our dues for their [ASTMS's] advice; they don't rule us, we rule them.' The other main development had come in the attitude of union members, which was more militant by 1976 largely because of frustrations generated by government incomes policy. Pay had become the dominant issue, not least for supervisors, whose differentials above shopfloor earnings had been eroded.

In the engineering company, the impetus for supervisory unionism, and the process by which it came about, was less clear-cut and dramatic. Mobilization of supervisors into union membership was more fragmentary. It was commented that at the beginning of mobilization among production supervisors they did not share a clear understanding of whether they wanted to be organized and, if so, which union they should join.

A combination of factors appears to have provided the impetus towards unionization among supervisors in the company. In 1968, while still an independent family firm, the company extended recognition to a shopfloor union for the first time. This was the organization of the toolroom, including its supervisors, by the AUEW. Organization of the production and maintenance sections by the TGWU, and to a much lesser extent by the AUEW, soon followed. The supervisors were at that time hourly-paid employees and some were already TGWU members. They felt that shopfloor unionization increased the danger of their being 'left behind' through the erosion of differentials; it had also provided an example of the additional muscle which unionization could provide *vis-à-vis* a management, whose approach to rewards and conditions was personalistic and *ad hoc* rather than standardized. As the (then) supervisor who played a leading role in recruiting his colleagues to ACTSS put it:

> 'At that particular time we thought we needed some muscle. Other people were using it and getting away with it. Possibly we were riding on a tide that suited us at that particular moment. And it's only fair to say that management at that time closed their eyes to quite a few things they shouldn't have done. So supervisors said why can't we get on the bandwagon – this is what we tried to do.'

A further spur for the supervisors to join a union was the increased challenge which shopfloor unionism provided to their own already limited authority through the way it emboldened employee action. One incident was related several times, in which the employees in a section voted to get rid of their supervisor.

At the end of 1971, the company was taken over by a large group operating principally in the non-ferrous metals, building products and cable manufacturing industries. Unlike the case of the food company, absorption into a larger group did not lead to any redundancies among supervisors, and our informants did not attach any great significance to the take-over as a factor in unionization. The next noticeable surge in membership in fact occurred in late 1973 and 1974. This was associated with a drive to secure 100 per cent membership which the local plant ACTSS officials instituted at the time, and which was later bolstered by the national move back to 'free collective bargaining' in 1974. It is not clear why the objective of a closed shop, with the intention of raising the union's bargaining effectiveness, was brought into prominence in 1973, particularly as senior management had not resisted the progress of supervisory unionization.

As with the food company, a few card-carrying activists played a central role in initiating the mobilization process. An early objective they held, which proved to be an immediate rallying point, was to stop management's policy of setting supervisors' rates of pay on an individual and *ad hoc* basis and to secure one rate and weekly-staff status. To quote the same leading activist again:

> 'Some people you dealt with in management at that time, you got a fair deal off them, but some you didn't . . . The supervisors, instead of going up asking for an interview with management, and being sorted out one or two at a time, they wanted some kind of representation – for money as well. You know, at that particular time we had the five-bob touch; they'd give one supervisor five shillings more than another and that caused more problems than enough. When we sorted the union out, each one of us put our docket on the table, and within five minutes everyone of us knew what everyone else was getting.'

Another decision consciously taken by only a few active ACTSS members was whether they should set up their own branch for supervisors, which they did. ACTSS is the staff side of the TGWU, which had already organized the production shopfloor, and joining ACTSS rather than the TGWU proper was never an issue, given pressure among supervisors at the time to secure staff status, which management rapidly conceded. Management had already concluded an agreement with ACTSS for production control staff, and it also preferred this choice of union for supervisors, modelling a new agreement on the one previously established. Similar to the situation in the food company, local branch affairs are now conducted independently of the district union office, with little contact between the two levels. The mobilization of union membership among supervisors in the engineering company centred around a few activists and domestic issues, and did not involve full-time external union officials. In both companies, the major surge of unionization among supervisors came after management recognition of shopfloor unions but before management recognition of the new supervisory and junior management union. Managerial recognition of white-collar unions *per se* does not appear to have provided a major impetus to supervisor unionization, although the absence of overt management hostility in either company to the development may have facilitated its progress significantly. The importance of managerial reactions has been emphasized by several writers (e.g. Bain, 1970; Marsh and Pedler, 1979).

This section has been concerned with the process of unionization among supervisors. As such it has exposed relatively immediate rather than long-term factors which account for growth in this sector of white-collar unionism. More immediate events can, however, reflect underlying causes and the following comments are offered with this in mind. In the food plant, the redundancies, which were such a dramatic break with the company's traditional culture, represented a shift in management attitude from regarding supervisors as a fixed cost to treating them more in terms of a variable cost. The merger had led management to look for improved profitability from the company's operations. The long-term trend has indeed been towards a declining rate of profit in British industry (Glyn and Sutcliffe, 1972) which, if it has encouraged other companies to undertake a similar reappraisal of the status of supervisory labour (and perhaps white-collar employment in general), may be a major contributory impetus towards supervisory unionism. It would, in effect, make a significant shift in supervisors' internal labour market position.

In the engineering company, the organization of shopfloor workers in turn encouraged organization among supervisors, who were in a particularly good position to witness the benefits it was providing for the members of their sections, and to be aware of the possible threat it posed to their differentials and to their already limited authority.

Bain (1970) claimed to find no evidence that proximity to unionized manual workers was related to white-collar union growth. Supervisory unionism in this company is an exception to that conclusion, and perhaps more exceptions could be found if future studies were to focus more closely upon the process of unionization rather than on broad correlations.

The meaning of unionism

This section examines the reasons which supervisors gave for their membership of a union. We have noted that in both companies there was a disengagement of the plant-based branches to which the supervisors belonged from the full-time organization of ASTMS and ACTSS. It is likely, therefore, that supervisors' views as to the instrumental, ideological and political functions which their union should perform will have a far greater effect upon the character of the union at branch level than upon the attitudes and policies expressed by its full-time officials, even those in the local district. So long as the branch is permitted to make its own decisions, inconsistencies in the character of the union at different levels can be tolerated by its members.

Each supervisor who was a union member was asked to say why he had joined. The most frequently-mentioned type of reason referred to a group norm of membership: 'because most people here are members' (45 per cent of supervisors said this). It was mentioned particularly often in the engineering plant, where active group pressures to join were also mentioned more often. Normative reasons, 'because I think everyone should be in a union' and 'because I found the union was doing a good job locally', were mentioned with relatively greater frequency by supervisors in the food plant. The most significant difference between the two sites lies in the fact that, judging by the supervisors' replies, membership of a union had become institutionalized in the food plant. As well as the stronger normative emphasis just noted, nearly all the mentions of management encouragement came from that site, and mentions of the necessity for union membership in order to get a job came only from there. Unionization of supervisors in the plant was, of course, complete. It is particularly interesting to recall that the main wave of unionization among production supervisors in the food plant had been generated by the desire to secure protection against a markedly changed management policy towards supervisory job security. Some

177

five years later, with unionism complete, and a recognized part of the company's institutional framework, the rationale for membership as expressed by individual members has shifted accordingly – very little mention was made of the need for protection.

In the engineering plant, where unionization had been more fragmentary and was not total, the norms and pressures of the majority were still being felt by some supervisors as coercive. One, for example, who said that membership of the union did not give him any benefit and that he joined because most other supervisors had, continued: 'I just feel that I am a member along with the rest of the supervisors. I don't want to be different, though I have my own opinions.' Another supervisor mentioned that his colleagues had 'badgered' him into joining.

The main contrast between supervisors in charge of production and non-production sections lay in the need felt by some of the latter (especially in the engineering sections) to belong to their union (mainly the craft-oriented AUEW) in order to obtain or retain their jobs. This was also true of a small group of supervisors in the food plant on the production side who were in charge of printing and card-box making and were members of the craft printing unions. A higher proportion of non-production supervisors also mentioned reasons for having joined their union of a normatively approving kind. It may be recalled that non-production supervisors were generally much longer-standing members of their union.

The most frequently mentioned benefits from union membership were (1) the securing of better pay and conditions (57 per cent mentioned this), (2) the benefits of collective action and representation *per se* (42 per cent) and (3) the security and protection provided (33 per cent). Supervisors in the food plant gave particularly heavy emphasis to the securing of better pay and conditions, which may have reflected the fact that negotiations over pay were active at the time of the interviews. Collective action was also mentioned relatively more frequently in that plant. In the engineering plant more union members claimed to derive no benefits from union membership – these were often supervisors who felt they had been pressured into joining by their colleagues. A few claimed that the union had been run for the benefit of a clique of founder-member activists whom the company had since promoted to management.

In an attempt to record on a standardized basis the meaning of unionism to individual supervisors, they were asked to indicate the extent of their agreement or disagreement with 20 statements, by rating each of these along five-point labelled Likert-type scales. The choice of statements was made with Blackburn's (1967) concept of union character, and its expression in terms of 'unionateness', in mind. Blackburn regarded a union or occupational association as possessing high 'unionateness' if it was strongly committed to the general principles and ideology of trade unionism and the labour movement, and prepared to use all that movement's powers. Appendix D lists the 20 statements in full, and taken together they attempt to express at the individual level the equivalent of union character at the organizational level. The statements concern:

(1) the perceived degree of advantage and necessity of belonging to a union, including the importance of independence from employers (union versus staff association);
(2) the appropriateness of belonging to different types of union: shopfloor unions, management unions, supervisory unions;
(3) opinion on the degree of union militancy;
(4) attitudes towards the political and labour movement connections of unions.

1 Advantage and necessity of union membership and independence from employers

Most supervisors thought that membership of a union was advantageous, particularly with respect to the way it was seen (1) to offer a chance of negotiating with management through strength (91 per cent agreed or strongly agreed with this statement); (2) to offer a better chance of securing good rewards and conditions of employment (83 per cent endorsed this).

Supervisors' views on nine of the 20 statements followed a similar pattern and clustered together. These nine statements (which are denoted by an asterisk in Appendix D) each expressed the necessity or otherwise of belonging to a union. One statement specifically dealt with independence from employers ('an internal staff association would be better than an outside union'), with which 67 per cent disagreed and only 19 per cent agreed. Another one of the nine statements contrasted the need for union membership against the backing which management gave supervisors: 73 per cent thought that they should rely on the union rather than on management. In neither plant, it may be recalled, had management actively attempted to prevent supervisors from joining a union, and 90 per cent took the view that union membership did not harm any career prospects open to them. For most supervisors, unionization represented a lessening of dependence on management, but not a breaking with it.

Aggregation of the nine statements appeared justified on both conceptual and statistical grounds. Conceptually the statements all concern the degree of advantage or necessity for supervisors to be union members, with reference to instrumental rather than ideological or political objectives. The measure which resulted from summing scores for the nine statements was therefore labelled 'necessity for union membership'. Statistical criteria for aggregation were also satisfied, since the composite measure had high internal scale reliability.[2] A position of 'unsure', midway between agreement and disagreement on this measure, would score 27. The mean score for all supervisors ($N = 147$) was 20.37, which indicates an overall tendency to agree that union membership is necessary for instrumental reasons. While there was no significant difference between production and non-production supervisors in the importance attached to union membership for instrumental reasons, supervisors at the food plant did tend to emphasize this more than did those at the engineering plant (see Table 8.1).

Endorsement of the necessity for union membership on instrumental grounds can be interpreted as a general measure of support for membership since, to anticipate for a moment, strong support was not forthcoming for union membership on ideological and political grounds. Viewed in this light, it is not surprising to find that support for union membership was linked with an expression of willingness to hold local union office,[3] with participation in national

Table 8.1

Supervisors: perceived necessity for union membership	Engineering plant	Food plant
Mean score (lower score indicates greater necessity)	22.94	19.05
Standard deviation	6.62	5.10
Number of supervisors	50	97
$t = 3.63$ $p < 0.001$		

union elections[4] and also, marginally, with participation in local union elections.[5] There was no association, however, between the support expressed for union membership and attendance at union meetings.

2 The appropriateness of belonging to different types of union

Among the sample of supervisors as a whole, a majority (67 per cent) thought that belonging to a union catering for managers offered the best chance of bettering their pay and conditions of employment. However, almost as many (66.5 per cent) thought that membership of a union restricted to supervisors would be desirable. Support for membership of a management union was substantially stronger in the food company, while support for membership of a supervisory union was stronger in the engineering company.[6] Production supervisors also tended to give stronger support for membership of a management union than did those in charge of non-production sections.[7] Only a minority of supervisors (27 per cent) thought that there were advantages to be gained from membership of a shopfloor union; this minority opinion was not particularly characteristic of either site or of any major group.

There was very strong agreement (94 per cent) with the statement that supervisors should have a union just for themselves, to protect their position in comparison with other groups. Hill (1976b: 136) found that a large majority among foremen in the London docks whom he studied took a similar view. One has to recall, however, that the majority of supervisors were not adverse to belonging to a union which also included managerial personnel. A large majority (87 per cent) preferred to be in a union which bargained directly and locally with their own company. Any support for national bargaining tended to come from non-production supervisors ($p = 0.04$).

In short, most supervisors preferred to belong to a union which organized employees at their own and higher levels in the company. They preferred to bargain directly with their company, which is consistent with the generally local orientation of their unionism.

3 Union militancy

A substantial majority of supervisors (86 per cent) disagreed with the statement that 'Trade unions are not militant enough'; in fact, only seven supervisors (5 per cent) positively agreed with it. Reaction against the idea of union militancy was marginally stronger among production supervisors (p = 0.08).

4 *Political and labour movement connections of unions*

Most supervisors were not opposed to membership of a union on normative grounds. When presented with the statement that: 'Really, supervisors shouldn't have to belong to a union', 68 per cent disagreed and only 25 per cent agreed. However, their approval of unions did not generally extend to an ideological involvement in politics. Nine supervisors out of ten (89 per cent) agreed that 'unions should restrict their activities to representing members instead of getting involved in political issues.' More disagreed than agreed with the statement that 'to me, it is just as important to join a union as part of the labour movement as it is to join for personal advantage' (50 per cent disagreed; 35 per cent agreed). The spread of opinions on the political and labour movement connections of unions was similar among supervisors in both companies and, overall, as between production and non-production supervisors. The 16 AUEW members in charge of maintenance sections were the main deviators from the general trend. Compared to members of ASTMS and ACTSS, they were less opposed to the involvement of unions in political issues (F = 5.46, p < 0.01); there was also a slight tendency for them to regard union links with the labour movement more favourably.

The views expressed by these supervisors suggest that their rationale of attachment to union membership is more dynamic and less homogeneous than has sometimes been recognized in discussions of white-collar unionism and its character. Comparison of the circumstances in which surges in unionization took place with the reasons advanced for union membership on the later occasion of our study indicates that supervisors redefine the priority order of functions which they perceive the union to perform for them in accordance with changes in the industrial relations context. Within the food plant, for example, the prime rationale of union membership for supervisors became transformed from protection against threats to job security, in which entry of the union also symbolized withdrawal of previously unquestioning dependence upon managerial goodwill, to the gaining of better pay and conditions of employment through collective bargaining.

Unionateness, as a conceptualization of union character to which members can subscribe in greater or lesser degree, was not a one-dimensional phenomenon for the supervisors. They generally acknowledged that it was necessary to belong to a union as a way of enhancing benefits and ensuring protection through local collective action *vis-à-vis* the employer. However, their union should not, in the opinion of most supervisors, share membership with shopfloor employees, engage in militant action or be involved with national politics. There is some parallel here with the opinions of National and Local Government Officers' Association (NALGO) members surveyed by Nicholson *et al.* (1980), most of whom wished their union branch to confine itself to defending their job and pay level, and few of whom valued the union as a link with the labour movement. Prandy *et al.* (1974) separated the original concept of unionateness into two components: (1) enterprise unionateness which is concerned with the pursuit of union members' interests as employees, and (2) society unionateness which concerns the union's behaviour in the wider society. This is akin to the distinction which most supervisors made between the value of union membership in dealing with their employer and the desirability of avoiding policies of militancy and political action. On the whole, supervisors appeared to take a pragmatic view of the need to secure assistance from a union, which did not signify an ideological estrangement from management or a left-wing political attachment.

Looking to management or to union?

We examined the social identification of the supervisors from several angles, both through attitudes and behaviour. The attitudinal indicators referred to (1) the degree of similarity supervisors saw between their own attitudes and behaviour and those of six other categories of people in the firm; (2) the value they placed on relationships with those people; (3) the degree of conflict they perceived within the firm; and (4) their comment on statements concerning 'the supervisor's role today', which referred to relationships with management and to supervisors' economic interests. The main behavioural indicator was the presence of social contacts with other groups.

As mentioned in Chapter 7, the pattern of supervisors' social contacts pointed to a closer identification with shopfloor workers than with managers. The attitudinal indicators, however, suggested the reverse. Supervisors gave high approval to the statements listed in Table 7.5 (page 162) which depicted their role as managerial, although on economic interests their overall stance was neutral. While nearly all supervisors perceived that there was conflict within their company, two-thirds (66 per cent) believed that it was resolved by give-and-take and co-operation. The supervisors tended to perceive most similarity in attitudes and behaviour ('speak, behave, dress') between themselves and other supervisors, their immediate superiors and shopfloor workers in that order. In evaluating relationships their overall order of priority was (1) immediate superior, (2) shopfloor workers and (3) senior management.

In terms of their attitudes at least, the bulk of these supervisors looked towards management (especially their immediate superiors) rather more strongly than they did in other directions. What emerges quite clearly, however, is that this willingness to identify with management, and to adopt a managerial conception of their role, does not represent a trade-off with the value they place upon belonging to a union. The need which supervisors felt to belong to a union was no weaker among those who identified more closely with management, be this senior management or their immediate superior. Nor was it any weaker among those supervisors who expressed a preference for belonging to a management union. It has to be recalled that supervisors were articulating support for union membership for instrumental and pragmatic reasons, and that, in the food plant especially, their own immediate superiors were normally members of the same union. In the supervisors' opinion, then, there was no serious inconsistency between drawing upon the strength of union membership in order to secure better conditions of employment and protection, while at the same time maintaining a closer identification with management than with the shopfloor. The two unions to which most supervisors belonged were, of course, white-collar ones, not catering for a manual-worker membership.

In order to understand the impact which management has upon supervisors' attachment to the union, it may be necessary to move from the somewhat vague and diffuse notion of identification in order to focus upon more specific workplace phenomena. This is suggested by two additional findings. First, the supervisors who express the strongest need to belong to a union are also often among the less satisfied with their job both in general terms[8] and especially in terms of conditions of employment.[9] Secondly, stronger support for union membership is expressed on average by supervisors with between 11 and 20 years' service as a supervisor – the relationship with length of time in the job is curvilinear. Those who have been promoted to supervisor within the past ten years tend to express least support for unionism, and also to express somewhat higher job satisfaction. This could point to promotion being regarded for a while as a mark of support and confidence from management, which then becomes less credible for those who have remained at the same level for some years. It is an aspect of attachment to management and to union that deserves further investigation.

In some respects, supervisors' views about the *type* of union to which they preferred to belong did appear to depend upon the nature of their social identification. Those who favoured belonging to a management union took the view that any conflict within their company was not fundamental in nature, and they tended to believe that supervisors in their company had been accepted into management. They had relatively more social contact with staff specialists and with their immediate superiors than had other supervisors.[10] They also tended to have closer working contacts both with their immediate superiors and with managers further up in the hierarchy. In contrast, supervisors who did not see themselves sharing the attitudes and behaviour of their immediate superior, and who had less frequent working contacts with that manager, tended to favour belonging to a union restricted to other supervisors. These relationships, for which the level of statistical confidence exceeded the 95 per cent level, point to some degree of consistency among the supervisors between how strongly they are committed to management and how much they prefer to be in a union with a managerial membership. When one recalls that 'management' in both these respects was predominantly their immediate superior, then the basis for this consistency becomes reasonably clear.

Following Lockwood's (1958) study of clerical workers, there has been much discussion of the proposition that unionization among white-collar workers is a consequence of their relatively declining class position and their growing class consciousness (see especially Bain *et al.*, 1973; Crompton, 1976). This raises questions as to whether the class backgrounds and presently-perceived class positions of supervisors bear any relation to their views on trade unionism. The brief answer, we found, was yes, but only in limited respects.

Supervisors whose father's main employment had been in manual, rather than white-collar, work tended to express marginally greater support for a few aspects of unionism, namely belonging to a union rather than a staff association, confining membership to supervisors, and bargaining directly with the employer. No other differences exceeded the 95 per cent level of confidence. The minority (35) of supervisors who had some previous experience of white-collar employment tended to be more lukewarm about belonging to a shopfloor union, and keener on belonging to a supervisors' or managers' union. There is a suggestion in such findings that previous association with persons in white-collar jobs, either through upbringing or work experience, may encourage supervisors to favour belonging to unions which represent a higher status membership. There was, however, little evidence from which to conclude that previous white-collar affiliations weaken the need supervisors feel to belong to a collective organization representing their interests.

The major link between support for union membership and perception of class refers back to the distinction between pyramid and diamond class structures made in Chapter 7. Supervisors who saw the British class structure as a pyramid tended to express greater support for union membership than those who viewed the class structure as a diamond (see Table 8.2).

A pyramid structure implies that people from a working, lower-class or manual background have individually less chance to better themselves through upward social mobility than is the case with a diamond shape. This may point to the rationale in supervisors' minds

Table 8.2

Supervisors: perceived necessity for union membership	Those seeing the class structure as:	
	A pyramid	A diamond
Mean score (lower score indicates greater necessity)	19.06	21.58
Standard deviation	5.42	6.20
Number of supervisors	51	59

$t = 2.24$ $p = 0.025$

when those who viewed society as a pyramid tended to place greater emphasis on the need to join in collective action for purposes of betterment and self-help. Emphasis on the need to belong to a union, we are suggesting, is associated, for these supervisors, with how they perceive the chances in society for individual as opposed to collective betterment. It was not, however, associated with the level in society (i.e. the class *per se*) in which supervisors placed themselves. In other words, willingness to belong to a union did not appear to reflect class consciousness for most of the supervisors – rather it was seen to be necessary for the pragmatic purposes of improving their conditions of employment and protecting their position.

Where class consciousness, in the limited sense of identifying with a particular class level, may be more relevant is in predicting the level of active commitment to trade unionism. Those supervisors who saw their class as located in the lower half of the stratification hierarchy, and who described themselves as working-class, tended to attend union meetings and to vote in elections more frequently than did others, though the associations were statistically weak ($p = 0.067$ and 0.049 respectively).

Conclusion

Investigation of the circumstances of unionization among supervisors in the two Birmingham plants revealed as operative factors, respectively, a deteriorating internal labour market position and proximity to manual workers for whom unionism was providing readily observable benefits. Bain (1970) did not give primary emphasis to such factors in his influential model of white-collar union growth, although he was writing of a period before the squeeze on profits and the operation of incomes policies lent these factors their recent significance.

Enquiry into the meaning which unionism held for the supervisors, and comparison with the circumstances of their initial unionization, suggest that their rationale for union membership is more responsive to changed conditions, and less homogeneous, than has sometimes been implied in discussions of unionism and its character. The large majority of supervisors defined the role of trade unions in an essentially pragmatic manner with reference to the local workplace context, which can of course change substantially over time. The distinction offered by Prandy *et al.* (1974), between enterprise and society unionateness in the perspectives of union members, appears to be found in the views of the supervisors. In the main they supported the former but not the latter.

A clear difference emerged within supervisors' opinions between the necessity they attach to belonging to a union and the union character of which they approve (type of membership, degree of militancy, political involvement). The importance they attached to membership of a union appeared to vary according to how supervisors perceived the structure of the class system as a whole, and also according to their length of service as a supervisor. Their views regarding the appropriate *type* of union appeared to have some association with whether or not they had previously experienced white-collar employment, and the extent to which they identified (in a classic white-collar mode) with management within the company. Thus sociological factors to do with class and with identification within the competing interests of the firm are in some degree linked to the part which supervisors wish the union to play in their worklife. Closer attention should be given in future research to connections such as these, within the supervisor's perceptual world, between his social identity in the workplace and society, on the one hand, and his rationale towards trade unionism, on the other hand.

The rationale which most of the supervisors had about belonging to a union is not of the traditional proletarian type based upon an identification with a lower and socially exploited class of shopfloor workers. They generally saw no incompatibility between a commitment to union membership and identification with management. The strongest point of identification was, however, with their own middle-manager superiors rather than with senior management, alias 'the company'. It was collective strength in relation to the company, rather than against their own immediate superiors, which the union mainly offered. Indeed, many of their own managers belonged to the same white-collar union, especially in the food plant. Membership of this kind of union was therefore quite compatible with a continued identification by supervisors with that part of management with which they had the closest contact.

PART IV

Conclusion

9

Lost managers – will they be found?

It is difficult to see how the supervisor's status can change significantly until top management decide whether they want the supervisor to become a real part of the management process or to be retained as a kind of glorified handyman or management's whipping boy when things go wrong. (Institute of Personnel Management (IPM), *Profile of a Supervisor* (1975: 18))

This study's findings and 'the problem of the supervisor'

Supervision is widely regarded as a problem area in British industry, and it has both economic and welfare aspects. On the economic side, it has now become clear that low productivity in industry is not simply the result of inadequate investment. It is also due to the poor utilization of investment at the point of production, and part of this deficiency is likely to reside in management's failure to find a better approach towards the central role of shopfloor supervision. At the same time, the substantial unionization of supervisors in Britain since the mid-1960s, coupled with other expressions of their dissatisfaction and concern, points to a problem of supervisors' welfare. Any problem of personal welfare commands attention in its own right, but, in the case of supervisors, discontent may well exacerbate productive inefficiencies if it means that supervisors believe they no longer have a job to which it is worth giving their wholehearted commitment. Should this commitment fail, supervisors would be 'lost' to management in a very serious way. The economic role which supervisors are expected to perform cannot therefore be treated as a question apart from the threats to their status, security or satisfaction which supervisors may perceive they face. In effect, the so-called 'problem of the supervisor' means both that he *is* a problem and that he *has* a problem.

Conclusion

The study we have reported does not indicate that management has lost their supervisors' commitment to its production objectives of output, quality and low cost. It does, however, suggest that the problems supervisors face, which are in large measure of management's making, have become sufficiently severe as to place serious strains upon the future commitment of supervisors. These problems, as *supervisors* tend to perceive them, include an inadequate appreciation by management of what their jobs entail, an imbalance between their authority and responsibility, tension and stress resulting from multiple conflicts and pressures especially in production departments, unfairness in the level of their rewards and benefits, and generally a gap between the sentiments expressed by management and what they see to be the realities of their job and position. Even if management has not yet 'lost' the supervisor, these problems lead many supervisors to conclude that *they* have lost the managerial role and standing their predecessors enjoyed.

The scope of supervisors' jobs did not in the main extend to having authority and influence over establishing the basic parameters of their sections' activities. At the same time, many supervisors reported that their workload had risen in recent years. The extent of their workload was a problem which bothered them more than most in their job. As one supervisor put it, 'We have the responsibility but not the control', echoing the words of the American machine shop foreman quoted by Burawoy (1979: 105).[1] The upper limits of supervisors' authority did not qualify them in any way for the description of manager, and the fact that they may nevertheless be held as accountable as full managers would be for their sections' performance represents an imbalance that can encourage a cautious and defensive attitude to doing their job. This reaction was most noticeable among supervisors who adopted what we called the 'neutral' strategy of coping with the pressures and strains in their position.

Within the limited scope of their overall discretion, there was also considerable inconsistency in the authority and influence which supervisors enjoyed over certain decisions. This was the case even among supervisors working within the same department in the same factory. Both managers and supervisors professed to be concerned at this inconsistency, especially in the food plant where the matter was discussed at length when our findings were reported. The variations involved were not accounted for to any substantial extent by the supervisor's immediate task situation or by the nature of formal definition and procedure applied to his job and to his section. A great deal of the variation in the scope of supervisors' jobs appeared to be the result of informal accommodations over the course of time, or simply haphazard. A single stereotyped model of 'the' supervisor would certainly not apply to those we studied. It is interesting to note in this connection that the journal *Works Management* concluded, after visits to some half-a-dozen British factories, that 'there is no consensus of agreement on the role and responsibilities of the front-line manager' (Page, 1977: 76).

The question of what supervisory roles actually encompassed exposed a gap in understanding between supervisors and their own managers. There was often considerable disagreement between the two parties over the extent of the supervisor's authority and influence. Our findings on a range of matters, including priorities, the reporting of task contacts between manager and supervisor, and the rating of supervisors' performance, suggest that many managers do not have a good understanding of how supervisors go about their jobs or of the difficulties they may face.

While supervisors continued to give priority to management's main economic objectives, they have to be regarded as 'lost managers' in two aspects of carrying out their jobs. First, they had lost much of the managerial authority which supervisors once generally possessed, while their accountability for getting the work done satisfactorily by employees had not diminished appreciably. Second, supervisors now had to cope with the demands of their jobs without necessarily receiving either a full understanding of, or support for, their actions from managers. There was in this respect a divide between managers and supervisors which, in supervisors' eyes, placed them in a vulnerable position where an absence of initiative would seem the safest tactic for them to adopt. As a recent report put it, 'the much quoted "front line" role of the supervisors may simply mean they collect bullets rather than medals' (IDS, 1979: 2).

The awarding of 'medals', in other words the recognition, reward and status received, is another aspect for which we have to ask whether the supervisor is now a lost manager. Supervisors in the plants we investigated felt they had a need to defend their standard of living and job security against challenge, or at least apparent indifference, from management. In consequence, they had joined a trade union in large numbers. Additionally, judging by the extent of their authority over others, their work situation generally and their labour market position, these supervisors had objectively become members of the same social class as factory workers. If supervisory unionization manifests a shift in the supervisor's perception of where his best interests lie, and if in any case his social class position has today declined to a point where he is in much the same boat as collectively-organized employees, does this not indicate that, in sharp contrast to earlier times, he is no longer the 'company's man'? There have, after all, been reports from some companies of supervisors taking the side of manual workers in arguments with senior management (e.g. IDS, 1979: 2).

This question has, we found, to be examined very closely, with particular attention to the subjective interpretations that supervisors give both to their class position and to membership of a union. Around half the supervisors in our study perceived that they enjoyed a middle-class status and even more thought they were in the same social category as managers. Their answers to direct questions on social identification indicated that by 'management' these supervisors had their immediate superiors in mind rather than senior management. All the supervisors had, of course, chosen to be promoted into positions which in formal terms separated them from the shopfloor. It was also clear that the great majority believed they ought to enjoy managerial status, despite the doubts some had as to where their interests actually lay. It is understandable therefore why so many supervisors claimed a social class position which the sociologist would conclude is at variance with objective reality, and why it was *disappointment* with the gap between their desired managerial status and their perception of the reality which predicted more than any other feature a lowering in the level of social class to which they claimed membership. In effect, the extent to which supervisors were 'lost' to management in terms of their social identification was associated with the extent to which they perceived they had lost access to management.

Supervisors generally took a pragmatic view of their trade union membership. This was seen as a necessity in order to safeguard and further their interests in times when these could no longer be assured by their employer. Union membership was directed primarily against the 'company' and not against the middle managers, some of whom were members of the same union, who were 'management' to supervisors in the context of everyday work. Belonging to a trade union was compatible with identifying with middle management and with acceptance of the workplace objectives transmitted by this level of management. The supervisors did not on the whole approve of union militancy or of those union political activities which imply the assumption of a fundamental conflict with the employer. The overall conclusion which may be drawn for the majority of supervisors is that membership of a trade union did not express alienation from management, but it did indicate a belief that they had lost the protection of management. It was a further manifestation of the thread which has run through many of our findings, namely that supervisors experience a distancing and rejection from management.

The perspective we have tried to portray is largely the supervisor's own. We believe that this has sometimes been overlooked and that it is fruitless to discuss ways of dealing with the 'problem of the supervisor' unless we understand how he, the central actor, sees things. What impresses us from a close encounter with the Birmingham supervisors is that they continue to display a level of goodwill towards managerial purposes which is remarkable when set alongside the appearances of managerial neglect towards them. The question is how long such goodwill can continue without a determination by management to face up to the problem and the choices of action involved.

The quotation which opens this chapter is one of several recent exhortations to senior management to recognize the problem of the supervisor and do something about it. These take the view that management has control over the parameters of supervisors' work situations, over the definition of their responsibilities, and over the condition of their status. It therefore has the ability to create supervisory jobs which will motivate the people in them and, if necessary, attract a better quality of recruit. The problem of the supervisor, according to this argument, is one of management's own making. It has to decide whether or not supervisors are to be full first-line managers, and to iron out the inconsistencies in whatever role they are given.

The difficulty with statements of this kind is that they more successfully express intention than the means whereby these can be fulfilled. A practical issue which is in danger of being overlooked is whether the intention to make the supervisor into a manager refers to a change in his tasks or to a change in his status within the organization, or both. Does the root of the problem lie in the erosion of the supervisor's work role or in the undermining of his status? One also has to ask whether there is yet sufficient understanding of the supervisor's present role for major changes to be contemplated. While they do not admit of any easy or certain answers, questions such as these need to be considered in any serious discussion of the supervisory problem which aims to uncover the policy options that are available and the considerations relevant to choosing between them.

The question of supervisory status

Much of the uncertainty about the appropriate role for supervision in British industry derives from the way in which a once clearly recognizable occupational position – that of shop foreman in manufacturing or labour master in construction – has over the years become submerged within the developing idiosyncratic organizational structures of different firms. This has created a lack of clarity about the functions remaining to supervisors and ambivalence about their status. The comprehensive set of managerial tasks contained in the stereotype of the old-style foreman has become transformed into several different stereotypes of the contemporary supervisor, each one suggesting a different role and status in the system of productive relationships. According to the modern view, supervision now has to be organizationally defined: it should vary according to the circumstances of each organization and can no longer constitute an occupational role maintaining its own consistent features across different organizations. An organizational definition of supervision means that its key components are adjusted to the parameters of specific organizational units: technological ones which mould the system of work and bureaucratic ones which define areas of specialized responsibility and specify standard procedures. This is basically a 'contingency' or 'situational' view of supervision, very much in line with the currently dominant mode of thinking about organizational design.

The question of supervisory status has to be considered in the light of this historical shift away from an occupational role. The argument that supervisors are part of management is clearly making an assertion about their status. It nevertheless flies in the face of a contingency view which holds that while it may be appropriate for supervisors to play a managerial role in some situations, it may be appropriate for them to play a much more limited role in others. In seeking to reverse the decline in the foundations of supervisors' status, by giving them clear authority over shopfloor operations, closer communication with senior management, and favourable differentials, those who claim supervisors for management are implicitly referring back to the occupational status enjoyed by the foreman of yesteryear. The findings we reported in Chapter 5 could be said to justify this emphasis on the need to restore the supervisor's status. For the dissatisfaction which supervisors expressed in their jobs was centred on the status aspects, namely their pay relative to that of other groups, their opportunities for promotion and their benefits and privileges. The maintenance and improvement of these status elements also constituted an important reason in supervisors' minds for remaining members of a trade union. Should one conclude, then, that the improvement of the status of supervisors is a priority step towards lessening the 'problem' of the supervisor? Can this be done in spite of the contingency view that the function performed by supervisors must vary to suit the situation?

It is difficult to envisage making changes to the status of supervisors, outside narrow limits, without making complementary changes to their tasks and function. The status of supervisors must fundamentally depend upon their function within the organization or, to use the more exact terminology of Marxist writers, upon their relation to the mode of production. Are supervisors to perform a function delegated from ownership ('capital'), with control over the operating parameters of their sections and accountability for results? Or are supervisors just to perform another kind of labour function confined to securing supplies, progress chasing or providing technical advice? The granting of managerial status implies that supervisors will be given functions that are managerial. Otherwise their rewards and benefits would run ahead of their level of work, which is a recipe for dissatisfaction among other groups in the organization. A resolution of the status issue therefore depends upon decisions as to the function of supervision.

Cases do arise which correspond to the 'man-in-the-middle' stereotype, where supervisors are given responsibilities for which neither their authority nor their rewards and privileges are commensurate. These are the circumstances where the raising of supervisors' status has a good chance of decreasing their dissatisfaction and strengthening their identification with management. The food plant we investigated provides an example. A large number of supervisors in the food plant were given higher job gradings and rewards in 1978 after our study there was completed. The upgraded supervisors are now formally designated as first-line managers, and an attempt was made to check that their level of work was in line with their raised status. The results of this adjustment of status so as to match function more closely appear, according to informal reports, to be of the kind predicted above. This example is consistent with the general argument that it is realistic only to contemplate changes to supervisors' status if these are commensurate with the function and level of work that the supervisors are expected to perform.

It is not clear, however, that the enhancement of supervisors' status will by itself do much to affect their involvement in their jobs, even though it may reduce their dissatisfaction with management. Many of the supervisors we studied were not happy about their status, but they were quite satisfied with those intrinsic aspects of their jobs which some psychologists (particularly Herzberg *et al.*, 1959) stress as the more relevant points of reference for motivating people to do their job well. The supervisors surveyed by the BIM (1976) also expressed general satisfaction with the content of their jobs, while considering that their status had declined. There is little reason to conclude from our investigation that the majority of supervisors are not involved in their work. It has to be borne in mind, however, that our studies were conducted in small and large batch production systems where, it has been suggested (Bowey, 1973), the intrinsic challenge of supervisors' jobs and hence their involvement in them, tends to be greater compared with more automated and process-type systems.

Difficulties in designating supervisory roles

The point has often been made that a prerequisite for redesigning work roles or work systems is a thorough understanding of the present situation, so that the full extent of its requirements may be met by the new design (e.g. Hackman and Suttle, 1977). This applies equally to changes which may be contemplated in the supervisor's role. In plants such as the ones we studied, several factors stood in the way of improving management's understanding of what supervision entailed.

The supervisor is located at the interface of the management control system and the shopfloor. He is therefore liable to experience role conflict and pressures. Chapter 5 noted that for production supervisors in the batch plants we investigated the heaviest pressures arose from concern over work quality, technical problems, break-downs and labour problems. Both production and non-production supervisors experienced problems of coping with changes in plans and with unevenness of work. One strategy for coping with these pressures, especially when the supervisor is caught between conflict-ing expectations (often arising from within management), is to keep the conflict latent by 'colluding' with the workgroup. This means holding certain things back from management's attention and attempting to handle them within the section. The contingencies which arise within production systems may force supervisors to break or stretch certain rules, such as work schedules, line speeds or maintenance procedures, in order to meet the overriding expectations of role-senders that outputs will be achieved, employee earnings maintained, and so on. Supervisors in these circumstances have to order rules and expectations into a priority list and if necessary sacrifice some, while in contrast management tends to treat each one as having much more equal priority. Clearly, this kind of disparity between managerial and supervisory priorities can stand in the way of managers attaining a better understanding of the supervisory role. It may misleadingly encourage an underestimation of the difficulties inherent in supervisory jobs, and also lead to an unduly depressed evaluation of supervisors' competences. The fact that managerial ratings of supervisors' performances were only weakly related to supervisors' own assessments serves to remind one of the gap in perceptions that can exist between the two parties.

Managers, in the factories we studied, inhabited an ordered paper world of plans, targets and variances; an illusion which supervisors struggled to turn into some semblance of reality. If, on the basis of a poor understanding of the part supervisors are playing, management were to set out to develop supervisory roles formally into a reflection of their own, this would run the risk of leaving a vacuum in which the necessary degree of informal interpretive flexibility for handling contingencies and disturbances could go by default. As Fores (1977) has remarked, the school of thought which holds that supervisors should act more like managers implies that they are to sit at a desk, plan and make decisions. Not only is this quite unlike anything for which the supervisor's experience has equipped him, it also completely ignores the problem that things planned do not simply translate into things done: 'So, for the goods to be turned out at all someone has to fill in the gaps: this someone can only be the foreman' (p. 2).[2]

The argument that supervision should be a managerial role has therefore to be examined extremely carefully, and in so doing management has to take pains to overcome the barriers to understanding the tasks supervisors actually perform and their functional relations to the management system. The significant variety in the scope of supervisors' jobs, judged by their authority and influence in decision making, and the difficulty in ascribing much of this variation to easily recognizable organizational parameters, serves to emphasize still more how difficult it is to define what are appropriate supervisory roles.

Seeking a rationale behind supervisory roles

We have already asked, in Chapter 4, whether a rationale could be found in our investigation for the considerable degree of variation in supervisors' jobs. We concluded that, in the plants concerned, only a small amount of this variation could be predicted by the task system and organizational structuring of each section. Even this limited degree of prediction made reference to features specific to each section or department, since a designation of whole plants in terms of certain broad types of production system could not account for the considerable variation among supervisors' jobs within each plant. In addition, we concluded that some of the variation has to be ascribed to informal factors, lying outside the normal purview of organizational design, such as the supervisor's own capability for coping with change and uncertainty, and the relationship between each supervisor and his immediate superior.

It is difficult to ascertain whether the degree of variation in supervisors' jobs, which our study and others have found, is the mark of a good supervisory system. One of the problems here, as Chapter 6 indicated, lies in the difficulty of agreeing on what constitutes good supervisory performance; our findings suggest that it is not sufficient to rely upon managers' ratings. There is a supposition from contingency theory that variations in supervision represent functional adaptations to different operational circumstances. Our analyses have not yet thrown any clear light on this proposition, though the fact that variations in supervisory coping behaviour were not all closely allied to contextual factors casts some doubt on it.

Another consideration is that a high level of variation among supervisors' jobs within one plant or organization carries with it certain clear disadvantages. It makes for difficulties in formally designating the content of supervisory roles, and it has other consequences which neither managers nor supervisors welcome. For variation among supervisors' jobs:

(1) makes appraisal of supervisors more difficult because comparisons between supervisors in different sections become less meaningful;

(2) makes it more difficult to mount supervisory training schemes, because appropriate training is specific to single, or small numbers of, jobs;

(3) reduces mobility because supervisory expertise is localized to each section; this also makes it more difficult to transfer or replace a supervisor. In so far as a company is localizing expertise in this way and relying upon long experience, the development of supervisors through job mobility and training is inhibited and serious problems may arise if they are called upon to adjust to radically new technologies;

(4) is likely to encourage inequity in the balance between reward and effort and/or responsibility;

(5) will increase the supervisor's isolation within the managerial structure of the organization because only his immediate superior will have some knowledge of what he does in his job, and even that, we have suggested, is limited knowledge. This, coupled with point 3 above, will greatly lessen any opportunities for a supervisor to make his abilities known and to create career and promotion opportunities for himself.

It would be unwise therefore to conclude that a high degree of variation between supervisory jobs is necessarily beneficial. The fact that it is widely reported suggests that, within a given technological and organizational system, some degree of latitude is available in the shaping of supervisory jobs. Those involved in discussions of how to develop supervision might decide to use this element of design choice to move towards a greater standardization of supervisory jobs and conditions. There must, on the other hand, be limits on how far standardization can go. It was apparent in the plants we studied that the operational problems of individual sections differed, the uncertainties present in the systems of production called forth a variety of informal *ad hoc* adaptations by supervisors, and the capabilities of individual supervisors were not the same. Factors such as these militate both against standardization and the accompanying attempt to define supervisors' jobs closely.

It is, however, necessary to place the conclusions of our study in a broader perspective. The rather precise mode of questioning which we employed on matters such as supervisory decision making will tend to emphasize any specific variations there may be between supervisors. While from a practical point of view the content of individual supervisory jobs cannot be ignored, a broadening of perspective from jobs to whole plants may reveal that the difference in the type of supervisory roles which predominate in different modes of production is more significant than the variation among such roles within a given production system. In addition, this broader basis of comparison may suggest that variation in supervisors' jobs is likely to be particularly marked in the types of production systems that we studied. The wider comparison we now make refers primarily to the jobs of production supervisors.

Our investigations were located within small and large batch systems. The preliminary studies in the metal plants also involved batch systems. Joan Woodward's research has suggested that there is more variation in the organizational arrangements adopted in these types of production system than in either unit or process systems (Woodward, 1970). Reeves and Turner (1972) concluded that batch production generates a particularly high level of complexity and uncertainty, and that it is a major part of production supervisors' jobs in these circumstances to cope with the re-scheduling of work, the unforeseen shortages, breakdowns and other contingencies to which batch production is especially liable. This fluid, crisis-prone working environment is clearly not readily subject to standardization or formalization and it is likely to encourage variety among supervisors' jobs. When, however, other systems of production are compared with the batch system, rather different characterizations of the supervisory role can be found. These are 'modal' characterizations and there is usually variation among particular supervisory jobs within each system.

Drawing primarily upon research by Thurley and Hamblin (1963), Reeves and Turner (1972), Bowey (1973), Thurley and Wirdenius (1973) and our own studies, it has been possible in Table 9.1 to draw up a scheme which relates salient dimensions of production systems to characteristics of supervisory roles likely to be found in the systems concerned.[3] It is more useful to base this analysis upon dimensions of work situations rather than whole 'systems' because of the variation within systems which renders the labels commonly applied to production systems too gross. 'Mass production', for example, could encompass more than one configuration of the dimensions shown in Table 9.1. Although this book has focused upon supervision in manufacturing, all the dimensions are in principle applicable to service operations as well.

The fact that many configurations of these production system dimensions are possible helps one to appreciate the variety in supervisory roles which is found in practice, both within and between plants. The commonly-made distinction between unit, batch, mass and process production systems is not sufficiently refined to take account of the combinations allowed by Table 9.1. However, unit systems of a one-off jobbing kind and small batch systems will often be placed high on dimensions 1, 2 and 3. It is likely, therefore, that in unit and small batch systems re-scheduling work, re-allocating manpower, managing inter-dependencies between sections, and quality control will be important components in the supervisory role. Mass production systems can be very diverse in nature (cf. Woodward, 1965, 1970), but they are likely to be high on dimension 4 or on dimension 5 combined with low variation in operations (dimension 1). In the latter case, supervisors may generally be left with relatively minor roles such as allocating materials, requisitioning maintenance work, and carrying out routine procedures. In the case of non-automated flow-line mass production, such as traditional automobile assembly plants, supervisors can have a more prominent role which is concerned with keeping the line going and at the highest possible speed where incentive payments to this end are not used (e.g. Beynon, 1973: 75–6). Process systems may often be low on dimensions 1, 2 and 3 and high on dimension 5. In such cases, it appears that supervision can either become a very limited monitoring role or else be built up into one which incorporates problem-diagnostic and developmental tasks, including the handling of crises should these occur.

The search for a rationale behind supervisory roles by reference to production systems can only be pursued so far. As we become better able to conceptualize and measure task systems at every level, so we

Table 9.1 *Dimensions of production systems and likely characteristics of supervisory roles*

Dimension of production system	Characteristics of supervisory roles likely to be present when work situation is *high* on the dimension
(1) Variation in operations	1.1 Dealing with problems of re-scheduling work and re-allocating manpower at the point of production. 1.2 Dealing with labour problems which re-allocating and stoppages generate. 1.3 Progress chasing, dealing with materials shortages.
(2) Complexity of work-flow system: differentiation of component units	Unless the process is automatically controlled, emphasis on managing balance and reciprocity between sections (co-ordination with supervisors in linked sections, exchange of resources, especially manpower, and intense exchange of information on workflows).
(3) Technical complexity of problems and difficulty of their solution	Stress on inspection and technically biased supervisory system *and/or* use of technical specialists to deal with problems such as quality control, monitoring of plant functioning.
(4) Level of mechanization	4.1 Concentration on inspecting machinery, and dealing with machine faults and breakdowns. 4.2 Dealing with problems caused by poor morale – e.g. absenteeism and consequent manpower adjustments; attempting to match employee effort to plant capability.[a]
(5) Level of automation	5.1 If combined with low variation in operations: bulk of role is monitoring and carrying out routine procedures combined with technological understanding to handle crises if these arise.

(*Contd.*)

Table 9.1   (*Contd.*)

Dimension of production system	Characteristics of supervisory roles likely to be present when work situation is *high* on the dimension
	5.2 If combined with development work: supervisory role may be to link new system designs with practical applications in the plant.
	5.3 If applied to large projects: monitoring combined with interpretation of data for resolving problems.

(*a*) Where incentive payments linked to output levels are not used.

may find that the contingencies they present for supervisory jobs are somewhat clearer and more influential than available research suggests. None the less, as Bowey's (1973: 413) comparative case studies and our research indicate, other characteristics of an organization can also influence the type of supervisory role most likely to exist. The following are examples. First, larger organizations generally utilize a more extensive division of labour and are more likely to have extracted tasks from supervision and allocated these to specialist departments. Second, if the rate of turnover among supervisors' immediate superiors is high, perhaps because their jobs are points of entry for young inexperienced career managers, then supervisors are likely to be left more initiative for dealing with systems and technical decisions (see Chapter 4). Third, the development of extensive formalization to prescribe the limits to supervisory discretion and to monitor supervisory performance may restrict the authority of supervisors. Fourth, the application of incentive payment systems linked to output, quality or other criteria is likely to reduce the supervisor's role in motivating employees' performance along those criteria. These features help to promote differences in typical supervisory roles between plants which have similar production systems.

It is possible, then, to point tentatively to the elements of a rationale behind supervisory roles which makes reference to technological and organizational parameters that are, to some extent, open to managerial control. There appears to be a lot of scope left within such parameters to choose between alternative supervisory role models according to other criteria, such as the philosophy management may have about job enrichment and the capabilities and expectations of supervisors themselves. The following section outlines the main role models that are available.

The choice of models for supervision

Although it is ideologically acceptable to management to claim the supervisor as a first-line manager, by no means every model which has been proposed for supervision is managerial in nature. The following are general characterizations of the main choices.

1 Abolish the role of first-line supervisor

This model envisages the delegation of responsibility for routine supervisory tasks to workgroup leaders. It has most frequently been implemented in connection with schemes which re-structure work in groups. Such groups are given the freedom to appoint their own leaders, who carry responsibility *vis-à-vis* management for arranging the group's internal organization, allocation of work and of people to jobs or equipment, the availability of materials, completion of routine paperwork, and possibly inspection and routine maintenance. The group leader is also expected to act as arbitrator when human problems arise and he or she should be trained to undertake personnel responsibilities, such as arranging necessary operative training. Under this scheme, the level of first-line supervision is abolished, or a small number of former supervisors are retained to serve as advisers to workgroups on technical matters, procedures, training, or the resolution of disputes between employees. In the latter role, the ex-supervisors are not expected to act on their own initiative, but rather on that of the workgroup.

The benefits expected from this model include economy in management resources and improvement of vertical communications by abolishing one hierarchical level, the provision of openings for untapped potential on the shopfloor, and the rendering of promotion from the shopfloor more attractive since the new first-line role would be much more substantially managerial. Moreover, the whole movement towards autonomous workgroups, to which this model is allied, is seen as meeting important social goals of improving the quality of working life and enhancing democracy at shopfloor level.

Attempts to apply this model in practice have often failed. Many of the early experiments with autonomous workgroups in Norway were not only introduced without the participation of supervisors but were implemented on the basis that the abolition of supervision was a mark of success. Among the problems which arose, however, was a paralysis when members of workgroups failed to resolve their own internal conflicts over matters such as work allocation. In Sweden, the development of new forms of work organization has more frequently proceeded with the participation of supervisors and has entailed a change in their role towards the lines of model 3 below – this is claimed to have greatly improved the chances of successful organizational development (Swedish Employers' Confederation, 1975). Even the transformation of supervisors into team or workgroup advisers can lead to problems. For example, in a biscuit manufacturing plant which has introduced autonomous work groups ('teams') of ladies responsible for wrapping and packing, occasions arise when they overlook a problem which will give rise to wastage. When this happens the team adviser, formerly a supervisor, has to decide whether to intervene immediately or leave matters until the operatives notice that something is wrong. If she were to intervene on every occasion, wastage might well be reduced, but the whole autonomous group working scheme would be threatened.

The more need there is for someone to cope with unforeseen contingencies on the shopfloor, to correct problems which arise from the limitations of management plans and procedures, and to manage interdependencies between different workgroups, the less plausible does the abolition of supervision become. If the jobs of supervisors have already decayed into the performance of minor allocating, servicing and monitoring tasks, then the case for abolition becomes stronger. Such tasks are in principle readily absorbed by employees, and if they constitute the main content of supervisors' jobs, it is unlikely that they will afford the supervisors much intrinsic motivation or much standing *vis-à-vis* employees over whom they are nominally in charge. This kind of shrunken supervisory role is more likely to arise in work situations which are low on dimensions 1, 2 and 3 and high on dimension 5 in Table 9.1, particularly a combination of high automation with low variation in operations.

Conclusion

2 Leave the role as it is, but make improvements

This model recognizes the unsatisfactory situation that many supervisors find themselves in today, including the fact that part of the problem arises from the double standards between management ideology and management practice. It is argued that the solution is not to attempt to dress supervisors up as managers if it is really supervision that is wanted. Rather, the logical course of action is to clarify the distinction between managerial and supervisory roles so that supervisors are no longer encouraged to have a set of expectations which does not accord with the reality of their level of work or their capabilities.

One example of this approach is provided by the research into role definition conducted by Jaques (1976) and his colleagues (BIOSS, 1977). They point out that the situation may arise where it is useful to group a particular set of activities under a single manager, but where that grouping overloads the manager and inhibits him from maintaining an adequate two-way relationship with each of his subordinates. This type of problem can often be overcome, it is argued, by providing the manager with one or more assistants to supervise the subordinates.

In this model, the supervisor may oversee the work of the subordinates, help them to overcome problems which arise, assist the manager in training, recruiting and assessing the subordinates, and in scheduling work, allocating employees to jobs, and setting out appropriate methods. The supervisor, however, does not have managerial accountability or authority regarding the work of the department and the appraisal of its employees. Supervisors act towards employees only in pursuit of their manager's policy. They can recommend, but he decides.

The brief description just offered agrees with the substance of the supervisory jobs that are often found in practice. Their definition is, however, frequently *ad hoc* and in large part informal. The implication of the model is that if a management thinks it appropriate to employ people strictly as *supervisors* then it should be clear about the nature of their role. It is less than managerial. It should stop confusing the issue by calling supervisors front-line or first-line managers; and if this is being done in an attempt to retain their loyalty, management would be well advised to find less confusing and more convincing ways of doing this.

In opting for a supervisory role, in the strict sense, management can endeavour to make improvements to the present often ambiguous and demoralizing situation. One of these would be a clarification with supervisors, managers and employees of the purpose, content and limits of the role of 'supervision'. This might help to resolve the problem of conflicting pressures to which many of the supervisors we studied were exposed. Then, if the matter at issue concerned managerial parameters, a decision would have to come from the person with managerial authority and the supervisor would not be accountable for it. Clarification of a distinctively supervisory role should help to avoid the problem pointed out by Roethlisberger (1945) long ago, namely holding supervisors responsible for functions over which they have no real authority. Another improvement which the attempt at clear role definition should encourage would be the identification and provision of information that is required for the role to be performed adequately – for example, information on appropriate work methods or on the destination of work done.

The approach behind this model is bureaucratic, in that it relies upon the clear definition of the supervisory role through formal organizational rules. It is appropriate to conditions of fairly routine work not involving a high degree of technical complexity. It is easier in such circumstances to define a supervisory role that is strictly limited in the ways described above. If unexpected and significant contingencies arise, as they do in more variable work systems, then it may not be so functional to deny the first-line supervisor the right to make a decision if his manager happens to be out of contact, or if indeed the supervisor is the more experienced person at handling the contingency. The model is also attractive when it is not possible to recruit people with more than modest capabilities into the post of supervisor. It is, of course, unlikely that people with more than modest abilities or ambition would wish to take up a limited supervisory role of this type, which might amount to little more than a life of progress chasing. Equally, if supervisors are managed by young inexperienced career managers in circumstances where the latter cannot, or will not, cope with shopfloor problems, the clear managerial – supervisory role distinction at the root of this model will be difficult to sustain.

The main attraction of this model lies in the clear and literal definition it provides of supervision. If the role of labour master and foreman has been reduced to that of supervision, then at least this approach makes no bones about it. It cuts through the fog about the function, and by implication the status, of supervisors *vis-à-vis* management. It clearly defines supervision as a specialized 'labour' role and not a 'management' one, and it should clear up any illusions that people promoted to supervision may have about this being an entry to a managerial career. The other models we describe, of course, also attempt to inject greater clarity into discussions about action choices for supervision, but this particular model provides a benchmark of what a strictly supervisory role is, against which other possibilities can be compared.

3 Develop into a first-line managerial role

Many of the supervisors we studied were taking the initiative in adjusting the day-to-day operations of their sections, and had a far closer knowledge of the sections' work, technology and employees than had their managerial superiors. Nevertheless, these supervisors did not have control over the parameters and boundary conditions of their sections. Their role was less than managerial.

This third model of supervision envisages a transformation from first-line supervision to first-line management. This would involve concentrating the role of first-line manager on to deciding major parameters of the section, such as the selection and training of employees, working on technical improvements and having a greater share in the determination of work methods, layout and choice of equipment. The first-line manager would also have more authority to agree on boundary conditions such as the scheduling of new work (e.g. batches) on to the section, re-allocation of manpower between his section and others, and handling relations with staff departments. The first-line manager concept moves the supervisor closer to the German 'Meister', whose role Fores *et al.* (1978) compare favourably to that of the problematic typical British model. One criterion for this model, suggested by a comparison with West Germany, is that first-line managers would have to have thorough technical training to combine with the benefit of experience. Most German foremen are qualified craftsmen and it is quite common for a production foreman to have had experience of working in maintenance functions. This clearly provides an important prop of expertise to his authority, and permits a greater concentration of specialized functions into line positions, which again enhances the foreman's authority and standing. The German foreman is a first-line manager who can, and is expected to, make decisions which in Britain may well be the prerogative of staff specialists. The German approach is therefore more economical of staff roles and this is reflected in the lower proportions of staff personnel which have been found in German compared to British companies (Maurice *et al.*, 1980).

A move towards this model would involve delegation of the progress chasing and minor disturbance-handling which can constitute a significant part of the supervisor's job, especially in systems which are not highly automated or integrated. Such duties could be delegated down to work groups. Where this is not feasible, an alternative is to delegate these to a new non-managerial role. An example would be the role of 'progress chaser'. The exact definition of this role would have to take account of needs in local production areas, but it would probably include routine tasks otherwise carried out by supervisors such as provision of materials and equipment, liaison with other links in the production chain, calling up of services, and record keeping. The basic purpose of the progress chaser would be to absorb routine problems which otherwise tie up the supervisor's time. The supervisor who had the appropriate skills could then give more attention to managerial tasks and possibly apply his skills over a wider physical area than hitherto. The need for him to be physically 'on call' throughout his shift should be reduced. Each progress chaser could probably serve several sections, and hence total manpower need not necessarily be greatly increased by this kind of development.

In the food plant, something of this progress-chaser role used to exist, at least informally. Floor-sweepers and record clerks were used by supervisors to run errands, check information and so forth. Economy drives in the intervening years had substantially reduced the numbers of such personnel. This was felt by some supervisors to have actually made it more difficult to develop their role into a managerial one, since their time had now to be devoted to carrying out these lower-level tasks themselves.

A danger in the creation of a further assistant-type role of this kind is that one may end up with some elements of the problem of the supervisor that the model is intended to resolve. The progress chaser would, like the supervisor in the previous model, depend for his limited authority on the first-line manager and possibly suffer the same ambiguities about whether he was going to be backed up that supervisors often complain of. The role is likely to be a pretty thankless one too, with little intrinsic satisfaction. Its content is so limited that it would not offer a training ground for promotion into management, although some technical knowledge and some interpersonal skills would be required. The balance between these skill requirements would depend on the labour intensity of the work area: in process areas, technical knowledge would assume relatively greater importance. Because the progress chaser role would only be of limited scope, would be liable to pressure and role conflict, and would add to manpower, it is not as attractive a way of delegating non-managerial tasks as is the possibility of their absorption by workgroups. Much depends therefore on whether the extension to workgroups of duties previously carried out by supervisors can be accomplished. Another relevant consideration is how much reliance has to be placed on progress chasing and similar activities. This is generally greatest in batch systems, but new computerized control systems, with input direct from the shopfloor, may obviate much of the need for these activities.

Two further considerations also point to possible limitations upon how far supervision can be developed into a full first-line managerial role. The first concerns the availability of people to fill this role, possessing an appropriate combination of qualifications and workplace experience. One important difference between most British production supervisors and most German *Meister* is that the former lack these credentials while the latter have them. A German foreman will usually have served a skilled apprenticeship, followed by several years' experience as a skilled worker, and will then have obtained a formal qualification in foremanship by examination. His status both as skilled worker and as accredited *Meister* is legally protected (Lawrence, 1980). Thus German companies have a supply of manpower to fill a first-line managerial role with competence and standing, while this is questionable for the British company. If, as Maurice *et al.* (1980) conclude, these differences in supervisory roles and quality of manpower reflect national systems of education, training, recruitment and promotion, then a widespread adoption in Britain of the German supervisory model may have to await changes in national institutions.

Secondly, batch production systems of the kind in which our investigations were located may involve such a degree of complexity and interdependence among the stages and components of production that full managerial control cannot be countenanced at individual section or department level. Supervisors in a batch production system may have a major role to play in handling the disturbances resulting from production contingencies, but they cannot expect to take action on their own account regarding the loading of work on to their sections. This view was held quite clearly by managers in the engineering plant. They argued that an unforeseen problem, such as a breakdown, created so many ramifications for other stages and batches in the production process that any one supervisor could not have sufficient knowledge to decide how to react in his own section. The dilemma here is that in a production system of this sort there may be so many disturbances to handle in his own section that a supervisor cannot readily come to grips with the complex wider system to a point at which he could share control in deciding how it should govern his section's pattern of work. As one manager in the engineering plant put it: 'one of the problems of supervisors in organizations of this sort is that if they are going to do their job of section supervision and control they have little opportunity to come into contact with the wider implications of running the organization.' If it is decided in circumstances such as these that supervisors cannot be granted full managerial discretion for planning their sections' work, then this should be reflected in diminished accountability for performance. It also does not preclude consultation with the supervisor about the possibly unforeseen consequences within his section of short-term re-scheduling, or about how his section's work would ideally be planned.

4 Technical supervision

In this model, the supervisor is primarily concerned with technical problems. Routine matters, such as requisitioning normal consumable items, can be delegated to employees. The next level of management would possibly handle the overall organization of the section and its co-ordination with others. The supervisor would, however, be closely involved in assessing the technical competence of new recruits.

There are two main variants to the technical role model. The first is appropriate to situations where craft skills are relied upon, such as maintenance work and woodworking, as in the manufacture of furniture and storage units. Here, the supervisor can be expected to have long craft experience and specialized skills not necessarily available to higher levels of management. He has probably kept up with any improvements to methods in his area of specialization. His workers, if they are skilled men, would not require or welcome close supervision, but they may need to consult an expert for judgement on alternative methods of tackling a job or for approval of work that is completed. The craft supervisor is also equipped with special knowledge in matters of specifying materials, equipment and plant to be purchased. In maintenance activities, craftsmen working at different places throughout the plant will require co-ordination with those from other sections and in the light of production priorities. In Chapter 3, we noted that the authority and influence of non-production supervisors tended to be relatively high with regard to decisions on these matters.

The second variant to technical supervision is that appropriate to technical and scientific areas of work. These did not come within the purview of our investigation, and we can only comment that technical supervision here is likely to bear a similarity to that in craft work, except that it may often be combined with carrying out work of a direct nature (particularly writing reports or working on a specialized problem). There may also be a greater need to co-ordinate members of the department as a team, because the integration of the complementary activities of a differentially specialized set of employees is likely to be a vital but taxing requirement. In our experience, problems of securing integration and motivation are particularly troublesome to those supervising this kind of group.

Both variants of the technical supervision model come closest to a situation in which supervisory roles are occupationally or professionally defined. These roles are defined by tradition or by professional and scientific rules. Their definition in such terms is relatively impervious to organizational rules of a bureaucratic kind, particularly in respect of technical decisions and the planning of work. The technical supervisor will usually experience conditions which encourage involvement in his work, though we found that supervisors in maintenance and service areas were only marginally more satisfied with the interest their work offered them than their production counterparts.[4]

Scope for the development of supervision

Over the past hundred years in Britain, the once clearly-recognizable occupational role enjoyed by the foreman as workshop manager has become transformed into the confusion of role conflicts, of specialist encroachments, and disparities between managerial theory and practice, which so often surround his contemporary equivalent, the supervisor. This is one sense in which he is the lost manager. The other significant sense of loss can be seen in the growing lack of confidence among unionizing supervisors that management any longer has a regard for their interests, or any wish to welcome them as colleagues.

The models of supervision just discussed point to alternative ways of handling the problem of supervision that has resulted. We have suggested some of the organizational contingencies which are relevant to choosing between the models. To these must be added the characteristics of the people involved in any change: the capabilities, willingness to assume greater responsibilities, and perception of how change will affect their standing, rewards and prospects, of the managers, supervisors, employees and others involved in any move towards adopting one of the models. All these are contingencies which will reduce the element of pure choice between transforming supervision into management, eliminating it, defining it more precisely as supervision, or moving towards a technical role model. So many different arrangements are possible, however, within this broad fourfold framework, and available research points to so much variation within given systems of production and organization, that to ignore the choice which remains would be foolish.

Much the same conclusion has to be reached when one looks ahead to supervision in the future. Thurley and Wirdenius (1973) attempt to take account of a wide range of technological, organizational, economic, social, political and value system changes and reach the pessimistic conclusion that 'the most likely direction of change is towards a situation where supervisors may tend to withdraw from their work roles either under the pressure of conflicting colleagues or because of the development of a bureaucratic situation' (pp. 213–14). They do insist, however, that this is not an inevitable trend of history and merely highlights the importance of viewing the question of supervision as a problem area. For instance, one lesson which can be learned from the introduction of automation, and applied to the introduction of microprocessing today, is that this comes in so many forms, each one of which may permit several organizational and job design applications. Again, deterministic predictions of its consequences for supervision are certainly not valid.

Conclusion

The more optimistic analysis offered by the Swedish Employers' Confederation (1975) contrasts somewhat with Thurley and Wirdenius's view, and this serves to reinforce the conclusion that the choice for supervision in the future is fairly open. The Confederation's envisaged 'lines of future development' are formulated in a context in which most Swedish firms have involved supervisors in discussions of organizational change and in which the introduction of new working methods and work organization have taken place with the active participation of supervisors. The role that is described as tending to emerge in Sweden contains the following assumptions which place it within the orbit of our model 3: (1) that employees and workgroups will always need a leader; (2) that supervisors will have to meet new demands as production situations develop; (3) that groups of production workers will increasingly handle 'fire-fighting' problems, which will relieve supervisors of routine tasks; (4) that supervisors will have to learn to consult with workers, to handle co-ordination between workgroups, and to be more concerned with how to develop the operations under their purview; and (5) that supervisors must be given the scope and backing to perform in this way by higher management, including appropriate personal development and training.

With the exception of work situations which are highly automated and open to precise cybernetic planning – feedback – control procedures, there would seem to be a continuing role to be performed by first-line supervisors or managers at the interface between the administrative and operating systems of organizations. The operating performance of many British firms does not compare well with that of overseas competitors, and one obvious route for managerial intentions to be more effectively translated into action lies through an improvement in supervision. The need to encourage supervisors to take a positive view towards improvements makes it essential that they are involved in discussions of changes. Perhaps an even more compelling reason for supervisors to be given a central role in such discussions, which can hardly avoid the question of their own roles, is the localization of valuable experience and detailed knowledge among individual supervisors, and evidence that even their immediate superiors do not have a firm basis of understanding about how the supervisors perform their roles. Thus a procedure whereby supervisors and others jointly tackle problems which affect their performance offers the best chance of attacking the issues in a positive way and of activating a learning process which will arrive at agreed and appropriate solutions, including an understanding of which model of supervision is to be preferred. Others, such as Thurley and Wirdenius (1973) and Jenkins (1978), have discussed the process of supervisory development in some detail. Embarkation on this road wisely acknowledges that management in complex and variable work systems cannot be presumed to have the knowledge to impose its own organizational definition upon supervision, even in the unlikely event that such an authoritarian approach would meet no resistance.

Having taken the view that management has opportunities to encourage a development of the supervisory role which may, in some cases, move it towards a more managerial function, along the lines described for Sweden, we must finally return to the question of whether it is now too late to do anything constructive. Have supervisors in British industry today moved too far from management and placed their hopes for the future exclusively with their unions? As Jenkins (1978: 144) comments: 'It is easier to act while, despite many frustrations, a measure of goodwill still exists between supervisors and their seniors than when intransigent unions of supervisors transform all issues into bargaining counters'.

The evidence from our investigation suggests that supervisors no longer feel they can rely upon management to look after their interests, but that they are not yet estranged from management. The great majority of the supervisors believed that it was necessary for them to belong to a union on pragmatic grounds. They did not, however, associate this view with a lessening of the identification they had with management or with a loss of belief in the managerial standing most of them thought it was proper that they should enjoy. Many supervisors thought it appropriate that they should belong to a management union, and it is further indicative that they were at pains to retain control over their union branch policies within the compass of the firm. All this suggests strongly that supervisors were not alienated from their managers, but that they felt – as many explicitly stated – they had been badly treated by their company.

There is no evidence in our research from which to conclude that a belated attempt to close the gap between managerial ideology and complementary supervisory expectations on the one hand, and the actual conditions of the supervisory role on the other, will now reduce the utility of union membership in supervisors' eyes. It may, however, make the difference between a constructive attitude towards improvement and an obstructive stance, and between the perception of a common purpose as opposed to an outlook based on antipathy and conflict. From management's point of view the prize for taking positive action to resolve 'the problem of the supervisor' appears very attractive, and if this action is based on a genuinely participative exploration of issues and alternatives the results for supervisors may not be bad either.

Appendix A *Sample of 16 supervisors in the food plant who were directly observed, showing type of section and sex of each supervisor*

Assortments division	Chocolate and moulding division	Printing and card box division	Trades division	Services division
Making units[1] – male	Making bars – male	Card cutting[3,8] – male	Electricians – male	Preparation of special samples – female
Make and wrap[5] – male	Make and wrap bars[2] – male	Card cutting[3,8] – male	Millwrights[4] – male	
Cut and wrap[5] – male	Wrap bars[2,7] – male		Lift installation[4] – male	
Packing[1,6] – female	Wrap neapolitans[7] – male			
Packing[6] – female	Wrap neapolitans[7] – female			

(1) Report to same manager
(2) Report to same manager
(3) Report to same manager
(4) Report to same manager

(5) Similar work in each section
(6) Similar work in each section
(7) Similar work in each section
(8) Fairly similar work in each section

Appendix B *Twelve statements on 'the supervisor's role today' which were evaluated by supervisors and managers*

(1) The supervisor is really a breed of his own; he has left the ranks of labour without being accepted into management.

(2) In industrial conditions today the economic interests of the supervisor are much the same as those of his workers.

(3) The supervisor is the first line of management and a line manager in every respect.

(4) The supervisor is a mediator between the two sides of industry.

(5) In effect the supervisor has become another specialist whose main concern is organizing and looking after his/her workers.

(6) There is not much left for the supervisor to do, except running errands.

(7) There are still plenty of opportunities for an able supervisor to be promoted into management.

(8) The supervisor is a key figure in resolving conflict on the shopfloor.

(9) An important contribution of the supervisor today is to act as a co-ordinator of people from different departments who affect the work in his section.

(10) The supervisor is in a position where he is pushed about from above and from below at the same time.

(11) The supervisor today has been replaced as leader of his workgroup by the shop-steward.

(12) The supervisor's main role is that of trouble-shooter.

Each of the above statements was accompanied by two seven-point scales. Labels attached to the ends of the scales and the method of subsequent scoring were as follows:

(1) Absolutely true in my firm   7 6 5 4 3 2 1   Not at all true in my firm

(2) Absolutely *should be* the case (i.e., I am completely in favour of the situation described by the statement – it is completely right and proper)   7 6 5 4 3 2 1   Definitely *should not be* the case (i.e. in my opinion this situation should not exist at all)

Interviewees were also invited to comment on each statement.

Appendices C and D

Appendix C *Items used to form the composite measure of supervisors' 'personal flexibility'*

Supervisors were asked during the second interview to assess how far they thought seven statements were true of themselves by means of the following five-point scale: definitely true; fairly true; true to some extent; not very true; definitely false (the order of the scale was reversed for some statements). The five statements below (out of a total of seven) were component items in the measure of 'personal flexibility':

(1) I prefer a job which is always changing.
(2) I enjoy finding myself in new and unusual circumstances.
(3) I like to have a regular pattern in my working day.
(4) I would generally prefer to do something I am used to rather than something that is different.
(5) I get a lot of pleasure from taking on new problems.

Each item was scored from 1 to 5, with preference for change/low routine scored high. The measure of 'personal flexibility' was formed by aggregating scores for the above five items. Its coefficient of internal reliability (K–R 8) was 0.86 and the mean item-total correlation was 0.73.

Appendix D *Twenty statements employed for assessing supervisors' views on trade unions*

During the second interviews, supervisors were asked to indicate how far they agreed or disagreed with each of 20 statements about trade unions, using a five-point scale: strongly agree, agree, unsure, disagree, strongly disagree, scored 1, 2, 3, 4 and 5 respectively. The 20 statements are listed below, and the nine asterisked were aggregated to form a measure of perceived 'necessity for union membership', with reversed scoring where appropriate.

(1) Ideally, supervisors should have their *own* union to protect their status, pay and conditions in comparison with other groups.
(2) Being part of a *shopfloor* union offers a better chance for supervisors to secure good rewards and conditions of employment.
(3) Being part of a *management* union offers a better chance for supervisors to secure good rewards and conditions of employment.
(4) I prefer to be in a union whose membership is restricted to supervisors rather than a union with other types of members.
(5) Really, supervisors shouldn't have to belong to a union.
(6)* In my case, good communication makes union representation unnecessary.

(Contd.)

221

(7)* People will always need the protection of union membership as an insurance against their employer.

(8)   Membership of a union would harm my career prospects.

(9)* In my sort of work it is necessary to be in a union so that my affairs are properly looked after.

(10)* Membership of a union offers the chance of negotiating through strength with management.

(11)* An internal staff association would be better than an outside union.

(12) I would always prefer to be in a union which bargained directly with my employers.

(13) Union members should stick together and help other groups less fortunate than themselves.

(14) Trade unions are not militant enough.

(15)* I prefer to handle my own affairs without interference from a union.

(16)* Union membership offers a better chance of securing good rewards and conditions of employment.

(17) Unions should restrict their activities to representing members instead of getting involved in political issues.

(18)* I could secure just as good benefits and working conditions outside the union as inside it.

(19)* Management will always back me up, so I don't need any support from elsewhere.

(20) To me, it is just as important to join a union as part of the labour movement as it is to join for personal advantage.

Notes

Chapter 2. The research setting and method of study (pp. 17–32)

1 The roles played by supervisors are examined in subsequent chapters. Superintendents did not have any formalized job descriptions. The role of superintendents was described to us as being 'to operate their own departments and to achieve the output demand required of those departments'.

2 The capital letter is used for Division here, since within the food factory the five main areas of activity were also designated as 'divisions' under the charge of 'divisional managers'.

3 Section managers typically had charge over supervisors and some clerical support staff. Their formal job objectives (in the production divisions) made reference to producing planned requirements at minimum cost to required standards. They were also held responsible for running-in any new plant, co-ordinating shift working, dealing with wages problems, ensuring the inflow and outflow of materials, and controlling the budget.

4 Except in the Assortments division where the schedulers' main reporting line was to production superintendents.

5 In the women's branch, where the local stewards were less forceful, supervisors could be brought into consultation with senior shop-stewards, though the section manager was more likely to be involved.

6 The food plant at one time only permitted female supervisors to supervise its many female operatives, but in recent years the numbers of female supervisors had fallen sharply. Brown *et al.* (1964) discuss the reluctance of married women to accept supervisory positions.

Chapter 3. One and many supervisory roles (pp. 35–62)

1 Only one correlation for either authority or influence exceeded 0.50, and for 16 decisions correlations between supervisor and manager did not even reach the 95 per cent level of confidence.

2 For these decisions, *within each plant*, the standard deviation of authority scores exceeded 1.6, the 25 percentile was greater than or equal to 4, and the 75 percentile less than or equal to 2.

Chapter 4. The shaping of supervisors' jobs (pp. 63–89)

1 Another major organizational difference between production and non-production supervisors was in the numbers of employees they supervised (span of control). Production supervisors' workgroups were on average twice the size of their non-production counterparts (35 as compared with 17). The average span of supervisory control was similar at both sites: engineering 33, food 28, which is higher than other surveys suggest is the general case (Toye, 1978).

2 Analysis of supervisors' replies indicated that this measure, which is the sum of responses to four questions, captures a central aspect of task variability. The measure has high internal reliability, with a K–R 8 coefficient of 0.84.

3 Personal flexibility was measured by seven questions with Likert-type five-point scales which each supervisor answered during his second interview. Scores on five of these questions (listed in Appendix C) were found to cluster together particularly closely and when aggregated the resulting measure of 'personal flexibility' has a K–R 8 value of 0.86 indicating high internal reliability.

Chapter 5. Coping and surviving (pp. 90–121)

1 But, as will be seen later in this chapter, this did not prevent certain supervisors from arranging *informal* exchanges of employees to cope with irregularities of workload, and with the approval of those employees. These exchanges did not therefore generate role conflict.

2 See Appendix B for the full list of these statements and method of scoring.

3 The section on 'market situation' in Chapter 7 provides evidence which indicates that supervisors' concerns about their relative pay and about promotion had some foundation.

4 The value of the K–R 8 coefficient of internal reliability is 0.88.

5 This is, of course, not to suggest that it is the pressures, problems and conflicts in the job which bring supervisors satisfaction – quite the reverse would be expected. It is to remark that the intrinsic nature of the work and the relationships involved can be satisfying despite the difficult conditions involved.

6 Correlation with perceived shortfall in line management status: $r = -0.30$, $p < 0.001$; and with perceived shortfall in acceptance into management: $r = -0.26$, $p < 0.001$.

7 Research which Schuler (1977) is conducting in the United States has begun to explore the ways in which individual differences among people working at various levels in organizations may influence their reactions to conflict and ambiguity in their jobs.

8 Kay (1963: 227) noted a rather similar set of responses to role conflict among foremen he studied in New Hampshire, USA.

Chapter 6. Assessing supervisory performance (pp. 122–40)

1 A comprehensive review of research on performance rating, which discusses these considerations at length, is Landy and Farr (1980).
2 Coefficient of internal reliability (K–R 8) = 0.93.
3 A hypothesis also favoured by Landy and Farr (1980) who report an absence of research results bearing directly upon it.
4 $r = 0.30, p < 0.01$ for correlation with the sum of five specific ratings; $r = 0.18, p < 0.05$ for correlation with the rating of general performance.
5 $r = 0.24, p < 0.01$ for correlation with the sum of five specific ratings; $r = 0.26, p < 0.01$ for correlation with the rating of general performance.
6 More precisely, predictor variables each having levels of confidence greater than the 95 per cent level in the equation. For fuller details of these equations see Child (1980a).

Chapter 7. Supervisors at the class divide (pp. 145–68)

1 It may be recalled from Chapter 5 that their levels of pay relative to other groups disturbed supervisors, and along with benefits and promotion opportunities contributed less to job satisfaction than did other conditions.

Chapter 8. Looking to management or to union? (pp. 169–88)

1 Contributors to this debate include Lockwood (1958); Bain (1970); Roberts *et al.* (1972); Bain *et al.* (1973); Crompton (1976, 1979) and Heritage (1980).
2 K–R (Kuder–Richardson) reliability coefficient = 0.87; mean item-total correlation = 0.65.
3 $p < 0.01$.
4 $p = 0.04$.
5 $p = 0.07$.
6 In both cases, $p < 0.001$.
7 $p < 0.01$.
8 $r = -0.28, p < 0.001$.
9 $r = -0.31, p < 0.001$.
10 For contact with immediate superiors, level of p was only 0.07.

Chapter 9. Lost managers – will they be found? (pp. 191–218)

1 'We have all the responsibility but no authority.'
2 In so far as the gap between things planned and things done results from the inadequate handling of complex information, it is possible that the application of micro-electronics to information processing will reduce the

problem, even in batch production systems where complexity can be extreme.

3 Thurley and Wirdenius (1980) in a recent unpublished paper regard supervisors as mostly engaged in controlling disturbances in the performance of a production system (the 'steering function'), and they argue that the relative importance of this function will vary for different production systems.

4 For differences in mean scores, $p = 0.07$.

Bibliography

Abell, P. 1975. Organizations as bargaining and influence systems: measuring intra-organizational power and influence. In P. Abell (ed.), *Organizations as Bargaining and Influence Systems*. London: Heinemann.

Abell, P. and D. Mathew. 1973. The task analysis framework in organizational analysis. In M. Warner (ed.), *The Sociology of the Workplace*. London: Allen and Unwin.

Alderson, S. 1976. The Jaquesian general theory. In J. Gray (ed.), *The Glacier Project: Concepts and Critiques*. London: Heinemann.

Bain, G. S. 1970. *The Growth of White-Collar Unionism*. Oxford: Clarendon Press.

Bain, G. S., R. D. Coates and V. Ellis. 1973. *Social Stratification and Trade Unionism*. London: Heinemann.

Bain, G. S. and R. Price. 1972. Who is a white-collar employee? *British Journal of Industrial Relations*, 10: 325–99.

Bates, D. and D. Hosking. 1977. *Factors which Influence the Success of Supervisory Training*. Engineering Industry Training Board. Occasional Paper no. 5, Watford.

Beal, E. 1963. In praise of job evaluation. *California Management Review*, 5: 9–16.

Bellamy, A. R. 1976. *Technology, Span of Control and Supervisory Style*. Unpublished PhD thesis, Purdue University, USA.

Bendix, R. 1956. *Work and Authority in Industry*. New York: Wiley.

Beynon, H. 1973. *Working for Ford*. Harmondsworth: Penguin.

Blackburn, R. M. 1967. *Union Character and Social Class*. London: Batsford.

Bowey, A. M. 1973. The changing status of the supervisor. *British Journal of Industrial Relations*, 11: 393–414.

Boyd, B. and B. Scanlon. 1965. Developing tomorrow's foremen. *Training Directors' Journal*, 19: 44–5.

Boyd, B. B. and J. M. Jensen. 1972. Perceptions of the first-line supervisor's authority: a study in superior–subordinate communication. *Academy of Management Journal*, 15: 331–42.

227

Bibliography

Brief, A. P., R. J. Aldag and M. Van Sell. 1977. Moderators of the relationships between self and superior evaluations of job performance. *Journal of Occupational Psychology*, 50:129–34.

British Institute of Management (BIM). 1976. *Front Line Management*. London.

Brown, R. K., J. M. Kirkby and K. F. Taylor. 1964. The employment of married women and the supervisory role. *British Journal of Industrial Relations*, 11: 23–41.

Brown, Lord W. 1960. *Exploration in Management*. London: Heinemann.

Brown, W. 1973. *Piecework Bargaining*. London: Heinemann.

Brunel Institute of Organization and Social Studies (BIOSS). 1977. Unpublished paper on Role definitions and Relationships, March.

Bulmer, M. 1975. Some Problems of Research into Class Imagery. In M. Bulmer (ed.), *Working Class Images of Society*. London: Routledge and Kegan Paul.

Burawoy, M. 1979. *Manufacturing Consent*. Chicago: University of Chicago Press.

Campbell, J. P., M. D. Dunnette, E. E. Lawler III and K. E. Weick. 1970. *Managerial Behavior, Performance and Effectiveness*. New York: McGraw-Hill.

Carchedi, G. 1975. On the economic identification of the new middle class. *Economy and Society*, 4: 1–86.

Child, J. 1969. *British Management Thought*. London: Allen and Unwin.

Child, J. 1973a. Predicting and understanding organization structure. *Administrative Science Quarterly*, 18: 168–85.

Child, J. 1973b. Strategies of control and organizational behavior. *Administrative Science Quarterly*, 18: 1–17.

Child, J. 1975. The industrial Supervisor. In G. Esland, G. Salaman and M. A. Speakman (eds.), *People and Work*. Edinburgh: Holmes McDougall.

Child, J. 1980a. Factors associated with the managerial rating of supervisory performance. *Journal of Management Studies*, 17: 275–302.

Child, J. 1980b. The meaning and process of supervisory unionism. *University of Aston Management Centre Working Paper* No. 172, February.

Child, J. and R. Mansfield. 1972. Technology, size and organization structure. *Sociology*, 6: 369–93.

Child, J., S. Pearce and L. King. 1980. Class perceptions and social identification of industrial supervisors. *Sociology*, 14: 363–99. (A more extended version of this paper appeared as Child, Pearce and King (1978), University of Aston Management Centre Working Paper no. 100.)

Cousins, J. and R. Brown. 1975. Patterns of paradox: shipbuilding workers' images of society. In M. Bulmer (ed.), *Working Class Images of Society*.

228

London: Routledge and Kegan Paul.

Crompton, R. 1976. Approaches to the study of white-collar unionism. *Sociology*, 10: 407–26.

Crompton, R. 1979. Trade unionism and the insurance clerk. *Sociology*, 13: 403–26.

Crossman, E. R. F. W. 1960. *Automation and Skill*. London: HMSO.

Crossman, E. R. F. W. 1969. *Human Factors in Technology*. Research Group Working Paper HFT 69–3, Department of Industrial Engineering and Operations Research, University of California, Berkeley.

Cummings, P. W. 1972. Measuring supervisors' responsibilities. *Training and Development Journal*, 26: 24–7.

De Cotiis, T. A. 1977. An analysis of the external validity and applied relevance of three rating formats. *Organizational Behavior and Human Performance*, 19: 247–66.

Department of Employment. 1976. *The Changing Structure of the Labour Force*. Project report by the Unit for Manpower Studies.

Dowell, B. E. and K. N. Wexley. 1978. Development of a work behavior taxonomy for first-line supervisors. *Journal of Applied Psychology*, 63: 563–72,

Dunkerley, D. 1975. *The Foreman: Aspects of Task and Structure*. London: Routledge and Kegan Paul.

Edwards, R. 1979. *Contested Terrain: The Transformation of the Workplace in the Twentieth Century*. London: Heinemann.

Ellis, T. and J. Child. 1973. Placing stereotypes of the manager into perspective. *Journal of Management Studies*, 10: 233–55.

Fletcher, C. 1969. Men in the middle: a reformulation of the thesis. *Sociological Review*, 17: 341–54.

Fletcher, C. 1973. The end of management. In J. Child (ed.), *Man and Organization*. London: Allen and Unwin.

Fores, M. 1977. Front line people: supervisors. Unpublished paper, February.

Fores, M., P. Lawrence and A. Sorge. 1978. Germany's front-line force. *Management Today*, March: 86–9, 158.

Gardner, B. B. and W. F. Whyte. 1945. The man in the middle: position and problems of the foreman. *Applied Anthropology*, 4: 1–28.

Ghiselli, E. E. 1971. *Explorations in Managerial Talent*. Santa Monica, California: Goodyear.

Glyn, A. and B. Sutcliffe. 1972. *British Capitalism, Workers and the Profit Squeeze*. Harmondsworth: Penguin.

Goldthorpe, J. H. 1970. Images of class among affluent manual workers. Department of Applied Economics, University of Cambridge (published in *Revue Française de Sociologie*, 11: 311–38).

Goldthorpe, J. H. (in collaboration with C. Llewellyn and C. Payne). 1980.

Mobility and Class Structure in Modern Britain. Oxford: Clarendon Press.

Gordon, M. 1976. Equitable payment by Elliott Jaques. Department of Psychology, University of California, Berkeley. Reported in S. Laner and E. Crossman, 'The current status of the Jaquesian time span of discretion concept – research and applications'. In J. Gray (ed.), *The Glacier Project: Concepts and Critiques*. London: Heinemann.

Government Social Survey. 1968. *Workplace Industrial Relations*. London: HMSO.

Gross, E. 1953. Some functional consequences of primary controls in formal work organizations. *American Sociological Review*, 18: 368–73.

Guest, R. H. 1956. Of time and the foreman. *Personnel*, 32: 478–86.

Gulowsen, J. 1972. A measure of work-group autonomy. In L. E. Davis and J. C. Taylor (eds.), *Design of Jobs*. Harmondsworth: Penguin.

Hackman, K. R. and J. L. Suttle. 1977. *Improving Life at Work*. Santa Monica, California: Goodyear.

Heritage, J. 1980. Class situation, white collar unionization and the 'double proletarianization' thesis: a comment. *Sociology*, 14: 283–94.

Herzberg, F., B. Mausner and B. B. Snyderman. 1959. *The Motivation to Work*. New York: Wiley.

Hill, J. 1976a. The time span of discretion. In J. Gray (ed.), *The Glacier Project: Concepts and Critiques*. London: Heinemann.

Hill, S. 1976b. *The Dockers: Class and Tradition in London*. London: Heinemann.

Homans, G. C. 1950. *The Human Group*. London: Routledge and Kegan Paul.

Incomes Data Services (IDS). 1979. *Supervisors' Pay*, Study no. 187.

Institute of Personnel Management (IPM). 1975. *Profile of a Supervisor*. London.

Institute of Supervisory Management. 1979. Personal communication, October.

Jaques, E. 1956. *Measurement of Responsibility*. London: Tavistock.

Jaques, E. 1967. *Equitable Payment*. Harmondsworth: Penguin, 2nd edition.

Jaques, E. 1976. *A General Theory of Bureaucracy*. London: Heinemann.

Jenkins, C. and B. Sherman. 1979. *White-Collar Unionism: The Rebellious Salariat*. London: Routledge and Kegan Paul.

Jenkins, D. 1978. The supervisor solution. *Management Today*, May: 74–7, 144, 147.

Kahn, R. L., D. M. Wolfe, R. P. Quinn, J. D. Snoek and R. A. Rosenthal. 1964. *Organizational Stress: Studies in Role Conflict and Ambiguity*. New York: Wiley.

Kay, B. R. 1963. Prescription and perception of the supervisory role. *Occupational Psychology*, 37: 219–27.

Bibliography

Kipnis, D. 1976a. *The Powerholders*. Chicago: University of Chicago Press.

Kipnis, D., P. J. Castell, M. Gergen and D. Mauch. 1976b. Metamorphic effects of power. *Journal of Applied Psychology*, 61: 127–35.

Kuder, G. and M. Richardson. 1937. The theory of the estimation of test reliability. *Psychometrika*, 2: 151–60.

Kuhn, J. W. 1961. *Bargaining in Grievance Settlement*. New York: Columbia University Press.

Landy, F. J. and J. L. Farr. 1980. Performance Rating. *Psychological Bulletin*, 87: 72–107.

Lawrence, P. 1980. *Managers and Management in West Germany*. London: Croom Helm.

Lennerlöf, L. 1966. *Dimensions of Supervision*. Stockholm: Swedish Council for Personnel Administration.

Lennerlöf, L. 1968. *Supervision: Situation, Individual, Behavior, Effect*. Stockholm: Swedish Council for Personnel Administration.

Lockwood, D. 1958. *The Blackcoated Worker*. London: Allen and Unwin.

Lynch, B. P. 1974. An empirical assessment of Perrow's technology construct. *Administrative Science Quarterly*, 19: 338–56.

Mackenzie, G. 1973. *The Aristocracy of Labour*. London: Cambridge University Press.

Mackenzie, G. 1975. World images and the world of work. In G. Esland, G. Salaman and M. A. Speakman (eds.), *People and Work*. Edinburgh: Holmes McDougall.

Mann, F. C. 1965. Toward an understanding of the leadership role in formal organizations. In R. Dubin, G. C. Homans, S. C. Mann and D. C. Miller (eds.), *Leadership and Productivity*. San Francisco: Chandler.

Mann, F. C. and J. K. Dent. 1954. The supervisor: member of two organizational families. *Harvard Business Review*, 32: 103–12.

Mant, A. 1979. *The Rise and Fall of the British Manager*. London: Pan.

Marples, D. L. 1967. Studies of managers – a fresh start?. *Journal of Management Studies*, 4: 282–99.

Marsh, R. and B. Pedler. 1979. Unionising the white-collar workers. *Employee Relations*, 1: 2–6.

Mathew, D. J. 1975. The logic of task analysis. In P. Abell (ed.), *Organizations as Bargaining and Influence Systems*. London: Heinemann.

Maurice, M., A. Sorge and M. Warner. 1980. Societal differences in organizing manufacturing units: a comparison of France, West Germany and Great Britain. *Organization Studies*, 1: 59–86.

Melling, J. 1980. 'Non-commissioned officers': British employers and their supervisory workers, 1880–1920. *Social History*, 5: 183–221.

Miller, R. 1976. Difficulties in the use of the time-span technique to measure level of work. In J. Gray (ed.), *The Glacier Project: Concepts and*

Critiques. London: Heinemann.

Mintzberg, H. 1973. *The Nature of Managerial Work*. New York: Harper and Row.

National Board for Prices and Incomes (NBPI). 1968. *Payment by Results*. Report no. 65. London: HMSO.

National Institute of Industrial Psychology (NIIP). 1951. *The Foreman*. London: Staples.

National Institute of Industrial Psychology (NIIP). 1957. *The Place of the Foreman in Management*. London: Staples.

Nealey, S. M. and F. E. Fiedler. 1968. Leadership functions of middle managers. *Psychological Bulletin*, 76: 313–29.

Nichols, T. and H. Beynon. 1977. *Living with Capitalism*. London: Routledge and Kegan Paul.

Nicholson, N., G. Ursell and P. Blyton. 1980. Social background, attitudes and behaviour of white-collar shop stewards. *British Journal of Industrial Relations*, 18: 231–9.

Nie, N. H., C. H. Hull, J. G. Jenkins, K. Steinbrenner and D. H. Bent. 1975. *Statistical Package for the Social Sciences*. New York: McGraw-Hill, 2nd edition.

Nunnally, J. C. 1978. *Psychometric Theory*. New York: McGraw-Hill, 2nd edition.

Ossowski, S. 1963. *Class Structure in the Social Consciousness*. London: Routledge and Kegan Paul.

Page, M. 1977. The supervisor: an endangered species. *Works Management*, July: 74–6.

Parkin, F. 1972. *Class Inequality and Political Order*. London: Paladin.

Partridge, B. E. 1979. Influence and responsibilities of first-line supervisors. *University of Aston Management Centre Working Paper*, no. 129, February.

Patten, T. H. 1968. The authority and responsibilities of supervisors in a multi-plant firm. *Journal of Management Studies*, 5: 61–82.

Perrow, C. 1967. A framework for the comparative analysis of organizations. *American Sociological Review*, 32: 194–208.

Perrow, C. 1970. *Organizational Analysis: A Sociological View*. Belmont, California: Wadsworth; London: Tavistock.

Pfeffer, J. and G. R. Salancik. 1975. Determinants of supervisory behavior: a role set analysis. *Human Relations*, 28: 139–54.

Pollard, S. 1968. *The Genesis of Modern Management*. Harmondsworth: Penguin.

Prandy, K., A. Stewart and R. M. Blackburn. 1974. Concepts and measures: the example of unionateness. *Sociology*, 8: 427–46.

Reeves, T. K. and B. A. Turner. 1972. A theory of organization and behavior in batch production factories. *Administrative Science Quarterly*, 17: 81–98.

Roberts, B. C., R. Loveridge and J. Gennard. 1972. *Reluctant Militants: A Study of Industrial Technicians*. London: Heinemann.

Roberts, K., F. G. Cook, S. C. Clark and E. Semeonoff. 1977. *The Fragmentary Class Structure*. London: Heinemann.

Roethlisberger, F. J. 1943. *Management and Morale*. Cambridge, Mass: Harvard University Press.

Roethlisberger, F. J. 1945. The foreman: master and victim of double talk. *Harvard Business Review*, 23: 283–98.

Roy, D. 1954. Efficiency and 'the fix': the informal intergroup relations in a piecework machine shop. *American Journal of Sociology*, 60: 255–66.

Schuler, R. S. 1977. The effects of role perceptions on employee satisfaction and performance moderated by employee ability. *Organization Behavior and Human Performance*, 18: 98–107.

Silverman, D. 1970. *The Theory of Organisations*. London: Heinemann.

Smith, C. T. 1978. Supervisors' Activities. Unpublished project dissertation, Department of Management Studies, University of Leeds.

Smith, F. 1878. *Workshop Management: A Manual for Masters and Men*. London: Wyman.

Smith, P. C. 1976. Behaviors, results and organizational effectiveness: the problem of criteria. In M. D. Dunnette (ed.), *Handbook of Industrial and Organizational Psychology*. Chicago: Rand McNally.

Swedish Employers' Confederation. 1975. *Job Reform in Sweden*. Stockholm.

Taylor, J. C. 1971. Some effects of technology in organizational change. *Human Relations*, 24: 105–23.

Thurley, K. E. and A. C. Hamblin. 1963. *The Supervisor and his Job*. London: HMSO.

Thurley, K. E. and H. Wirdenius. 1973. *Supervision: A Reappraisal*. London: Heinemann.

Thurley, K. E. and H. Wirdenius. 1980. The influence of the supervisor in organizations: a production system perspective. Paper given to the conference on Leadership and Managerial Behaviour, University of Aston Management Centre, May.

Toye, J. 1978. *Supervisors in Industry: A Survey of Research and Opinion*. Cambridge: Industrial Training Research Unit.

Van de Ven, A. H. and D. L. Ferry. 1980. *Measuring and Assessing Organizations*. New York: Wiley.

Wedderburn, D. and C. Craig. 1974. Relative deprivation in work. In D. Wedderburn (ed.), *Poverty, Inequality and Class Structure*. London: Cambridge University Press.

Weir, M. and S. Mills. 1973. The supervisor as a change catalyst. *Industrial Relations Journal*, 4: 61–9.

Williams, A. 1915. *Life in a Railway Factory*. London: Duckworth.

Woodward, J. 1958. *Management and Technology*. London: HMSO.

Bibliography

Woodward, J. 1965. *Industrial Organization: Theory and Practice*. London: Oxford University Press.

Woodward, J. (ed.). 1970. *Industrial Organization: Behaviour and Control*. London: Oxford University Press.

Wray, D. E. 1949. Marginal men of industry: the foremen. *American Journal of Sociology*, 54: 298–301.

Wright, E. O. 1976. Class boundaries in advanced capitalist societies. *New Left Review*, 98: 3–41.

Yanouzas, J. N. 1964. A comparative study of work organization and supervisory behavior. *Human Organization*, 23: 245–53.

Youngman, M. B. 1979. *Analysing Social and Educational Research Data*. Maidenhead: McGraw-Hill.

Name Index

Abell, P., 39, 65
Aldag, R. J., 124
Alderson, S., 37

Bain, G. S., 169, 176, 185, 187, 225
Bates, D., 13, 99, 122
Beal, E., 38
Bellamy, A. R., 76
Bendix, R., 5
Beynon, H., 46, 110, 112, 169, 203
Blackburn, R. M., 179, 183, 187
Blyton, P., 183
Bowey, A., 198, 205
Boyd, B., 36
Boyd, B. B., 48
Brief, A. P., 124
B. I. M., 8, 46, 99, 109, 145, 149, 198
Brown, R. K., 154, 155, 158, 223
Brown, Lord W., 35
Brown, W., 112
B. I. O. S. S., 54, 208
Bulmer, M., 158
Burawoy, M., 192

Campbell, J. P., 129, 132
Carchedi, G., 146
Castell, P. J., 132–136
Child, J., 7, 64, 74, 76, 78, 129, 150,
    158, 159, 164, 170, 225
Clark, S. C., 150
Coates, R. D., 185, 225
Cook, F. G., 150
Cousins, J., 154, 155, 158
Craig, C., 149
Crompton, R., 146, 147, 185, 225
Crossman, E. R. F. W., 8, 37
Cummings, P. W., 109

De Cotiis, T. A., 124

Dent, J. K., 90
Dowell, B. E., 41, 105
Dunette, M. D., 129, 132
Dunkerley, D., 148, 151

Edwards, R., 4, 6, 7
Ellis, T., 78
Ellis, V., 185, 225

Farr, J. L., 130, 225
Ferry, D. L., 66
Fiedler, F. E., 14
Fletcher, C., 8, 65, 154
Fores, M., 148, 199, 210

Gardner, B. B., 154
Gennard, J., 225
Gergen, M., 132, 136
Ghiselli, E. E., 129
Glyn, A., 176
Goldthorpe, J. H., 11, 30, 154, 155
Gordon, M., 38
Gross, E., 75
Guest, R. H., 105, 109
Gulowsen, J., 8

Hackman, J. R., 198
Hamblin, A. C., 12, 14, 64, 105, 202
Heritage, J., 225
Herzberg, F. B., 198
Hill, J., 29, 38
Hill, S., 64, 77, 81, 90, 109, 111, 112,
    156, 161, 170, 181
Homans, G. C., 133
Hosking, D., 13, 99, 122

Incomes Data Services, 148, 193, 194
Institute of Personnel Management,
    149, 191

Name Index

Jaques, E., 35, 37, 38, 208
Jenkins, C., 169
Jenkins, D., 217
Jenson, J. M., 72

Kahn, R. L., 98
Kay, B. R., 224
King, L., 150, 158
Kipnis, D., 132, 136
Kirkby, J. M., 223
Kuder, G., 52
Kuhn, J. W., 112

Landy, F. J., 130, 225
Lawler, E. E., 111, 129, 132
Lawrence, P., 148, 210, 212
Lennerlöf, L., 38, 39, 41, 69
Lockwood, D., 145, 146, 149, 150, 185, 225
Loveridge, R., 225
Lynch, B. P., 76

Mackenzie, G., 151, 152, 154
Mann, F. C., 41, 90
Mansfield, R., 64
Mant, A., 9, 137
Marples, D. L., 105
Marsh, R., 176
Mathew, D. J., 65, 66
Mauch, D., 132, 136
Maurice, M., 211, 212
Mausner, B., 198
Melling, J., 5, 7
Miller, R., 38
Mills, S., 12
Mintzberg, H., 105

National Board for Prices and Incomes, 112
National Institute of Industrial Psychology, 12, 29, 35, 36, 43, 64
Nealey, S. M., 14
Nichols, T., 46, 112, 169
Nicholson, N., 183
Nie, N. H., 125
Nunnally, J. C., 52

Ossowski, S., 150

Page, M., 193
Parkin, F., 145
Patten, T. H., 36, 41
Pearce, S., 150, 158

Pedler, B., 176
Perrow, C., 66–68, 69, 71, 76
Pfeffer, J., 123
Pollard, S., 5
Prandy, K., 183, 187
Price, R., 169

Quinn, R. P., 98

Reeves, T. K., 63, 64, 94, 202
Richardson, M., 52
Roberts, B. C., 225
Roberts, K., 150, 166, 171
Roethlisberger, F. J., 8, 209
Rosenthal, R. A., 98
Roy, D., 112

Salancik, G. R., 123
Scanlon, B., 36
Schuler, R. S., 224
Semeonoff, E., 150
Sherman, B., 169
Silverman, D., 54
Smith, C. T., 110
Smith, F., 5
Smith, P. C., 122
Snoek, J. D., 98
Snyderman, B. B., 198
Sorge, A., 148, 210, 211, 212
Stewart, A., 183, 187
Sutcliffe, B., 176
Suttle, J. L., 198
Swedish Employers Confederation, 12, 207, 216

Taylor, J. C., 8
Taylor, K. F., 223
Taylor, F. W., 6
Thurley, K. E., 3, 12, 14, 17, 35, 42, 54, 55, 64, 69, 76, 77, 105, 122, 127, 202, 205, 215, 216, 217, 226
Toye, J., 224
Turner, B. A., 63, 64, 94, 202

Ursell, G., 183

Van de Ven, A. H., 66
Van Sell, M., 124

Warner, M., 211, 212
Wedderburn, D., 149
Weick, K., 129, 132
Weir, M., 12
Wexley, K. N., 41, 105

Name Index

Whyte, W. F., 154
Williams, A., 5
Wirdenius, H., 3, 17, 35, 42, 54–5, 64, 69, 76, 77, 202, 215, 216, 217, 226
Wolfe, D. M., 98, 105, 122, 127
Woodward, J., 13, 14, 64, 65, 76, 110, 202, 203
Wray, D. E., 8
Wright, E. O., 147

Yanonzas, J. N., 64, 90
Youngman, M. B., 121

Subject Index

ambiguity, facing supervisors, 97–100, 196; in class position, 146, 150; *see also* uncertainty

authority of supervisors, 4, 5, 7, 8, 10, 11, 14, 30, 36–62, 67, 71–2, 74–5, 76–8, 81–9, 99, 147–8, 192; defined, 36–7; measurement of, 37–42; simplified measurement of, 51–3; over system, technical and people decisions, 39–42; assessed by supervisors, 42–5; assessed by managers, 47–9, 57–8; variation in, 50–1; historical changes in, 4–8; association with supervisors' level of influence, 42–6, 48–9; compared with supervisors' responsibilities, 9, 46–7, 192; and relation with manager, 78, 81–2, 89; and organizational context, 74–5, 79–82, 86; and task system, 71–2, 79–81, 82–3, 84–5, 87–8; and personal attributes, 77–9, 89; challenge to posed by shopfloor unionization, 7, 174

breakdowns in production, 24, 70–1, 85, 91, 92, 94; and pressure on the supervisor, 94, 95–6, 98

class, social: of supervisors, 11, 15, 145–50; assessed by authority and work situation, 147–8; assessed by labour market position, 148–9; supervisors' perceptions of, 150–66; association between indicators of class perceptions, 158–60; class perceptions and supervisors' backgrounds, 160–1; class perceptions and identification at work, 161–4; class perceptions and

managerial policies, 166; relevance of occupational role and social relationships for class perceptions, 161, 164; class consciousness and attitudes towards trade unions, 185–7; *see also* labour market, status

communications: between supervisors and other groups, 109–10; and ratings of supervisors' performance, 133–4

companies (plants) studied, 18–29; differences between supervisors in, 50, 60, 68, 73–4, 98, 107–8, 110–11, 169–70, 171–8, 180, 224 (Chapter 4, note 1)

conflict, 48–50, 90–4, 103–4, 111, 113, 117–18, 184; *see also* role conflict, trade unions

contingency (situational) analysis, 12–13, 14, 200–6; *see also* organizational context, task system, technology, managers, payment, personal attributes

control, managerial, 4, 6, 7, 23, 27; *see also* authority, discretion, influence

coping strategies of supervisors, 104–18, 137, 199; 'management-oriented', 111–14, 115–16; 'neutral', 111–14, 116–17; 'workgroup-oriented', 111–15; *see also* priorities

decisions, as reference for assessing supervisors' authority, 38–41; classification of, 40–2

design, of supervisors' jobs, 35, 54–5, 82–3, 198–214; a rationale for, 200–6; choice of models for, 206–14

discretion, 35, 36–7, 75, 112; authority as discretion, 36–7; time span of discretion, 37–8 disturbance handling, 9, 71, 77, 93–4, 98, 127; *see also* breakdowns in production, uncertainty

formalization, 47, 48, 72–5, 205
functional foremanship, 6

influence of supervisors, 14, 30, 36, 39–62, 67, 71–2, 74–5, 76–8, 81–9, 99, 192; measurement of, 39–42; simplified measurement of, 51–3; over system, technical and people decisions, 39–42; assessed by supervisors, 42–5; assessed by managers, 47–9, 57–8; variation in, 50–1; and supervisors' authority, 39, 42–6, 48–9; and relation with manager, 78, 81–2, 89; and organizational context, 74–5, 79–82; and task system, 71–2, 79–81, 82–3, 84–5, 87–8; and personal attributes, 77–9, 89; as predictor of ratings of supervisors' performance, 127–9, 135, 138

job satisfaction of supervisors, 15, 100–4, 184–5, 197; with different aspects of the job, 101–2; and conflict, 103–4, 119; and 'job tension', 100, 103–4, 119; and pressures, 102–4, 119; and stress, 103–4, 119

labour market: supervisors' changing position in, 5–8, 10; contemporary market situation, 148–9, 176; *see also* class, social
'lost managers', 191–2, 193, 194, 214–15

management: ideology on supervision, 8–9, 145, 150; supervisors' identification with, 8–9, 157, 162–3, 183–4, 188; supervisors' acceptance of management's objectives, 110, 192; supervisors' desire for a managerial role, 162–3; supervisors' attitudes towards management and attachment to trade unions, 183–7
managers: assessments of supervisors' authority and influence, 47–9; views on the supervisory role, 49, 59; disagreement with supervisors' view of their role, 48–50, 124, 131–2, 135, 143, 193; influence on supervisors' activities, 12–13; understanding of supervisor's activities, 9–10, 111, 118; view of the 'effective' supervisor, 136–7; *see also* conflict, role conflict, supervisors, trade unions
markets and products: of companies studied, 21–4, 25–6

observation of supervisors at work, 31, 51, 75, 79–82, 114–17; sample of supervisors observed, 219
organizational context, and supervisors' jobs, 64, 72–5; *see also* formalization

payment: incentive systems (piecework), 5, 7, 24, 28, 79, 94, 96, 109, 112, 204–5; supervisors' earnings, 5, 24, 28, 148–9; workers' earnings, 24, 28, 94, 97, 148; supervisors' differentials over workers, 148, 174
performance of supervisors, 15, 27, 72, 74, 75, 83, 122–40; formal assessment, 27, 72, 74, 75, 83; rating scales, 123–4; problems of assessment 122–3; managers' ratings, 123–35; supervisors' self-ratings, 123; limited agreement between managers' and supervisors' ratings, 124, 126; subjectivity of managers' ratings, 135–6; mangers' ratings and supervisors' 'personal flexibility', 127; and supervisors' influence, 127–9; and managers' qualities, 129–30; and differences in opinion between managers and supervisors, 131–2; and differences in personal profiles between managers and supervisors, 132; and quality of relations between managers and supervisors, 132–4
personal attributes, and supervisors' jobs, 77–9; and ratings of supervisors' performance, 127–9; supervisors' 'personal flexibility', 77–8, 127, 135, 221
pressures experienced by supervisors, 83, 91–8, 102, 117, 119; and production planning problems, 94

priorities in supervisors' jobs, 21, 23, 27, 83, 104–14, 120, 131; managers' and supervisors' priority ratings compared, 111; emphasis on quality and workflow, 106–9; *see also* coping strategies

redundancy, 8, 11, 19; and unionization of supervisors, 171–2, 175

research, approach to: data collection, 30–1; design and method, 17–21, 29–31; perspective and assumptions, 13–16; samples, 22, 29–30, 219

responsibilities of supervisors, 46–7; *see also* authority, influence

role conflict, 8, 83, 91–4, 118, 119; caught between management and workers ('man in the middle'), 8, 91–2; conflicting pressures from management, 92–3; conflict with one other party, 93

scientific management, 6

shop stewards, 7, 8, 24, 28, 93, 112

social identification of supervisors, 10, 13, 15–16, Chapters 7 and 8 passim

social class, *see* class, social

socio-technical system, 80; *see also* task system, technology

status of supervisors, 4, 5, 10, 11, 19, 150, 194, 195–8; in relation to supervisory functions, 197; concept of status, 146; supervisors' dissatisfaction with status, 100, 102

stress, experienced by supervisors, 8, 15, 90, 98–100

supervision: definitions of, 35–6; dimensions of, 41–2, 52; historical transformation, 4–11, 14; as an occupation, 13, 196–7; 'problem of supervision', 8, 12, 16, 191–6; in West German industry, 210–12; choice of models for, 206–14; future possibilities for, 214–18; *see also* contingency analysis, design, supervisors

supervisors: career and promotion prospects 9, 10, 102, 149; commitment to their role, 11, 191–2; double standards towards, 8–9; goodwill to management, 195, 217; job security, 149; leadership, 7,

41–2; lifestyle, 5; managerial role, 8, 46, 54, 195–6, 199–200, 210–13; 'men in charge', 4, 18; 'men in the middle', 5, 8, 47, 90–1, 102, 117, 197; 'marginal men', 4, 8, 90, 102, 117, 157; 'men on the way out', 8, 206–7; numbers in Great Britain, 3; occupational role, 196–7; production and non-production compared, 50–1, 61, 98, 107–8, 110–11, 170–1, 178, 180, 182, 224 (Chapter 4, note 1); role as 'buffer', 137; role in industrial relations, 24–5, 28; role in production planning, 24, 26–7; social origins, 11, 16, 160–1, 186; social relations with managers, 132–3, 147–8; spans of control, 14, 64, 224 (Chapter 4, note 1); and staff personnel, 6–7, 19, 71; style, 132, 139; task contacts with managers, 81, 114, 115, 116, 133–4; task contacts with workers, 114, 115, 116; views on the supervisory role, 47, 56, 92, 161–2, 167–8, 183–5, 220; women supervisors, 29, 223; *see also other entries in index*

task (production) system, 14, 65–72; in plants studied, 23–7; classification of and supervision, 66–8; measurement of, 68–70; complexity of tasks, 69–71, 203–5; difficulty of tasks, 66, 68, 76–7, 203–5; variability of tasks, 66, 68–71, 75, 76–7, 79–80, 203–5; task characteristics and supervisors' jobs, 63–72, 76–7, 79–82; *see also* technology

technology, 6, 7, 9, 12–13, 63–72, 75, 79–82, 202–3; different concepts of, 64–5; batch technology, 18, 23–4, 26–7, 29, 63–4, 202; *see also* breakdowns in production, task system

tensions, in supervisors' jobs, 98–100, 103–4

trade unions: shopfloor, 7, 24, 28; supervisory, 8, 11, 13, 16, 19, 169–88; supervisors' membership and participation in, 169–71, 180–1; process of supervisory unionization, 171–7; key activists and unionization, 171–3, 174–6; pay and unionization, 174, 175, 178;

redundancy and unionization, 171–2, 175; shopfloor organization and unionization, 174–5, 176; reasons given for membership, 177–83; attitudes towards union membership, 179–83; attitudes to union and management, 183–7; attitudes to union and class consciousness, 185–7; instrumentalism, 180, 184, 187; unionateness, 179, 183

training of supervisors, 13, 98–9

uncertainty, in supervisors' work, 9, 75, 79, 80, 82, 97; *see also* ambiguity, breakdowns in production, disturbance handling, task system

variation, between supervisors' jobs, 12, 13, 15, 50–5, 60, 63–81, 82, 83, 107, 108, 110, 111, 112, 114, 192, 200–2